MATHS FRAMEWORKING

Complete success for Mathematics at KS3

YEAR 8

PUPIL BOOK 2

KEVIN EVANS KEITH GORDON TREVOR SENIOR BRIAN SPEED

Contents

CHAPTER 1

Number and Algebra 1

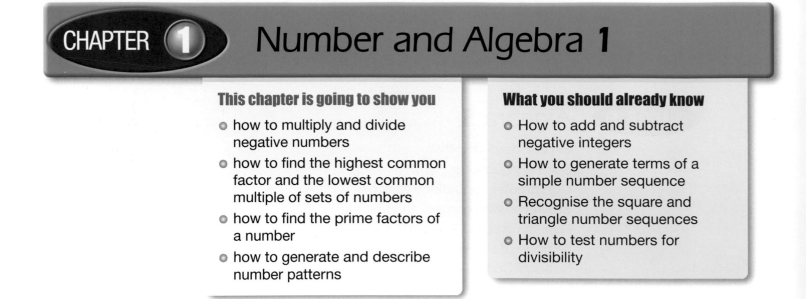

This chapter is going to show you

- how to multiply and divide negative numbers
- how to find the highest common factor and the lowest common multiple of sets of numbers
- how to find the prime factors of a number
- how to generate and describe number patterns

What you should already know

- How to add and subtract negative integers
- How to generate terms of a simple number sequence
- Recognise the square and triangle number sequences
- How to test numbers for divisibility

Multiplying and dividing negative numbers

Example 1.1 Work out the answers to **a** $-2 \times +4$ **b** -6×-3 **c** $-15 \div -5$ **d** $+6 \times -4 \div -2$

a $2 \times 4 = 8$, and $- \times +$ is equivalent to $-$, so $-2 \times +4 = -8$

b $6 \times 3 = 18$, and $- \times -$ is equivalent to $+$, so $-6 \times -3 = +18$

c $15 \div 5 = 3$, and $- \div -$ is equivalent to $+$, so $-15 \div -5 = +3$

d $+6 \times -4 = -24$, $-24 \div -2 = +12$

Example 1.2 Find the missing number in **a** $\boxed{} \times 3 = -6$ **b** $-12 \div \boxed{} = 3$

a The inverse problem is $\boxed{} = -6 \div +3$, so the missing number is -2

b The inverse problem is $\boxed{} = -12 \div +3$, so the missing number is -4.

Example 1.3 Work out **a** $-3 \times -2 + 5$ **b** $-3 \times (-2 + 5)$

a Using BODMAS do -3×-2 first, $-3 \times -2 + 5 = +6 + 5 = +11$

b This time the bracket must be done first, $-3 \times (-2 + 5) = -3 \times +3 = -9$

Exercise 1A

1 Work out

  a $-7 + 8$ **b** $-2 - 7$ **c** $+6 - 2 + 3$ **d** $-6 - 1 + 7$ **e** $-3 + 4 - 9$
  f $-3 - 7$ **g** $-4 + -6$ **h** $+7 - +6$ **i** $-3 - 7 + -8$ **j** $-5 + -4 - -7$

2 In these 'walls', subtract the right-hand from the left-hand number to find the number in the brick below.

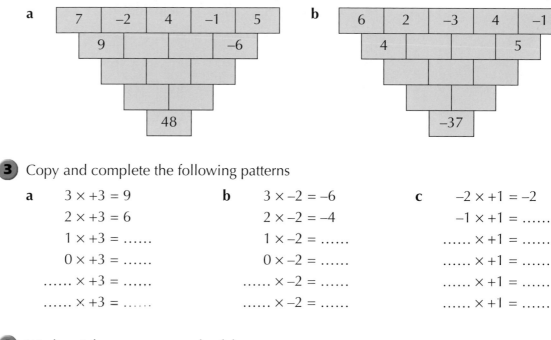

a

7	−2	4	−1	5

9			−6

48

b

6	2	−3	4	−1

4			5

−37

3 Copy and complete the following patterns

a
$3 \times +3 = 9$
$2 \times +3 = 6$
$1 \times +3 = ...$
$0 \times +3 = ...$
$...... \times +3 = ...$
$...... \times +3 = ...$

b
$3 \times -2 = -6$
$2 \times -2 = -4$
$1 \times -2 = ...$
$0 \times -2 = ...$
$...... \times -2 = ...$
$...... \times -2 = ...$

c
$-2 \times +1 = -2$
$-1 \times +1 = ...$
$...... \times +1 = ...$
$...... \times +1 = ...$
$...... \times +1 = ...$
$...... \times +1 = ...$

4 Work out the answer to each of these

a $+2 \times -3$ b $-3 \times +4$ c $-5 \times +2$ d -6×-3
e $-3 \times +8$ f $-4 \times +5$ g -3×-4 h -6×-1
i $+7 \times -2$ j $+2 \times +8$ k $+6 \times -10$ l $+8 \times +4$
m -15×-2 n $-6 \times -3 \times -1$ o $-2 \times +4 \times -2$

5 The answer to the question on this blackboard is −12.

Using multiplication and/or division signs write down at least 5 different calculations that give this answer.

$= -12$

6 Work out the answer to each of these

a $+12 \div -3$ b $-24 \div +4$ c $-6 \div +2$ d $-6 \div -3$
e $-32 \div +8$ f $-40 \div +5$ g $-32 \div -4$ h $-6 \div -1$
i $+7 \div -2$ j $+12 \div +6$ k $+60 \div -10$ l $+8 \div +4$
m $-15 \div -2$ n $-6 \times -3 \div -2$ o $-2 \times +6 \div -3$

7 Copy and complete the following multiplication grids

a

×	−2	3	−4	5
−3	6			
6				
−2				
5				

b

×	−1	−3	4	
−2		6		
		12		
−5				
7			−42	

c

×				−8
−2		−12		
	−15		21	
4			28	
	−30			

3

8 Find the missing number in each calculation. (Remember that the numbers without a + or − sign in front of them are actually positive, as we don't always show every positive sign when writing a calculation.)

a $2 \times -3 = \boxed{}$ **b** $-2 \times \boxed{} = -8$ **c** $3 \times \boxed{} = -9$

d $\boxed{} \div -5 = -15$ **e** $-4 \times -6 = \boxed{}$ **f** $-3 \times \boxed{} = -24$

g $-64 \div \boxed{} = 32$ **h** $\boxed{} \times 6 = 36$ **i** $-2 \times 3 = \boxed{}$

j $\boxed{} \times -6 = -48$ **k** $-2 \times \boxed{} \times 3 = 12$ **l** $\boxed{} \div -4 = 2$

m $5 \times 4 \div \boxed{} = -10$ **n** $-5 \times \boxed{} \div -2 = -10$ **o** $\boxed{} \times -4 \div -2 = 14$

9 Work out

a -2×-2 **b** -4×-4 **c** $(-3)^2$ **d** $(-6)^2$

e Explain why it is impossible to get a negative answer when you square any number.

10 Work out the following

a $2 \times -3 + 4$ **b** $2 \times (-3 + 4)$ **c** $-2 + 3 \times -4$ **d** $(-2 + 3) \times -4$

e $-5 \times -4 + 6$ **f** $-5 \times (-4 + 6)$ **g** $-12 \div -6 + 2$ **h** $-12 \div (-6 + 2)$

11 Put brackets in each of these to make them true

a $2 \times -5 + 4 = -2$ **b** $-2 + -6 \times 3 = -24$ **c** $9 - 5 - 2 = 6$

Extension Work

This is an algebraic Magic square.

What is the 'Magic expression' that every row, column and diagonal adds up to?

Find the value in each cell when $a = 7$, $b = 9$, $c = 2$

Find the value in each cell when $a = -1$, $b = -3$, $c = -5$

$a + c$	$c - a - b$	$b + c$
$b + c - a$	c	$a + c - b$
$c - b$	$a + b + c$	$c - a$

HCF and LCM

Remember that:

HCF stands for Highest Common Factor

LCM stands for Lowest Common Multiple

Look at the diagrams opposite. What do you think they are showing?

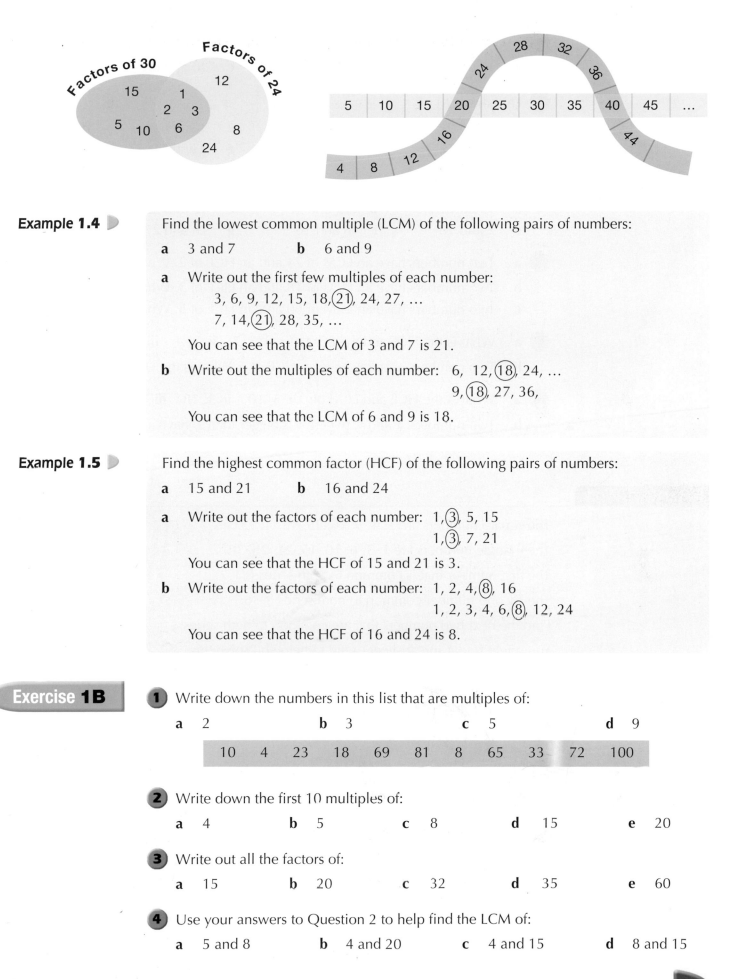

Example 1.4 ▷ Find the lowest common multiple (LCM) of the following pairs of numbers:

    a   3 and 7   **b**   6 and 9

    a   Write out the first few multiples of each number:

        3, 6, 9, 12, 15, 18, (21), 24, 27, …

        7, 14, (21), 28, 35, …

    You can see that the LCM of 3 and 7 is 21.

    b   Write out the multiples of each number: 6, 12, (18), 24, …

                                     9, (18), 27, 36,

    You can see that the LCM of 6 and 9 is 18.

Example 1.5 ▷ Find the highest common factor (HCF) of the following pairs of numbers:

    a   15 and 21   **b**   16 and 24

    a   Write out the factors of each number: 1, (3), 5, 15

                                       1, (3), 7, 21

    You can see that the HCF of 15 and 21 is 3.

    b   Write out the factors of each number: 1, 2, 4, (8), 16

                                       1, 2, 3, 4, 6, (8), 12, 24

    You can see that the HCF of 16 and 24 is 8.

Exercise 1B

1   Write down the numbers in this list that are multiples of:

    a 2   **b** 3   **c** 5   **d** 9

        10   4   23   18   69   81   8   65   33   72   100

2   Write down the first 10 multiples of:

    a 4   **b** 5   **c** 8   **d** 15   **e** 20

3   Write out all the factors of:

    a 15   **b** 20   **c** 32   **d** 35   **e** 60

4   Use your answers to Question 2 to help find the LCM of:

    a 5 and 8   **b** 4 and 20   **c** 4 and 15   **d** 8 and 15

5 Use your answer to Question 3 to help find the HCF of:

    a 15 and 20   **b** 15 and 60   **c** 20 and 60   **d** 20 and 32

6 Find the LCM of:

    a 5 and 9   **b** 5 and 25   **c** 3 and 8   **d** 4 and 6

    e 8 and 12   **f** 12 and 15   **g** 9 and 21   **h** 7 and 11

7 Find the HCF of:

    a 15 and 18   **b** 12 and 32   **c** 12 and 22   **d** 8 and 12

    e 2 and 18   **f** 8 and 18   **g** 18 and 27   **h** 7 and 11

8 **a** Two numbers have an LCM of 24 and an HCF of 2. What are they?

    b Two numbers have an LCM of 18 and an HCF of 3. What are they?

    c Two numbers have an LCM of 60 and an HCF of 5. What are they?

9 **a** What is the HCF and the LCM of: **i** 5, 7 **ii** 3, 4 **iii** 2, 11?

    b Two numbers, x and y, have an HCF of 1. What is the LCM of x and y?

10 **a** What is the HCF and LCM of: **i** 5, 10 **ii** 3, 18 **iii** 4, 20?

    b Two numbers, x and y, (where y is bigger than x) have an HCF of x. What is the LCM of x and y?

Extension Work

The square numbers are 1, 4, 9, 16, 25, 36, ...

The triangle numbers are 1, 3, 6, 10, 15, 21, 28, 36, ...

The first number that is common to both series is 1.

The second number common to both series is 36.

Find the next two numbers that are common to both series.

You might find a spreadsheet useful to help you solve this.

Powers and roots

Look at these cubes. Is cube B twice as big, four times as big or eight times as big as cube A? How many times bigger is cube C than cube A?

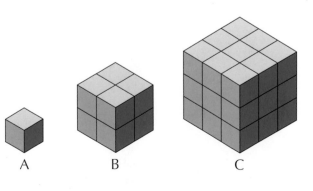

A   B   C

Example 1.6 ▷ Use a calculator to work out: **a** 4^3 **b** 5.5^2 **c** -3^4

  a $4^3 = 4 \times 4 \times 4 = 64$

  b $5.5^2 = 5.5 \times 5.5 = 30.25$ (most calculators have a button for squaring, usually marked x^2)

  c $-3^4 = -3 \times -3 \times -3 \times -3 = +9 \times +9 = 81$

Example 1.7 ▷ Use a calculator to work out: **a** $\sqrt{12.25}$ **b** $\sqrt{33124}$

  a Depending on your calculator, sometimes you type the square root before the number, and sometimes the number comes first. Make sure you can use your calculator. The answer is 3.5.

  b The answer is 182.

Exercise 1C

1 The diagrams at the beginning of this section show cubes made from smaller 1 cm cubes. Copy and complete this table.

Length of side	1 cm	2 cm	3 cm	4 cm	5 cm	6 cm	7 cm	8 cm	9 cm	10 cm
Area of face	1 cm²	4 cm²	9 cm²							
Volume of cube	1 cm³	8 cm³	27 cm³							

2 Use the table in Question 1 to work out:

  a $\sqrt{4}$ **b** $\sqrt{64}$ **c** $\sqrt{81}$ **d** $\sqrt{100}$ **e** $\sqrt{25}$
  f $\sqrt[3]{27}$ **g** $\sqrt[3]{125}$ **h** $\sqrt[3]{1000}$ **i** $\sqrt[3]{512}$ **j** $\sqrt[3]{729}$

3 You can see from the table in Question 1 that 64 is a square number (8^2) and a cube number (4^3)

  a One other cube number (apart from 1) in the table is also a square number. Which is it?

  b Which is the next cube number that is also a square number?
  (Hint: Look at the pattern of cube numbers so far, e.g. 1^3, 4^3, ...)

4 Find two values of x that make the following equations true:

  a $x^2 = 36$ **b** $x^2 = 121$ **c** $x^2 = 144$ **d** $x^2 = 2.25$
  e $x^2 = 196$ **f** $x^2 = 5.76$ **g** $x^2 = 2.56$ **h** $x^2 = 3600$

5 Use a calculator to find the value of:

  a 13^2 **b** 13^3 **c** 15^2 **d** 15^3 **e** 21^2 **f** 21^3
  g 1.4^2 **h** 1.8^3 **i** 2.3^3 **j** 4.5^2 **k** 12^3 **l** 1.5^3

6 Use a calculator to find the value of:

  a 2^4 **b** 3^5 **c** 3^4 **d** 2^5 **e** 4^4 **f** 5^4
  g 7^4 **h** 8^3 **i** 2^7 **j** 2^9 **k** 2^{10} **l** 3^{10}

7 Without using a calculator write down the values of: (Hint: use the table in question 1 and some of the answers from Question 6 to help you).

  a 20^2 **b** 30^3 **c** 50^3 **d** 20^5 **e** 70^2 **f** 200^3

8 $10^2 = 100$, $10^3 = 1000$, copy and complete the following table.

Number	100	1000	10 000	100 000	1 000 000	10 000 000
Power of 10	10^2	10^3				

9 Work out: **a** 1^2 **b** 1^3 **c** 1^4 **d** 1^5 **e** 1^6
  f write down the value of 1^{223}

10 Work out: **a** $(-1)^2$ **b** $(-1)^3$ **c** $(-1)^4$ **d** $(-1)^5$ **e** $(-1)^6$
  f write down the value of: **i** $(-1)^{223}$ **ii** $(-1)^{224}$

Extension Work

How many squares are there on a chessboard?

The answer is not 64!

For example in this square [figure] there are five squares

Four this size [figure] and one this size [figure]

in this square [figure] there are 14 squares

nine this size [figure] four this size [figure] and one this size [figure]

By drawing increasingly larger 'chessboards', work out how many squares there are and see if you can spot the pattern.

A computer spreadsheet is useful for this activity.

Prime factors

What are the prime factors of 120 and 210?

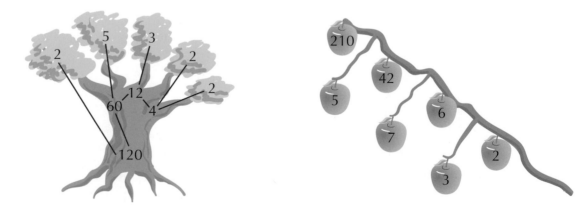

Example 1.8 ▷

Find the prime factors of 18.

Using a prime factor tree, split 18 into 3×6 and 6 into 3×2

So, $18 = 2 \times 3 \times 3 = 2 \times 3^2$

```
        18
       /  \
      3    6
          / \
         3   2
```

Example 1.9 ▷

Find the prime factors of 24.

Using the divide method

```
2 | 24
2 | 12
2 | 6
3 | 3
    1
```

So, $24 = 2 \times 2 \times 2 \times 3 = 2^3 \times 3$

Example 1.10 ▷

Use prime factors to find the highest common factor (HCF) and lowest common multiple (LCM) of 24 and 54.

$24 = 2 \times 2 \times 2 \times 3$, $54 = 2 \times 3 \times 3 \times 3$

You can see that 2×3 is common to both lists of prime factors.

Put these in the centre, overlapping, part of the diagram.

Put the other prime factors in the outside of the diagram.

The product of the centre numbers, $2 \times 3 = 6$, is the HCF

The product of all the numbers, $2 \times 2 \times 2 \times 3 \times 3 \times 3 = 216$, is the LCM.

24   2   2   3   54
    2   3   3

Exercise 1D

1 These are the prime factors of some numbers. What are the numbers?

    a $2 \times 2 \times 3$ **b** $2 \times 3 \times 3 \times 5$ **c** $2 \times 2 \times 3^2$ **d** $2 \times 3^3 \times 5$ **e** $2 \times 3 \times 5^2$

2 Using a prime factor tree, work out the prime factors of:

    a   8   **b**   10   **c**   16   **d**   20   **e**   28

    f   34   **g**   35   **h**   52   **i**   60   **j**   180

3 Using the division method work out the prime factors of:

    a   42   **b**   75   **c**   140   **d**   250   **e**   480

4 Using the diagrams below work out the HCF and LCM of:

    a

30   72
   5   2   2
     3   3   2

30 and 72

    b

50   90
   5   2   3
     5   3

50 and 90

    c

48   84
   2   2
   2   3   7
     2

48 and 84

5 The prime factors of 120 are $2 \times 2 \times 2 \times 3 \times 5$. The prime factors of 150 are $2 \times 3 \times 5 \times 5$.

Put these numbers into a diagram like those in Question 4.

Use the diagram to work out the HCF and LCM of 120 and 150.

6 The prime factors of 210 are $2 \times 3 \times 5 \times 7$. The prime factors of 90 are $2 \times 3 \times 3 \times 5$.

Put these numbers into a diagram like those in Question 4.

Use the diagram to work out the HCF and LCM of 210 and 90.

7 The prime factors of 240 are $2 \times 2 \times 2 \times 2 \times 3 \times 5$. The prime factors of 900 are $2 \times 2 \times 3 \times 3 \times 5 \times 5$.

Put these numbers into a diagram like those in Question 4.

Use the diagram to work out the HCF and LCM of 240 and 900.

8 Use prime factors to work out the HCF and LCM of:

    a   200 and 175   **b**   56 and 360   **c**   42 and 105

Extension Work

1 Show that 60 has 12 factors.
Find three more numbers less than 100 that also have 12 factors.

2 Show that 36 has nine factors.
There are seven other numbers less than 100 with an odd number of factors.
Find them all. What sort of numbers are they?

3 There are 69 three-digit multiples of 13. The first is 104 and the last is 988.
Five of these have a digit sum equal to 13.
For example, 715 is a multiple of 13 and $7 + 1 + 5 = 13$.
Find the other four.

You may find a computer spreadsheet useful for this activity.

Sequences 1

Example 1.11

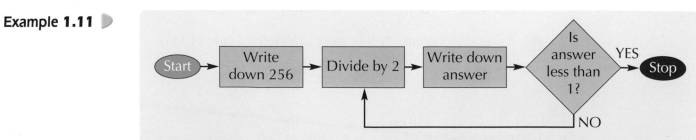

Follow the above flow diagram through and write down the numbers generated.
These are 256, 128, 64, 32, 16, 8, 4, 2, 1, 0.5

Example 1.12 ▷

For each of the following sequences, **i** describe how it is being generated, and
ii find the next two terms.

a 2, 6, 10, 14, 18, 22, ...
i the sequence is going up by 4
ii next two terms are 26, 30

b 1, 3, 9, 27, 81, 243, ...
i each term is multiplied by 3
ii next two terms are 729, 2187

Exercise 1E

1 Follow these instructions to generate sequences:

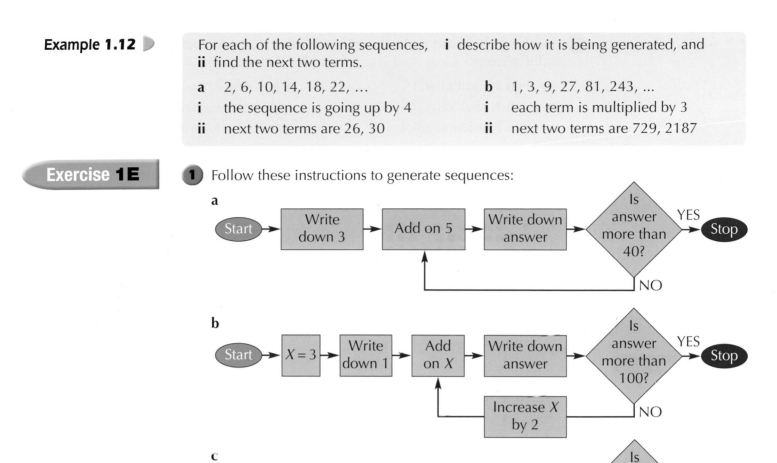

a

b

c

2 **a** What is the sequence of numbers generated by the flow diagram in Question 1, part b, called?

b Draw a flow diagram to generate the triangle numbers 1, 3, 6, 10, 15, 21. (Hint: look at the differences between consecutive terms and compare with those in the sequence from Question 1, part b.)

3 **a** Describe in words the sequence of numbers generated by the flow diagram in Question 1, part c.

b Draw a flow diagram to generate the sequence of powers of 2 (2, 4, 8, 16, 32, 64, ...).

4 Describe how the sequences below are generated:

a 1, 4, 7, 10, 13, 16, ...
b 1, 4, 16, 64, 256, 1024, ...
c 1, 4, 8, 13, 19, 26, ...
d 1, 4, 9, 16, 25, 36, ...

5 Write down four sequences beginning 1, 5, ..., and explain how each of them is generated.

6 Describe how each of the following sequences is generated and write down the next two terms:

a 40, 41, 43, 46, 50, 55, ...
b 90, 89, 87, 84, 80, 75, ...
c 1, 3, 7, 13, 21, 31, ...
d 2, 6, 12, 20, 30, 42, ...

7 You are given a start number and a multiplier. Write down at least the first six terms of the sequences (e.g. start 2 and multiplier 3 gives 2, 6, 18, 54, 162, 486, …).

   a   start 1, multiplier 3   **b**   start 2, multiplier 2

   c   start 1, multiplier −1   **d**   start 1, multiplier 0.5

   e   start 2, multiplier 0.4   **f**   start 1, multiplier 0.3

8 The following patterns of dots generate sequences of numbers.

   i   Draw the next two patterns of dots.

   ii Write down the next four numbers in the sequence.

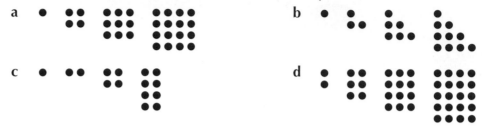

a   **b**

c   **d**

Extension Work

Fibonacci numbers

You will need a calculator.

The Fibonacci sequence is: 1, 1, 2, 3, 5, 8, 13, 21, …

It is formed by adding together the previous two terms, that is 5 = 3 + 2, 8 = 5 + 3, etc.

Write down the next five terms of the sequence.

Now divide each term by the previous term, that is 1 ÷ 1 = 1, 2 ÷ 1 = 2, 3 ÷ 2 = 1.5, 5 ÷ 3 = …

You should notice something happening.

You may find a computer spreadsheet useful for this activity.

If you have access to the Internet, find out about the Italian mathematician after whom the sequence is named.

Sequences 2

Paving slabs 1 metre square are used to put borders around square ponds. For example

1 × 1 m² pond
8 slabs

2 × 2 m² pond
12 slabs

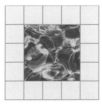

3 × 3 m² pond
16 slabs

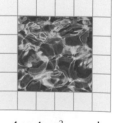

4 × 4 m² pond
20 slabs

How many slabs would fit around a 5 × 5 m² pond? What about a 100 × 100 m² pond?

Example 1.13 ▷ Using the rules given, generate the sequences:

a First term 5, increase each term by a constant difference of 6.

b First term 32, multiply each term by $-\frac{1}{2}$.

c First term 3, subtract 1 then multiply by 2.

a The sequence is 5, 5 + 6 = 11, 11 + 6 = 17, …, which gives 5, 11, 17, 23, 29, 35, …

b The sequence is $32 \times -\frac{1}{2} = -16$, $-16 \times -\frac{1}{2} = 8$, etc., which gives 32, –16, 8, –4, 2, –1, $\frac{1}{2}$, $-\frac{1}{4}$, …

c The sequence is $(3 - 1) \times 2 = 4$, $(4 - 1) \times 2 = 6$, $(6 - 1) \times 2 = 10$, etc., which gives 3, 4, 6, 10, 18, 34, 66, …

Exercise 1F

1 For the following arithmetic sequences, write down the first term a, and the constant difference d:

a 4, 9, 14, 19, 24, 29, …   **b** 1, 3, 5, 7, 9, 11, …

c 3, 9, 15, 21, 27, 33, …   **d** 5, 3, 1, –1, –3, –5, …

2 Given the first term a and the constant difference d, write down the first six terms of each of these sequences:

a $a = 1$, $d = 7$ **b** $a = 3$, $d = 2$ **c** $a = 5$, $d = 4$

d $a = 0.5$, $d = 1.5$ **e** $a = 4$, $d = -3$ **f** $a = 2$, $d = -0.5$

3 The following flow diagram can be used to generate sequences:

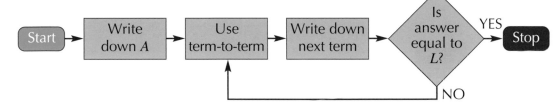

For example, if $A = 8$, the term-to-term rule is 'halve' and $L = 0.25$, the sequence is:

     8, 4, 2, 1, 0.5, 0.25

Write down the sequences generated by:

	A	Term-to-term rule	L
a	1 000 000	Divide by 10	1
b	1	Add 3, 5, 7, 9, 11, etc.	225
c	1	Double	1024
d	10	Subtract 5	–25
e	3	Add 2	23
f	1	Multiply by –2	1024
g	48	Halve	0.75
h	1	Double and add 1	63
i	2	Times by 3 and subtract 1	365
j	0	Add 1, 2, 3, 4, 5, 6, etc.	55

4 Write down a first term A and a term-to-term rule that you can use in the flow diagram in Question 3 so that:

    a   each term of the sequence is even;

    b   each term of the sequence is odd;

    c   the sequence is the five times table;

    d   the sequence is the triangle numbers;

    e   the numbers in the sequence all end in 1;

    f   the sequence has alternating odd and even terms;

    g   the sequence has alternating positive and negative terms.

5 The nth term of sequences are given by the rules below. Use this to write down the first five terms of each sequence:

    a $2n - 1$ **b** $2n + 3$ **c** $2n + 2$ **d** $2n + 1$

    e   What is the constant difference in each of the sequences in **a-d**?

6 The nth term of sequences are given by the rules below. Use this to write down the first five terms of each sequence:

    a $3n + 1$ **b** $3n + 2$ **c** $3n - 2$ **d** $3n - 1$

    e   What is the constant difference in each of the sequences in **a-d**?

7 The nth term of sequences are given by the rules below. Use this to write down the first five terms of each sequence:

    a $5n - 1$ **b** $5n + 2$ **c** $5n - 4$ **d** $5n + 3$

    e   What is the constant difference in each of the sequences in **a-d**?

Extension Work

In Questions 5, 6 and 7 above, there is a connection between the constant difference for the sequence and the number in front of n in the expression for the nth term. Can you see what it is?

Look at these sequences:

    nth term: $3n + 2$ Sequence 5, 8, 11, 14, 17, 20,...

    nth term: $4n - 1$ Sequence 3, 7, 11, 15, 19, 23, ...

    nth term: $10n + 5$ Sequence 15, 25, 35, 45, 55, 65, ...

Do they all have the same connection between their constant difference and the number in front of n?

Now can you spot a connection between the expression for the nth term and the first number of the sequence?

Here are some examples:

    i nth term $2n - 1$, first term 1   **ii** nth term $3n - 2$, first term 1

    iii nth term $5n - 1$, first term 4   **iv** nth term $9n - 3$, first term 6

If you spot the connection, then you should be able to write down the nth term of these sequences:

    a 3, 5, 7, 9, 11, ...   **b** 2, 7, 12, 17, 22, ...

    c 6, 10, 14, 18, 22, ...   **d** 1, 3, 5, 7, 9, ...

    e 4, 7, 10, 13, 16, ...   **f** 1, 7, 13, 19, 25, ...

Solving problems

An Investigation

At the start of the last section you were asked to say how many slabs would be needed to go round a square pond.

1 × 1 pond
8 slabs

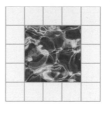

2 × 2 pond
12 slabs

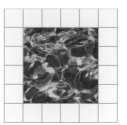

3 × 3 pond
16 slabs

4 × 4 pond
20 slabs

To solve this problem you need to: Step 1, break the problem into simple steps;
Step 2, set up a table of results;
Step 3, predict and test a rule;
Step 4, use your rule to answer the question.

Step 1 is already done with the diagrams given.

Step 2

Pond side	Number of slabs
1	8
2	12
3	16
4	20

Step 3 Use the table to spot how the sequence is growing.

In this case, it is increasing in 4s.

So a 5 × 5 pond will need 24 slabs (see right).

We can also say that the numbers of slabs (S) is 4 times the pond side (P) plus 4, which we can write as:

$$S = 4P + 4$$

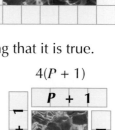

There are many other ways to write this rule, and many ways of showing that it is true.

For example: $4P + 4$ $2(P + 2) + 2P$ $4(P + 1)$

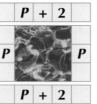

Step 4 We can now use any rule to say that for a 100 × 100 pond,
4 × 100 + 4 = 404 slabs will be needed.

Do the following investigations. Make sure you follow the steps above and explain what you are doing clearly. In each investigation you are given some hints.

1 Write a rule to show how many square slabs it takes to make a border around rectangular ponds.

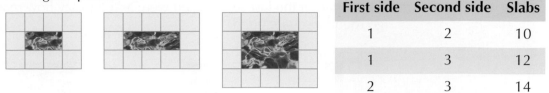

First side	Second side	Slabs
1	2	10
1	3	12
2	3	14

2 The final score in a football match was 5–4. How many different half-time scores could there have been?

For a match that ended 0–0, there is only one possible half-time result (0–0).

For a match that ended 1–2, there are six possible half-time scores (0–0, 0–1, 0–2, 1–0, 1–1, 1–2)

Take some other low-scoring matches, such as 1–1, 2–1, 2–0, etc., and work out the half-time scores for these.

Set up a table like the one in Question 1.

3 There are 13 stairs in most houses. How many different ways are there of going up the stairs in a combination of one step or two steps at a time?

Take one stair. There is only 1 way of going up it (1).

Take two stairs. There are two ways of going up (1+1, 2).

Before you think this is going to be easy, look at five stairs. There are eight ways of going up them (1+1+1+1+1, 1+1+1+2, 1+2+1+1, 1+1+2+1, 1+2+2, 2+1+2, 2+2+1, 2+1+1+1).

Work out the number of ways for three stairs and four stairs. Draw up a table and see if you can spot the rule!

What you need to know for level 5

- How to multiply and divide decimals by 10, 100 and 1000
- How to add, subtract, multiply and divide using negative and positive numbers
- How to solve problems using mathematics
- How to use simple formulae

What you need to know for level 6

- How to find the prime factor decomposition of a number
- How to find the least common multiple and the highest common factor of two or more numbers
- How to describe in words the rule for the next term or the nth term of a sequence where the rule is linear

National Curriculum SATs questions

LEVEL 5

1   *1996 Paper 2*

Windmills

This is a series of patterns with grey and black tiles.

 Pattern number 1

 Pattern number 2

 Pattern number 3

a   How many grey tiles and black tiles will there be in pattern number 8?

b   How many grey tiles and black tiles will there be in pattern number 16?

2   *2002 Paper 1*

Copy and complete these calculations by filling in the missing numbers in the boxes using only negative numbers.

☐ – ☐ = 5   ☐ – ☐ = –5

3   *1999 Paper 2*

Jeff makes a sequence of patterns with black and grey triangular tiles.

Pattern number 1   Pattern number 2   Pattern number 3

The rule for finding the number of tiles in pattern number N in Jeff's sequence is:

number of tiles = $1 + 3N$

a   The 1 in this rule represents the black tile.

What does the $3N$ represent?

b   Jeff makes pattern number 12 in his sequence.

How many black tiles and how many grey tiles does he use?

LEVEL 6

4   *2000 Paper 1*

a   Two numbers multiply together to make –15. They add together to make two.

What are the two numbers?

b   Two numbers multiply together to make –15, but add together to make –2.

What are the two numbers?

c   The square of 5 is 25. The square of another number is also 25.

What is that other number?

5 *1998 Paper 1*

This is a series of patterns with grey and white tiles.

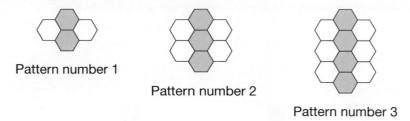

Pattern number 1

Pattern number 2

Pattern number 3

The series of patterns continues by adding 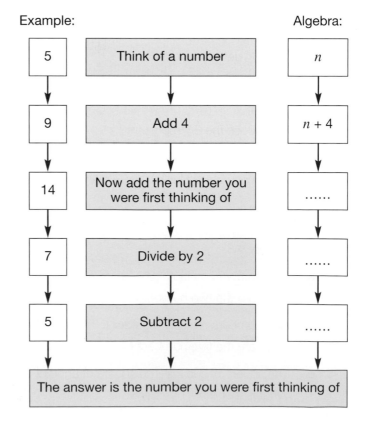 each time.

a Copy and complete this table:

pattern number	number of grey tiles	number of white tiles
5		
16		

b Copy and complete this table by writing expressions:

pattern number	expression for the number of grey tiles	expression for the number of white tiles
n		

c Write an expression to show the total number of tiles in pattern number n. Simplify your expression.

6 *2002 Paper 1*

You can often use algebra to show why a number puzzle works. Copy this puzzle and fill in the missing expressions.

Example: Algebra:

5	Think of a number	n
9	Add 4	$n + 4$
14	Now add the number you were first thinking of	......
7	Divide by 2	......
5	Subtract 2	......

The answer is the number you were first thinking of

CHAPTER 2

Shape, Space and Measures **1**

This chapter is going to show you

- how to identify alternate and corresponding angles
- how to calculate angles in triangles and quadrilaterals
- how to classify shapes using their properties
- how to calculate exterior angles of polygons
- how to construct angle bisectors and perpendicular lines

What you should already know

- How to identify parallel and perpendicular lines
- How to measure angles
- How to estimate acute, obtuse and reflex angles
- How to measure and draw shapes accurately using a ruler and protractor

Alternate and corresponding angles

Look at the picture of the railway. Can you work out why the angle between the arms of the signals and the post are both the same?

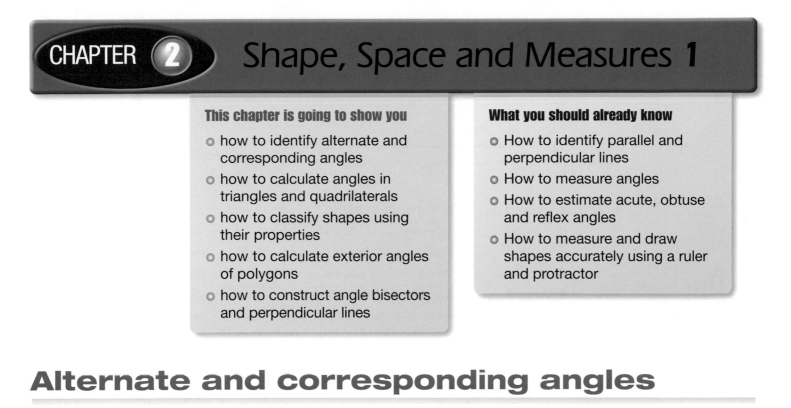

Example 2.1 ▷   Look at the diagram

    a   Name pairs of angles that are alternate angles.

    b   Name pairs of angles that are corresponding angles.

    a   The alternate angles are b and g, and d and e.

    b   The corresponding angles are a and e, b and f, c and g, and d and h.

1 Copy and complete the following sentences:

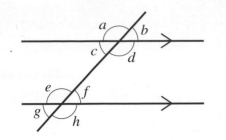

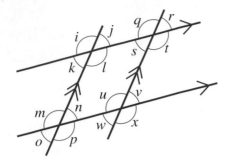

a   *a* and … are corresponding angles.
b   *b* and … are corresponding angles.
c   *c* and … are corresponding angles.
d   *d* and … are corresponding angles.
e   *e* and … are alternate angles.
f   *f* and … are alternate angles.

g   *k* and … are corresponding angles.
h   *u* and … are corresponding angles.
i   *l* and … are corresponding angles.
j   *r* and … are corresponding angles.
k   *n* and … are alternate angles.
l   *s* and … are alternate angles.

2 Work out the size of the lettered angles in these diagrams:

a

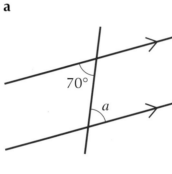

70°

a

b

75°

85°

b

c

c

42°

d

e

d

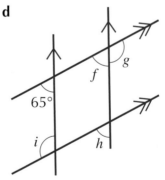

65°

f

g

i

h

e

l

k

33°

82°

m

j

f

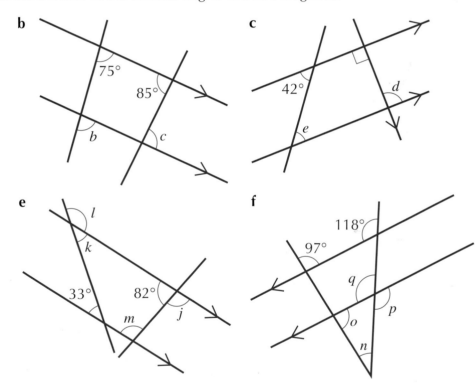

118°

97°

q

o

p

n

Extension Work

Prove that the angles in a triangle add up to 180°. Hint: Use parallel lines, as shown above, to help you.

Now use this result to prove that the angles in a quadrilateral add up to 360°.

2 Copy the table below and put each of these quadrilaterals in the correct column: square, rectangle, parallelogram, rhombus, kite, arrowhead and trapezium.

Rotational symmetry of order one	Rotational symmetry of order two	Rotational symmetry of order four

3 A quadrilateral has four right angles and rotational symmetry of order two. What type of quadrilateral is it?

4 A quadrilateral has rotational symmetry of order two and no lines of symmetry. What type of quadrilateral is it?

5 Rachel says:

A quadrilateral with four equal sides must be a square.

Is she right or wrong? Explain your answer.

6 Robert says:

A quadrilateral with rotational symmetry of order two must be a rectangle

Is he right or wrong? Explain your answer.

7 Sharon knows that a square is a special kind of rectangle (a rectangle with 4 equal sides). Write down the names of other quadrilaterals that could also be given to a square.

8 The three-by-two rectangle below is to be cut into squares along its grid lines:

This can be done in two different ways:

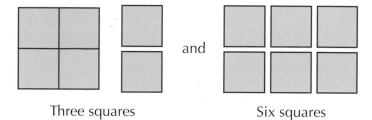

and

Three squares   Six squares

Use squared paper to show the number of ways different sizes of rectangles can be cut into squares.

1   The tree classification diagram below shows how to sort a set of triangles:

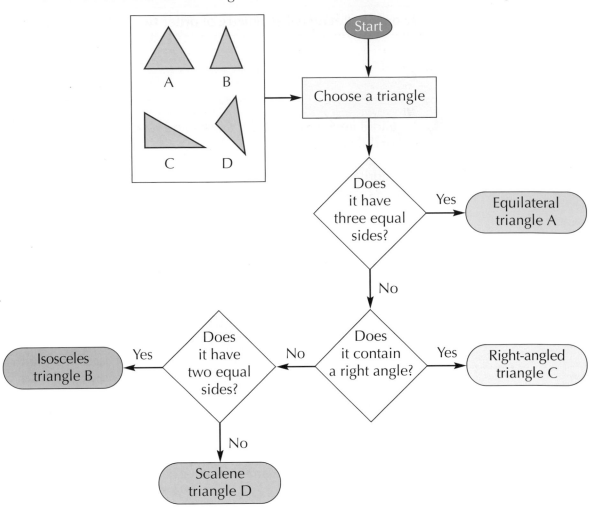

Draw a tree classification diagram to sort a given set of quadrilaterals. Make a poster to show your diagram and display it in your classroom.

2   The instructions below are to draw the parallelogram shown.

REPEAT TWICE:

    [FORWARD 10
    TURN RIGHT 120°
    FORWARD 6
    TURN RIGHT 60°]

Write similar instructions to draw different quadrilaterals. Choose your own measurements for each one. If you have access to a computer, you may be able to draw the shapes by using programs such as LOGO.

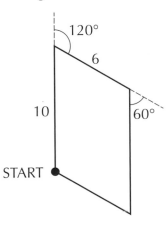

Constructions

The following examples are four important geometric constructions. Carefully work through them yourself. They are useful because they give exact measurements and are therefore used by architects and in design and technology. You will need a sharp pencil, straight edge (or ruler), compasses and a protractor. Leave all your construction lines on the diagrams.

Example 2.6 ▷ *To construct the mid-point and the perpendicular bisector of the line AB:*

- Draw a line segment AB of any length.
- Set compasses to any radius greater than half the length of AB.
- Draw two arcs, with the centre at A, one above and one below AB.
- With compasses set at the same radius, draw two arcs with the centre at B, to intersect the first two arcs at C and D.
- Join C and D to intersect AB at X. X is the mid-point of the line AB.
- The line CD is the perpendicular bisector of the line AB.

Example 2.7 ▷ *To construct the bisector of the angle ABC:*

- Draw an angle (∠) ABC of any size.
- Set compasses to any radius and, with the centre at B, draw an arc to intersect BC at X and AB at Y.
- With compasses set to any radius, draw two arcs with the centres at X and Y, to intersect at Z.
- Join BZ.
- BZ is the bisector of the angle ABC.
- Then ∠ABZ = ∠CBZ.

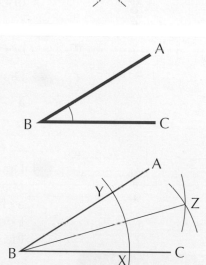

Example 2.8 ▷ *To construct the perpendicular from a point P to a line segment AB:*

- Set compasses to any suitable radius and draw arcs from P to intersect AB at X and Y.
- With compasses set at the same radius, draw arcs with the centres at X and Y to intersect at Z below AB.
- Join PZ.
- PZ is perpendicular to AB.

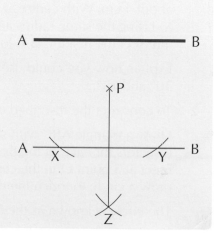

Example 2.9 ▷ *To construct the perpendicular from a point Q on a line segment XY:*

- Set compasses to a radius that is less than half the length of XY with the centre at Q. Draw two arcs on either side of Q to intersect XY at A and B. (You may have to extend the line XY slightly.)
- Set compasses to a radius that is greater than half the length of XY and, with the centres at A and B, draw arcs above and below XY to intersect at C and D.
- Join CD.
- CD is the perpendicular from the point Q.

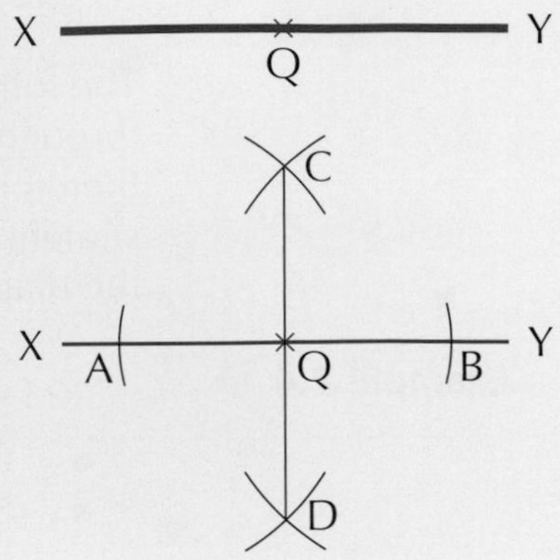

Exercise 2E

1 Draw a line AB 10 cm in length. Using compasses, construct the perpendicular bisector of the line.

2 Draw a line CD of any length. Using compasses, construct the perpendicular bisector of the line.

3 Using a protractor, draw an angle of 80°. Using compasses, construct the angle bisector of this angle. Measure the two angles formed to check that they are both 40°.

4 Using a protractor, draw an angle of 140°. Using compasses, construct the angle bisector of this angle. Measure the two angles formed to check that they are both 70°.

5 Draw a line XY that is 8 cm in length.

  a Construct the perpendicular bisector of XY.

  b By measuring the length of the perpendicular bisector, draw a rhombus with diagonals of length 8 cm and 5 cm.

6 Draw a circle of radius 6 cm and centre O. Draw a line AB of any length across the circle, as in the diagram (AB is called a chord). Construct the perpendicular from O to the line AB. Extend the perpendicular, if necessary, to make a diameter of the circle.

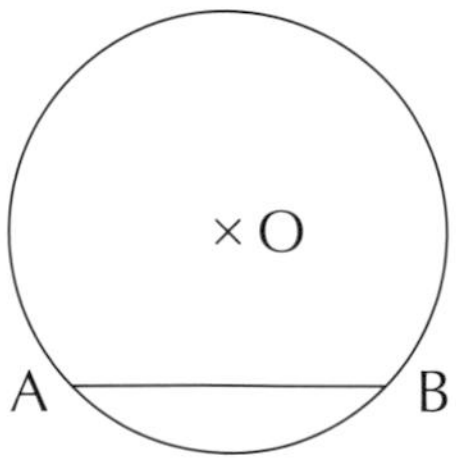

Extension Work

1 To construct an angle of 60°:

Draw a line AB of any length. Set your compasses to a radius of about 4 cm. With centre at A, draw a large arc to intersect the line at X. Using the same radius and, with the centre at X, draw an arc to intersect the first arc at Y. Join A and Y: ∠YAX is 60°.

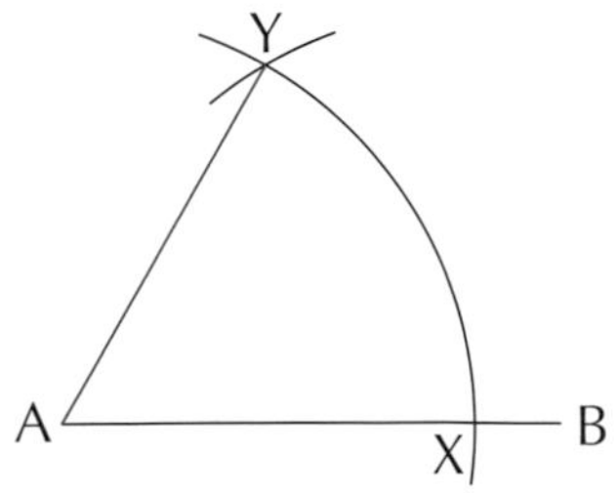

Explain how you could use this construction to construct angles of 30° and 15°.

2 To construct the inscribed circle of a triangle:

Draw a triangle ABC with sides of any length. Construct the angle bisectors for each of the three angles. The three angle bisectors will meet at a point O in the centre of the triangle. Using O as the centre, draw a circle to touch the three sides of the triangle.

The circle is known as the inscribed circle of the triangle.

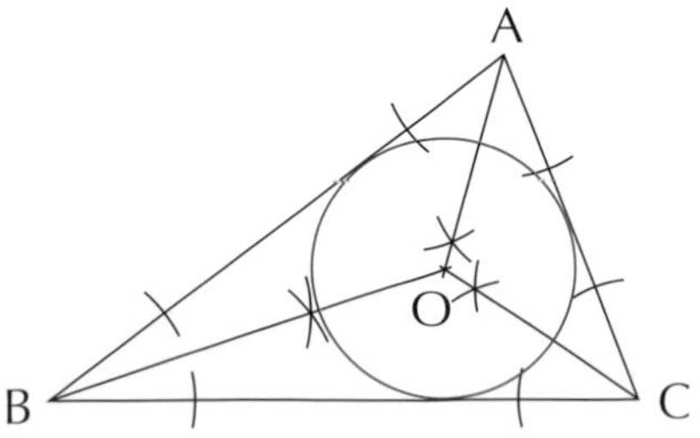

National Curriculum SATs questions

LEVEL 6

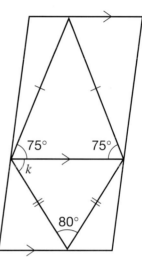

1 *2001 Paper 1*

The diagram (not drawn accurately) shows two isosceles triangles
inside a parallelogram.

a On a copy of the diagram, mark another angle that is 75°.
Label it 75°.

b Calculate the size of the angle marked k. Show your working.

2 *1997 Paper 1*

Kay is drawing shapes on her computer.

a She wants to draw the triangle shown.
She needs to know angles a, b and c.

Calculate angles a, b and c.

b Kay draws a rhombus:

Calculate angles d and e.

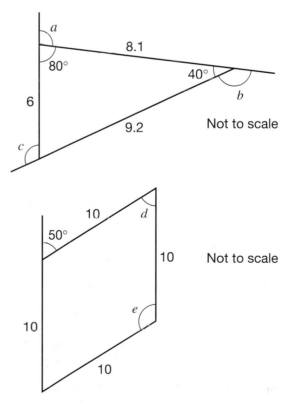

3   *1999 Paper 1*

The shape shown has three identical white tiles and three identical grey tiles.

The sides of each tile are all the same length. Opposite sides of each tile are parallel. One of the angles is 70°.

a   Calculate the size of angle *k*.

b   Calculate the size of angle *m*.
Show your working.

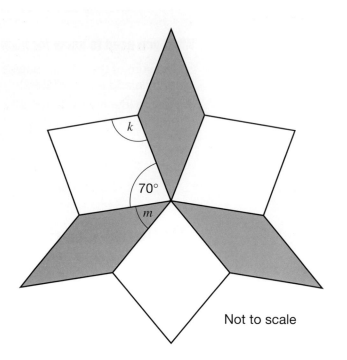

Not to scale

4   *2002 Paper 2*

The diagram shows a rectangle:

Work out the size of angle *a*. You must show your working.

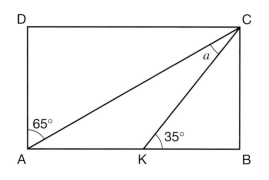

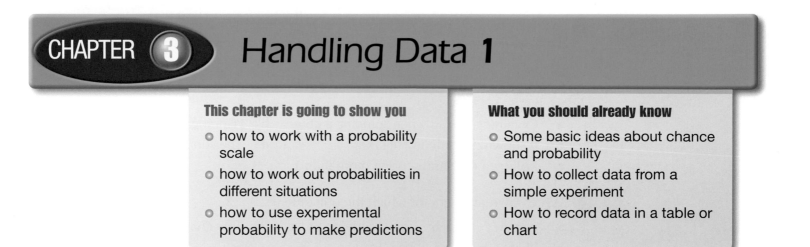

Handling Data 1

CHAPTER 3

This chapter is going to show you

- how to work with a probability scale
- how to work out probabilities in different situations
- how to use experimental probability to make predictions

What you should already know

- Some basic ideas about chance and probability
- How to collect data from a simple experiment
- How to record data in a table or chart

Probability

Look at the pictures. Which one is most likely to happen where you live today?

We use probability to decide how likely it is that different events will happen.

Example 3.1 ▶
Here are some words we use when talking about whether something may happen:

very likely, unlikely, certain, impossible, an even chance, very unlikely, likely

The two complete opposites here are impossible and certain, with an even chance (evens) in the middle, and so these can be given in the order:

impossible, very unlikely, unlikely, **evens**, likely, very likely, **certain**

Example 3.2 ▶
Which is more likely to happen: Flipping a tail on a coin or rolling a number less than 5 on a dice?

A coin can only land two ways (heads or tails), so provided the coin is fair, there is an even chance of landing on a tail.

On a dice there are four numbers less than 5 and two numbers that are not, so there is more than an even chance of rolling a number less than 5. So, rolling a number less than 5 is more likely than getting tails when a coin is flipped.

1

Impossible	Very unlikely	Unlikely	Evens	Likely	Very likely	Certain

Copy the probability scale above and put labels on it to show each of the following events:

a Obtaining a head when spinning a coin.   **b** Winning the lottery with one ticket.

c It snowing in July in England.   **d** The sun rising tomorrow.

e Rolling a dice and scoring more than 1.

2 Write down an event for which the outcome is:

a certain   **b** impossible   **c** fifty-fifty chance   **d** very unlikely

e likely   **f** very likely   **g** unlikely

3 Here are two grids:

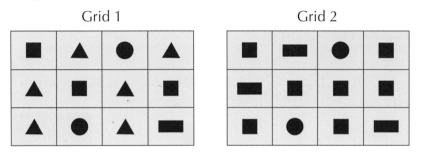

Grid 1   Grid 2

A shape is picked at random. Copy and complete the sentences:

a Picking a ...... from Grid ... is impossible.

b Picking a ...... from Grid ... is likely.

c Picking a ...... from Grid ... is unlikely.

d Picking a ...... from Grid ... is highly unlikely.

e Picking a ...... from Grid ... is fifty–fifty.

4 Bag A contains 10 red marbles, 5 blue marbles and 5 green marbles. Bag B contains 8 red marbles, 2 blue marbles and no green marbles. A girl wants to pick a marble at random from a bag. Which bag should she choose to have the better chance of:

Bag A   Bag B

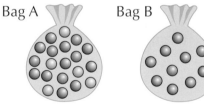

a a red marble?   **b** a blue marble?   **c** a green marble?

Explain your answers.

5 A coin is flipped 60 times. It lands on heads 36 times.

Do you think that the coin is biased? Explain your answer.

Extension Work

Carry out a survey by asking many people in your class to give you five different numbers between 1 and 20.

Record the results and write a brief report to say whether you think that each number has the same chance of being chosen.

Probability scales

The probability of an event:

$$P(\text{event}) = \frac{\text{Number of outcomes in the event}}{\text{Total number of all possible outcomes}}$$

Probabilities can be written as either fractions or decimals. They always take values between 0 and 1, including 0 and 1. The probability of an event happening can be shown on the probability scale:

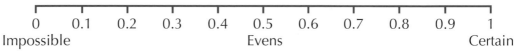

| 0 | 0.1 | 0.2 | 0.3 | 0.4 | 0.5 | 0.6 | 0.7 | 0.8 | 0.9 | 1 |

Impossible   Evens   Certain

If an event is the complete opposite of another event, such as raining and not raining, then the probabilities of each event add up to 1.

Look at the probability scale and see how many pairs of decimals you can find that add up to 1.

Example 3.3

The probability that a woman washes her car on Sunday is 0.7. What is the probability that she does not wash her car?

These two events are opposites of each other, so the probabilities add up to 1. The probability that she does not wash her car is 1 − 0.7 = 0.3.

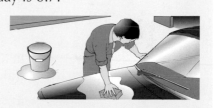

Example 3.4

A girl plays a game of tennis. The probability that she wins is $\frac{2}{3}$. What is the probability that she loses?

Probability of not winning (losing) $= 1 - \frac{2}{3}$
$= \frac{1}{3}$

Example 3.5

Here are the probabilities of different events happening. What are the probabilities of these events not happening?

a 0.4   **b** 0.8   **c** 0.75   **d** 0.16   **e** $\frac{1}{4}$ **f** $\frac{3}{5}$ **g** $\frac{3}{8}$

The probabilities of the events not happening are:

a 1 − 0.4 = 0.6   **b** 1 − 0.8 = 0.2   **c** 1 − 0.75 = 0.25

d 1 − 0.16 = 0.84   **e** $1 - \frac{1}{4} = \frac{3}{4}$ **f** $1 - \frac{3}{5} = \frac{2}{8}$ **g** $1 - \frac{3}{8} = \frac{5}{8}$

Exercise 3B

1 Here is a probability scale:

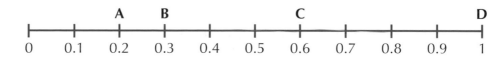

| | A | B | | | C | | | D |
| 0 | 0.1 | 0.2 | 0.3 | 0.4 | 0.5 | 0.6 | 0.7 | 0.8 | 0.9 | 1 |

The probability of events A, B, C and D happening are shown on the scale. Copy the scale and mark on it the probabilities of A, B, C and D not happening.

2 Copy and complete the table.

Event	Probability of event occurring (p)	Probability of event not occurring ($1 - p$)
A	$\frac{1}{4}$	
B	$\frac{1}{3}$	
C	$\frac{3}{4}$	
D	$\frac{9}{10}$	
E	$\frac{2}{15}$	
F	$\frac{7}{8}$	
G	$\frac{7}{9}$	

3 A card is chosen at random from a pack of 52 playing cards. Calculate the probability that it is:

a a black card   **b** an ace   **c** not an ace   **d** a diamond

e not a diamond   **f** not a 2   **g** not a picture   **h** not a king

I not a red card   **j** not an even number   **k** not the ace of spades

4 In a bus station there are 24 red buses, 6 blue buses and 10 green buses. Calculate the probability that the next bus to arrive is:

a green   **b** red   **c** red or blue   **d** yellow   **e** not green

f not red   **g** neither red nor blue   **h** not yellow

5 A bag contains 32 counters that are either black or white. The probability that a counter is black is $\frac{1}{4}$.

How many white counters are in the bag? Explain how you worked it out.

Extension Work

Design a spreadsheet to convert the probabilities of events happening into the probabilities that they do not happen.

Mutually exclusive events

You have a dice and are trying to throw numbers less than 4, but you are also looking for even numbers. Which number is common to both events?

When two events **overlap** like this, we say that the events are **not mutually exclusive**. This means they can both happen at once.

Example 3.6 ▶

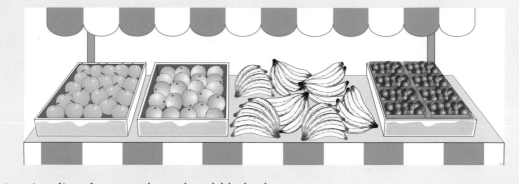

Here is a list of events about the old lady shown:

Event A: she chooses strawberries.
Event B: she chooses red fruit.
Event C: she chooses green apples.
Event D: she chooses red apples.
Event E: she chooses oranges.
Event F: she chooses bananas.
Event G: she chooses fruit with thick skins that need peeling.

She chooses one item only. State which of these pairs of events are mutually exclusive:

a A and B   **b** A and E   **c** B and C   **d** B and D   **e** E and F   **f** E and G

a   Strawberries are red fruit, so the events are **not mutually exclusive**.

b   Strawberries are not oranges, so the events are **mutually exclusive**.

c   Green apples are not red fruit, so the events are **mutually exclusive**.

d   Red apples are red fruit, so the events are **not mutually exclusive**.

e   Oranges are not bananas, so the events are **mutually exclusive**.

f   Oranges are fruits with thick skins that need peeling, so the events are **not mutually exclusive**.

Exercise 3C

1 A number square contains the numbers from 1 to 100:

Numbers are chosen from the number square. Here is a list of events:

Event A: A number chosen is greater than 50.

Event B: A number chosen is less than 10.

Event C: A number chosen is a square number (1, 4, 9, 16, …).

Event D: A number chosen is a multiple of 5 (5, 10, 15, 20, …).

Event E: A number chosen has at least one 6 in it.

Event F: A number chosen is a factor of 100 (1, 2, 5, 10, …).

Event G: A number chosen is a triangle number (1, 3, 6, 10, …).

1	2	3	4	5	6	7	8	9	10
11	12	13	14	15	16	17	18	19	20
21	22	23	24	25	26	27	28	29	30
31	32	33	34	35	36	37	38	39	40
41	42	43	44	45	46	47	48	49	50
51	52	53	54	55	56	57	58	59	60
61	62	63	64	65	66	67	68	69	70
71	72	73	74	75	76	77	78	79	80
82	82	83	84	85	86	87	88	89	90
91	92	93	94	95	96	97	98	99	100

State whether each of the following pairs of events are mutually exclusive or not:

a A and B **b** A and C **c** B and C **d** C and D
e B and F **f** C and F **g** C and G **h** D and E
i D and G **j** E and F **k** E and G **l** F and G

2 A sampling bottle contains 40 different coloured beads. (A sample bottle is a plastic bottle in which only one bead can be seen at a time.)

a After 20 trials a boy has seen 12 black beads and 8 white beads. Does this mean that there are only black and white beads in the bottle? Explain your answer.

b You are told that there are 20 black beads, 15 white beads and 5 red beads in the bottle. State which of the following events are mutually exclusive:

i Seeing a black bead and seeing a white bead.

ii Seeing a black bead and seeing a bead that is not white.

iii Seeing a black bead and seeing a bead that is not black.

iv Seeing any colour and seeing a red bead.

3 A till contains lots of 1p, 2p, 5p, 10p, 20p, 50p, £1 and £2 coins.

A woman is given two coins in her change. List all the different amounts of money that she could have received in her change.

4 Look back at Example 3.6. On one particular day the old lady decides to buy two types of fruit from bananas, apples, oranges or strawberries. List all the possible combinations that she could choose.

5 Each spinner is spun. Complete the table to show the different pairs of scores:

Spinner 1	Spinner 2	Total score
+2	0	2
+2	−1	1

Extension Work

Imagine a horse race between two horses (called A and B). They could finish the race in two different ways, AB or BA.

Now look at a three-horse race. How many ways can they finish the race?

Extend this problem to four horses, and so on. Put your results into a table. See if you can work out a pattern to predict how many different ways a 10 horse race could finish.

When you have finished this, then you can explore what the factorial (!) button does on a calculator (this may help you to solve the horse problem).

Calculating probabilities

Look at the spinners. Which one is most likely to land on red? Remember, the answer is not how many times a colour appears, but the probability that it will appear.

$$\text{Probability of event} = \frac{\text{Number of successes}}{\text{Total number of outcomes}}$$

Sometimes you will look at more than one event happening. To do this you can use diagrams, called **sample spaces**, to help you. Look at the sample space for a coin and a dice:

	1	2	3	4	5	6
Head	H, 1	H, 2	H, 3	H, 4	H, 5	H, 6
Tail	T, 1	T, 2	T, 3	T, 4	T, 5	T, 6

You can now work out the probability of throwing both a head and a 6.

Example 3.7 ▷ An ice-cream man sells 10 different flavours of ice cream. A girl picks a tub at random (without looking). What is the probability that the girl picks her favourite flavour?

She has only one favourite, so the probability that she picks that one out of 10 flavours = $\frac{1}{10}$.

Example 3.8 ▷ The contents of Toni's shopping bags are: bag 1 – tins of spaghetti and tins of beans; bag 2 – white bread and brown bread. One item is picked from each bag. List all the combinations that could be chosen.

Beans and white bread

Spaghetti and white bread

Beans and brown bread

Spaghetti and brown bread

Exercise 3D

1) A set of cards is numbered from 1 to 50. One card is picked at random. Give the probability that it:

    a   is even   **b**   has a 7 on it   **c**   has a 3 on it

    d   is a prime number   **e**   is a multiple of 6   **f**   is a square number

    g   is less than 10   **h**   is a factor of 18

2) Two pupils are chosen from a class with an equal number of boys and girls.

    a   Write down the four possible combinations that could be chosen.

    b   Jo says that the probability of choosing two boys is $\frac{1}{3}$. He is wrong. Explain why he is wrong.

3) A bag contains apples, bananas and pears. Two fruits are chosen at random. List the possible outcomes.

4 Jacket potatoes are sold either plain, with cheese or with beans. Clyde and Delroy each buy a jacket potato.

a Copy and complete the table:

Clyde	Delroy
plain	plain
plain	cheese

b Give the probability of:

i Clyde choosing plain

ii Delroy choosing plain

iii both choosing plain

iv Clyde choosing plain and Delroy choosing beans

v Clyde choosing beans and Delroy choosing cheese

vi both choosing the same

vii both not choosing plain

viii both choosing different

5 Two dice are rolled and the scores are added together. Copy and complete the sample space of scores.

	1	2	3	4	5	6
1	2	3				
2	3					

a What is the most likely total?

b Give the probability that the total is:

i 4   **ii** 5   **iii** 1   **iv** 12   **v** less than 7

vi less than or equal to 7   **vii** greater than or equal to 10

viii even   **ix** 6 or 8

Make up your own question using two different spinners as follows. Draw the spinners and put different numbers on each section. Now make a sample space diagram and write three of your own questions followed by the answers.

Experimental probability

Will the train be late again today?

Look at the picture. How could you estimate the probability that a train will be late?

You could keep a record of the number of times that the train arrives late over a period of 10 days, and then use these results to estimate the probability that it will be late in future.

$$\text{Experimental probability} = \frac{\text{Number of events in trials}}{\text{Total number of trials carried out}}$$

Example 3.9 ▷

An electrician wants to estimate the probability that a new light bulb lasts for less than 1 month. He fits 20 new bulbs and 3 of them fail within 1 month. What is his estimate of the probability that a new light bulb fails?

3 out of 20 bulbs fail within 1 month, so his experimental probability = $\frac{3}{20}$

Example 3.10 ▷

A dentist keeps a record of the number of fillings she gives her patients over 2 weeks. Here are her results:

Number of fillings	None	1	More than 1
Number of patients	80	54	16

Estimate the probability that a patient does not need a filling (there are 150 records altogether).

$$\text{Experimental probability} = \frac{80}{150}$$
$$= \frac{8}{15}$$

Example 3.11 ▷

A company manufactures items for computers. The number of faulty items is recorded:

Number of items produced	Number of faulty items	Experimental probability
100	8	0.08
200	20	
500	45	
1000	82	

a Copy and complete the table.

b Which is the best estimate of the probability of an item being faulty? Explain your answer.

a

Number of items produced	Number of faulty items	Experimental probability
100	8	0.08
200	20	0.1
500	45	0.09
1000	82	0.082

b The last result (0.082), as the experiment is based on more results.

1 A boy decides to carry out an experiment to estimate the probability of a drawing pin landing with the pin pointing up. He drops 50 drawing pins and records the result. He then repeats the experiment several times. Here are his results:

Number of drawing pins	Number pointing up
50	32
100	72
150	106
200	139
250	175

a From the results, would you say that there is a greater chance of a drawing pin landing point up or point down? Explain your answer.

b Which result is the most reliable and why?

c From these data, how could he estimate the probability of a drawing pin landing point up?

d What would his answer be?

e How could he improve the experiment?

2 A girl wishes to test whether a dice is biased. She rolls the dice 60 times. The results are shown in the table:

Score	1	2	3	4	5	6
Frequency	6	12	10	9	15	8

a Do you think the dice is biased? Give a reason for your answer.

b How could she improve the experiment?

c From the results, estimate the probability of rolling a 1.

d From the results, estimate the probability of rolling a 1 or a 4.

3 The number of winning raffle tickets sold in a charity event is recorded.

a Copy and complete the table:

Number of tickets sold	Number of winning tickets	Experimental probability
50	7	$\frac{7}{50} = 0.14$
100	15	
200	32	
500	75	

b Which experimental probability is the most reliable? Give a reason for your answer.

Extension Work

Decide on an experiment of your own. Write down a report of how you would carry it out and how you would record your results.

National Curriculum SATs questions

LEVEL 5

1 *1999 Paper 1*

A coin has two sides, heads and tails.

a Chris is going to toss a coin.

What is the probability that Chris will get heads? Write your answer as a fraction.

b Sion is going to toss two coins.

Complete a table of two columns to show the different results he could get.

c Sion is going to toss two coins.

What is the probability that he will get tails with both his coins? Write your answer as a fraction.

d Dianne tossed one coin.

She got tails.

Dianne is going to toss another coin.

What is the probability that she will get tails again with her next coin? Write your answer as a fraction.

2 *2000 Paper 2*

In each box of cereal there is a free gift of a card.

You cannot tell which card will be in a box. Each card is equally likely.

There are four different cards: A, B, C or D

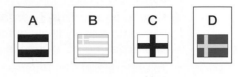

a   Zoe needs card A.

Her brother Paul needs cards C and D.

They buy one box of cereal.

What is the probability that the card is one that Zoe needs?

What is the probability that the card is one that Paul needs?

b   Then their mother opens the box. She tells them the card is not card A.

Now what is the probability the card is one that Zoe needs?

What is the probability that the card is one that Paul needs?

3   *1999 Paper 2*

Ann, Ben, Carl, Donna and Eric are friends.

They have four tickets for a concert.

The order in which they sit at the concert does not matter.

Ben must go to the concert.

If Eric goes to the concert, Donna must go too.

List all the different groups of four who could go to the concert. Remember, order does not matter.

LEVEL 6

4   *2000 Paper 1*

There are some cubes in a bag. The cubes are either red (R) or black (B). The teacher says:

> If you take a cube at random out of the bag, the probabiltiy that it will be **red** is $\frac{1}{5}$

a   What is the probability that the cube will be black?

b   A pupil takes one cube out of the bag. It is red.

What is the smallest number of black cubes there could be in the bag?

c   Then the pupil takes another cube out of the bag. It is also red.

From this new information, what is the smallest number of black cubes there could be in the bag?

d   A different bag has blue (B), green (G) and yellow (Y) cubes in it. There is at least one of each of the three colours.

The teacher says:

> If you take a cube at random out of the bag, the probabiltiy that it will be **red** is $\frac{3}{5}$

There are 20 cubes in the bag.

What is the greatest number of yellow cubes there could be in the bag? Show your working.

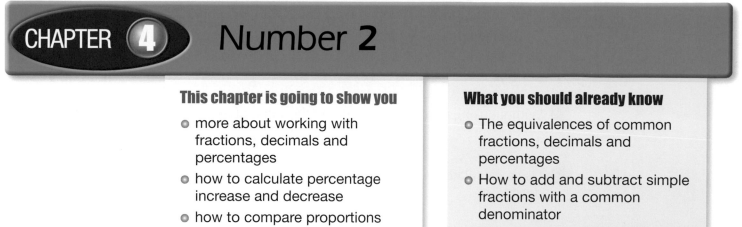

This chapter is going to show you

- more about working with fractions, decimals and percentages
- how to calculate percentage increase and decrease
- how to compare proportions using fractions and decimals

What you should already know

- The equivalences of common fractions, decimals and percentages
- How to add and subtract simple fractions with a common denominator
- How to calculate fractions and percentages of quantities

Fractions and decimals

These diagrams show shapes with various fractions of them shaded. Can you write them as a decimal, fraction and percentage?

Example 4.1 ▶

Work out the following decimals as fractions:

a   0.65

b   0.475

a $0.65 = \frac{65}{100} = \frac{13}{20}$ (cancel by 5)

b $0.475 = \frac{475}{1000} = \frac{19}{40}$

Example 4.2 ▶

Work out the following fractions as decimals:

a $\frac{2}{5}$

b $\frac{13}{60}$

c $\frac{4}{7}$

a $\frac{2}{5} = 0.4$ (you should know this)

b $\frac{13}{16} = 13 \div 16 = 0.8125$ (this is a terminating decimal because it ends without repeating itself)

c $\frac{4}{7} = 4 \div 7 = 0.571428571 \ldots = 0.\dot{5}7142\dot{8}$ (this is a recurring decimal because the six digits 5, 7, 1, 4, 2, 8 repeat infinitely; a recurring decimal is shown by the dots over the first and last recurring digits)

1 Write the following decimals as fractions with a denominator of 10, 100 or 1000 and then cancel to their simplest form if possible:

  a 0.24   **b** 0.45   **c** 0.125   **d** 0.348

  e 0.8   **f** 0.555   **g** 0.55   **h** 0.875

2 Without using a calculator, work out the value of these fractions as decimals:

  a $\frac{3}{5}$ **b** $\frac{3}{8}$ **c** $\frac{13}{20}$ **d** $\frac{18}{25}$

3 Use a calculator to work out, and then write down, the following terminating decimals:

  a $\frac{1}{2}$ **b** $\frac{1}{4}$ **c** $\frac{1}{5}$ **d** $\frac{1}{8}$

  e $\frac{1}{10}$ **f** $\frac{1}{16}$ **g** $\frac{1}{20}$ **h** $\frac{1}{25}$

  i $\frac{1}{40}$ **j** $\frac{1}{50}$

4 Use a calculator to work out, and then write down, the following recurring decimals:

  a $\frac{1}{3}$ **b** $\frac{1}{6}$ **c** $\frac{1}{7}$ **d** $\frac{1}{9}$

  e $\frac{1}{11}$ **f** $\frac{1}{12}$ **g** $\frac{1}{13}$ **h** $\frac{1}{14}$

  i $\frac{1}{15}$ **j** $\frac{1}{18}$

5 By looking at the denominators of the fractions in Questions 3 and 4, predict if the following fractions will be terminating or recurring decimals (and then work them out to see if you were correct):

  a $\frac{2}{3}$ **b** $\frac{4}{5}$ **c** $\frac{3}{7}$ **d** $\frac{2}{9}$

  e $\frac{3}{16}$ **f** $\frac{5}{8}$ **g** $\frac{7}{12}$ **h** $\frac{11}{14}$

  i $\frac{4}{15}$ **j** $\frac{39}{50}$

6 Describe, in words, a rule for the denominator of a terminating decimal.

7 Describe, in words, a rule for the denominator of a recurring decimal.

8 Give the larger of these pairs of fractions:

  a $\frac{7}{20}$ and $\frac{1}{3}$ **b** $\frac{5}{9}$ and $\frac{11}{20}$ **c** $\frac{7}{8}$ and $\frac{4}{5}$ **d** $\frac{2}{3}$ and $\frac{16}{25}$

9 Write the following lists of fractions in increasing order of size:

  a $\frac{2}{9}, \frac{13}{50}, \frac{6}{25}$ and $\frac{1}{4}$ **b** $\frac{5}{8}, \frac{3}{5}, \frac{17}{25}$ and $\frac{2}{3}$

10 a Work out $\frac{1}{9}, \frac{2}{9}, \frac{3}{9}$ and $\frac{4}{9}$ as recurring decimals.

  b Write down $\frac{5}{9}, \frac{6}{9}, \frac{7}{9}$ and $\frac{8}{9}$ as recurring decimals.

Extension Work

  a Work out the 'sevenths' (that is, $\frac{1}{7}, \frac{2}{7}, \frac{3}{7}, \frac{4}{7}, \frac{5}{7}, \frac{6}{7}$) as recurring decimals. Describe any patterns that you can see in the digits.

  b Work out the 'elevenths' (that is, $\frac{1}{11}, \frac{2}{11}, \frac{3}{11}, \frac{4}{11}, \frac{5}{11}, \frac{6}{11}, \frac{7}{11}, \frac{8}{11}, \frac{9}{11}, \frac{10}{11}$) as recurring decimals. Describe any patterns that you can see in the digits.

Adding and subtracting fractions

All of the grids below contain 100 squares. Some of the squares have been shaded in. The fraction shaded is shown below the square in its lowest terms. Use the diagrams to work out $1 - (\frac{1}{5} + \frac{7}{20} + \frac{22}{50} + \frac{1}{25})$.

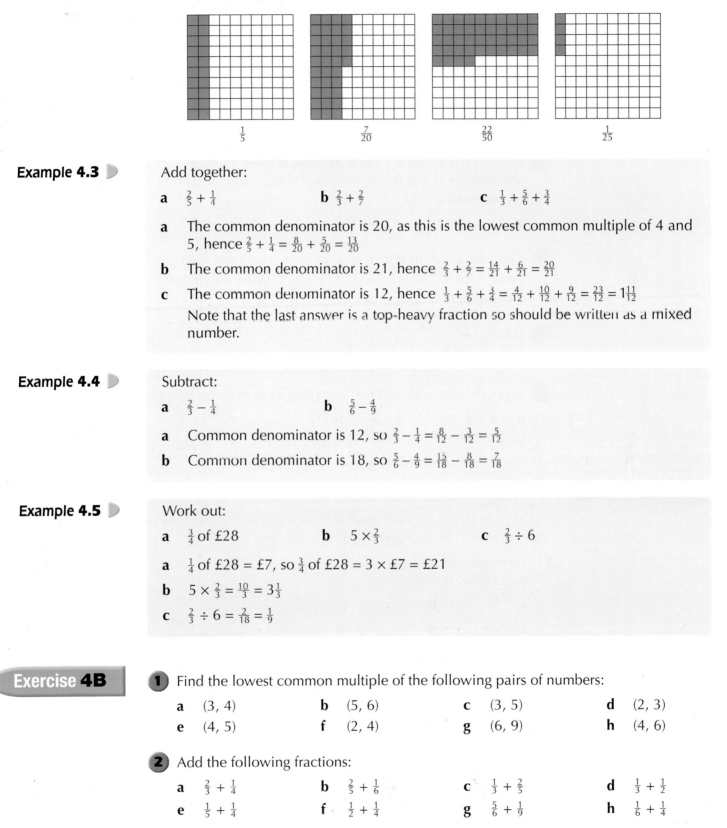

$\frac{1}{5}$ $\frac{7}{20}$ $\frac{22}{50}$ $\frac{1}{25}$

Example 4.3 ▷

Add together:

a $\frac{2}{5} + \frac{1}{4}$ **b** $\frac{2}{3} + \frac{2}{7}$ **c** $\frac{1}{3} + \frac{5}{6} + \frac{3}{4}$

a   The common denominator is 20, as this is the lowest common multiple of 4 and 5, hence $\frac{2}{5} + \frac{1}{4} = \frac{8}{20} + \frac{5}{20} = \frac{13}{20}$

b   The common denominator is 21, hence $\frac{2}{3} + \frac{2}{7} = \frac{14}{21} + \frac{6}{21} = \frac{20}{21}$

c   The common denominator is 12, hence $\frac{1}{3} + \frac{5}{6} + \frac{3}{4} = \frac{4}{12} + \frac{10}{12} + \frac{9}{12} = \frac{23}{12} = 1\frac{11}{12}$

Note that the last answer is a top-heavy fraction so should be written as a mixed number.

Example 4.4 ▷

Subtract:

a $\frac{2}{3} - \frac{1}{4}$ **b** $\frac{5}{6} - \frac{4}{9}$

a   Common denominator is 12, so $\frac{2}{3} - \frac{1}{4} = \frac{8}{12} - \frac{3}{12} = \frac{5}{12}$

b   Common denominator is 18, so $\frac{5}{6} - \frac{4}{9} = \frac{15}{18} - \frac{8}{18} = \frac{7}{18}$

Example 4.5 ▷

Work out:

a $\frac{3}{4}$ of £28   **b** $5 \times \frac{2}{3}$ **c** $\frac{2}{3} \div 6$

a $\frac{1}{4}$ of £28 = £7, so $\frac{3}{4}$ of £28 = 3 × £7 = £21

b $5 \times \frac{2}{3} = \frac{10}{3} = 3\frac{1}{3}$

c $\frac{2}{3} \div 6 = \frac{2}{18} = \frac{1}{9}$

Exercise 4B

1   Find the lowest common multiple of the following pairs of numbers:

    a   (3, 4)   **b**   (5, 6)   **c**   (3, 5)   **d**   (2, 3)

    e   (4, 5)   **f**   (2, 4)   **g**   (6, 9)   **h**   (4, 6)

2   Add the following fractions:

    a $\frac{2}{3} + \frac{1}{4}$ **b** $\frac{2}{5} + \frac{1}{6}$ **c** $\frac{1}{3} + \frac{2}{5}$ **d** $\frac{1}{3} + \frac{1}{2}$

    e $\frac{1}{5} + \frac{1}{4}$ **f** $\frac{1}{2} + \frac{1}{4}$ **g** $\frac{5}{6} + \frac{1}{9}$ **h** $\frac{1}{6} + \frac{1}{4}$

3 Subtract the following fractions:

a $\frac{1}{3} - \frac{1}{4}$ **b** $\frac{2}{5} - \frac{1}{6}$ **c** $\frac{2}{5} - \frac{1}{3}$ **d** $\frac{1}{2} - \frac{1}{3}$

e $\frac{2}{5} - \frac{1}{4}$ **f** $\frac{1}{2} - \frac{1}{4}$ **g** $\frac{5}{6} - \frac{1}{9}$ **h** $\frac{5}{6} - \frac{3}{4}$

4 Convert the following fractions to equivalent fractions with a common denominator, and then work out the answer, cancelling down or writing as a mixed number if appropriate:

a $\frac{1}{3} + \frac{1}{4}$ **b** $\frac{1}{6} + \frac{1}{3}$ **c** $\frac{3}{10} + \frac{1}{4}$ **d** $\frac{1}{8} + \frac{5}{6}$

e $\frac{4}{15} + \frac{3}{10}$ **f** $\frac{7}{8} + \frac{5}{6}$ **g** $\frac{7}{12} + \frac{1}{4}$ **h** $\frac{3}{4} + \frac{1}{3} + \frac{1}{2}$

i $\frac{2}{3} - \frac{1}{8}$ **j** $\frac{5}{6} - \frac{1}{3}$ **k** $\frac{3}{10} - \frac{1}{4}$ **l** $\frac{8}{9} - \frac{1}{6}$

m $\frac{4}{15} - \frac{1}{10}$ **n** $\frac{7}{8} - \frac{5}{6}$ **o** $\frac{7}{12} - \frac{1}{4}$ **p** $\frac{3}{4} + \frac{1}{3} - \frac{1}{2}$

5 Convert the following fractions to equivalent fractions with a common denominator, and then work out the answer, cancelling down or writing as a mixed number if appropriate:

a $1\frac{1}{3} - \frac{7}{8}$ **b** $2\frac{2}{3} + \frac{4}{7}$ **c** $1\frac{2}{3} + 2\frac{1}{4}$ **d** $3\frac{2}{3} - 1\frac{1}{5}$

6 Copy the diagram shown and shade in (using separate parts of the diagram): $\frac{1}{12}$, $\frac{5}{24}$, $\frac{1}{8}$, $\frac{1}{4}$ and $\frac{1}{6}$. Write down the answer, in its simplest form, to $1 - (\frac{1}{12} + \frac{5}{24} + \frac{1}{8} + \frac{1}{4} + \frac{1}{6})$.

7 Work out:

a $\frac{5}{8}$ of £32   **b** $\frac{3}{16}$ of 64 kg   **c** $\frac{2}{3}$ of £45   **d** $\frac{5}{6}$ of 240 cm

8 Work out (cancelling down or writing as mixed numbers as appropriate):

a $5 \times \frac{3}{4}$ **b** $7 \times \frac{4}{5}$ **c** $9 \times \frac{2}{3}$ **d** $4 \times \frac{7}{8}$

e $\frac{3}{4} \div 5$ **f** $\frac{4}{5} \div 8$ **g** $\frac{2}{3} \div 6$ **h** $\frac{5}{9} \div 7$

Extension Work

The ancient Egyptians only used unit fractions, that is fractions with a numerator of 1. So they would write $\frac{5}{8}$ as $\frac{1}{2} + \frac{1}{8}$.

1 Write the following as the sum of two unit fractions:

a $\frac{3}{8}$ **b** $\frac{3}{4}$

c $\frac{7}{12}$ **d** $\frac{2}{3}$

2 Write the following as the sum of three unit fractions:

a $\frac{7}{8}$ **b** $\frac{5}{6}$

c $\frac{5}{8}$ **d** $\frac{23}{24}$

Percentages

Example 4.6 ▷ Without using a calculator find:

a   The percentage of 25 that 18 is   b   The percentage of 300 that 39 is

a   Write as a fraction $\frac{18}{25}$. Multiply the top and bottom by 4, which gives $\frac{72}{100}$. So 18 is 72% of 25.

b   Write as a fraction $\frac{39}{300}$. Cancel the top and bottom by 3, which gives $\frac{13}{100}$. So 39 is 13% of 300.

Example 4.7 ▷ Find:

a   What percentage of 80 is 38?   b   What percentage of 64 is 14?

a   Write as a fraction $\frac{38}{80}$. Convert to a percentage by dividing through and multiplying by 100, which gives $47\frac{1}{2}$%.

b   Write as a fraction $\frac{14}{64}$. Convert to a percentage by dividing through and multiplying by 100, which gives 22% (rounded off from 21.875).

Example 4.8 ▷ Ashram scored 39 out of 50 in a Physics test, 56 out of 70 in a Chemistry test and 69 out of 90 in a Biology test. In which science did he do best?

Convert each mark to a percentage:

Physics   = 78%
Chemistry = 80%
Biology   = 77% (rounded off)

So Chemistry was the best mark.

Exercise 4C

1 Without using a calculator, work out what percentage the first quantity is of the second for the following:

a   32 out of 50   b   17 out of 20   c   24 out of 40   d   16 out of 25
e   122 out of 200   f   93 out of 300   g   640 out of 1000   h   18 out of 25

2 Use a calculator to work out what percentage the first quantity is of the second (round off to the nearest percent if necessary):

a   33 out of 60   b   18 out of 80   c   25 out of 75   d   26 out of 65
e   56 out of 120   f   84 out of 150   g   62 out of 350   h   48 out of 129

3 In the SATs test, Trevor scored 39 out of 60 in Maths, 42 out of 70 in English and 54 out of 80 in Science. Convert all these scores to a percentage. In which test did Trevor do best?

4 In a Maths exam worth 80 marks, 11 marks are allocated to Number, 34 marks are allocated to Algebra, 23 marks are allocated to Shape and 12 marks are allocated to Data Handling. Work out the percentage allocated to each topic (round the answers off to the nearest percent) and add these up. Why is the total more than 100%?

5 A table costs a carpenter £120 to make. He sells it for £192.

    a   How much profit did he make?

    b   What percentage was the profit of the cost price?

6 A dealer buys a painting for £5500. He sells it at a loss for £5000.

    a   How much did he lose?

    b   What percentage of the original price was the loss?

7 Mr Wilson pays £60 a month to cover his electricity, gas and oil bills. Electricity costs £24, gas costs £21 and the rest is for oil. What percentage of the total does each fuel cost?

8 My phone bill last month was £45. Of this, £13 went on Internet calls, £24 went on long-distance calls and the rest went on local calls. What percentage of the bill was for each of these types of call?

9 Last week the Smith family had a bill of £110.57 at the Supermarket. £65.68 was spent on food, £35.88 on drinks and £9.01 on cleaning products. Work out what percentage of the total bill was for food, drinks and cleaning products (round off the answers to the nearest percent). Add the three percentages up. Why do they not total 100%?

10 Fred drove from Barnsley to Portsmouth. The total distance was 245 miles. 32 miles of this was on B roads, 145 miles on A roads and 68 miles on motorways. What percentage of the journey was on each type of road?

Extension Work

    1   Write down 20% of 100.

    2   Write down 20% of 120.

    3   If £100 is increased by 20%, how much do you have?

    4   If £120 is decreased by 20%, how much do you have?

    5   Draw a poster to explain why a 20% increase followed by a 20% decrease does not return you to the value you started with.

Percentage increase and decrease

SPORTY SHOES

$\frac{1}{3}$ off all trainers

SHOES-FOR-YOU

30% off all trainers

Which shop gives the better value?

Example 4.9 ▷

a A clothes shop has a sale and reduces its prices by 20%. How much is the sale price of:

  i a jacket originally costing £45?   **ii** a dress originally costing £125?

  i 20% of 45 is 2 × 10% of 45 = 2 × 4.5 = 9. So the jacket costs
    £45 − £9 = £36.

  ii 20% of 125 is 2 × 10% of 125 = 2 × 12.50 = 25. So the dress costs
    £125 − £25 = £100.

b A company gives all its workers a 5% pay rise. How much is the new wage of:

  i Joan, who originally earned £240 per week?

  ii Jack, who originally earned £6.60 per hour?

  i 5% of 240 is $\frac{1}{2}$ × 10% of 240 = $\frac{1}{2}$ × 24 = 12. So Joan now earns
    £240 ┃ £12 = £252 per week.

  ii 5% of 6.60 is $\frac{1}{2}$ × 10% of 6.60 = $\frac{1}{2}$ × 66p = 33p. So Jack gets
    £6.60 + 33p = £6.99 per hour.

Exercise 4D

Do not use a calculator for the first four questions.

1 A bat colony has 40 bats. Over the breeding season the population increases by 30%.

  a How many new bats were born?
  b How many bats are there in the colony after the breeding season?

2 In a wood there are 20 000 midges. During the evening bats eat 45% of the midges.

  a How many midges were eaten by the bats?
  b How many midges were left after the bats had eaten?
  c What percentage of midges remain?

3 Work out the final amount when:

  a £45 is increased by 10%   **b** £48 is decreased by 10%
  c £120 is increased by 20%   **d** £90 is decreased by 20%
  e £65 is increased by 15%   **f** £110 is decreased by 15%
  g £250 is increased by 25%   **h** £300 is decreased by 25%
  i £6.80 is increased by 235%   **j** £5.40 is decreased by 15%

4 **a** In a sale all prices are reduced by 15%. Give the new price of items that previously cost:

    i £17.40   **ii** £26   **iii** £52.80   **iv** £74

  b An electrical company increases its prices by 5%. Give the new price of items that previously cost:

    i £230   **ii** £130   **iii** £385   **iv** £99

You may use a calculator for the rest of this exercise.

5 A petri dish contains 2400 bacteria. These increase overnight by 23%:

  a How many extra bacteria are there?
  b How many bacteria are there the next morning?

6 A rabbit colony has 230 rabbits. As a result of disease, 47% die off:

   a How many rabbits die from disease?

   b How many rabbits are left after the disease?

   c What percentage of the rabbits remain?

7 Work out the final price in euros when:

a €65 is increased by 12%		**b** €65 is decreased by 14%	
c €126 is increased by 22%		**d** €530 is decreased by 28%	
e €95 is increased by 132%		**f** €32 is decreased by 31%	
g €207 is increased by 155%		**h** €421 is decreased by 18%	
i €6.82 is increased by 236%		**j** €5.40 is decreased by 28%	

8 **a** In a sale all prices are reduced by $12\frac{1}{2}$%. Give the new price of items that previously cost:

      i £23.50   **ii** £66   **iii** £56.80   **iv** £124

   b An electrical company increases its prices by $17\frac{1}{2}$% so that they include value-added tax (VAT). Give the price with VAT of items that previously cost:

      i £250   **ii** £180   **iii** £284   **iv** £199

Extension Work

The government charges you VAT at $17\frac{1}{2}$% on most things you buy. Although this seems like an awkward percentage to work out, there is an easy way to do it without a calculator! We already know that it is easy to find 10%, which can be used to find 5% (divide the 10% value by 2), which can in turn be used to find $2\frac{1}{2}$% (divide the 5% value by 2), and 10% + 5% + $2\frac{1}{2}$% = $17\frac{1}{2}$%.

Find the VAT on an item that costs £24 before VAT is added.

10% of £24 = £2.40, 5% of £24 is £1.20, and $2\frac{1}{2}$% of £24 is £0.60.

So $17\frac{1}{2}$% of £24 = £2.40 + £1.20 + £0.60 = £4.20.

Work out the VAT on items that cost:

a £34   **b** £44   **c** £56   **d** £75   **e** £120   **f** £190

Real-life problems

Percentages occur in everyday life in many situations. You have already met percentage increase and decrease. Percentages are also used when buying goods on credit, working out profit and/or loss and paying tax.

Example 4.10   A car that costs £5995 can be bought on credit by paying a 25% deposit and then 24 monthly payments of £199.

   a How much will the car cost on credit?

   b What is the extra cost as a percentage of the usual price?

   a The deposit is 25% of £5995 = £1498.75. The payments are 24 × £199 = £4776. Therefore, the total paid = £1498.75 + £4776 = £6274.75.

   b The extra cost = £6274.75 − £5995 = £279.75. This as a percentage of £5995 is (279.75 ÷ 5995) × 100 = 4.7%

Example 4.11 ▷ A jeweller makes a brooch for £250 and sells it for £450. What is the percentage profit?

The profit is £450 – £250 = £200, which as a percentage of £250 is
200 ÷ 250 × 100 = 80%.

Example 4.12 ▷ Jeremy earns £18 000. His tax allowance is £3800. He pays tax on the rest at 22%. How much tax does he pay?

Taxable income = £18 000 – £3800 = £14 200. The tax paid is 22% of £14 200 = (£14 200 × 22) ÷ 100 = £3124.

Exercise 4E

1 A mountain bike that normally costs £479.99 can be bought using three different plans:

Plan	Deposit	Number of payments	Each payment
A	20%	24	£22
B	50%	12	£20
C	10%	36	£18

a Work out how much the bike costs using each plan.
b Work out the percentage of the original price that each plan costs.

2 A shop buys a radio for £55 and sells it for £66. Work out the percentage profit made by the shop.

3 A CD costs £10.99. The shop paid £8.50 for it. What is the percentage profit?

4 A car that costs £6995 can be bought by paying a 15% deposit, followed by 23 monthly payments of £189 and a final payment of £1900.

a How much will the car cost using the credit scheme?
b What percentage of the original cost is the extra cost on the credit scheme?

5 Work out the tax paid by the following people:

Person	Income	Tax allowance	Tax rate
Ada	£25 000	£4700	22%
Bert	£32 000	£5300	25%
Carmine	£10 000	£3850	15%
Derek	£12 000	£4000	22%
Ethel	£45 000	£7000	40%

6 A shop sells a toaster for £19.99 in a sale. It cost the shop £25. What is the percentage loss?

7 a What is £10 decreased by 10%?

b Decrease your answer to **a** by 10%.

c What is £10 decreased by 20%?

d A shirt in a clothes shop is reduced from its original price by 20% because it has a button missing. The shop is offering a further 15% off all marked prices in a sale. John the shop assistant says:

I don't need to work out the two reductions one after the other, I can just take 35% off the original price.

Is John correct? Explain your answer.

8 An insurance policy for a motorbike is £335. It can be paid for by a 25% deposit and then five payments of £55.25.

a How much does the policy cost using the scheme?

b What percentage is the extra cost of the original cost of the policy?

9 Mrs Smith has an annual income of £28 000. Her tax allowance is £4500. She pays tax at 22%.

a How much tax does she pay?

b It is discovered that her tax allowance should have been £6000. How much tax does she get back?

10 A TV costs £450. The shop has an offer '40% deposit and then 12 equal payments, one each month, for a year'.

a How much is the deposit?

b How much is each payment?

11 Which of these schemes to buy a three-piece suite worth £999 is cheapest?

Scheme A: No deposit followed by 24 payments of £56.

Scheme B: 25% deposit followed by 24 payments of £32.

Give a reason why someone might prefer scheme A.

What you need to know for level 5

- Equivalent fractions, decimals and percentages for a wider range and how to convert between them.
- How to calculate simple percentages.
- How to calculate simple fractions of quantities and how to multiply a fraction by an integer.

What you need to know for level 6

- How to use equivalent fractions, decimals and percentages to solve problems.
- How to add and subtract fractions with different denominators.
- How to calculate one quantity as a percentage of another.

National Curriculum SATs questions

LEVEL 5

1 *1998 Paper 1*

This is how Caryl works out 15% of 120 in her head.

a Show how Caryl can work out $17\frac{1}{2}$% of 240 in her head.

b Work out 35% of 520. Show your working.

> 10% of 120 is 12
> 5% of 120 is 6
> so 15% of 120 is 18

2 *2001 Paper 1*

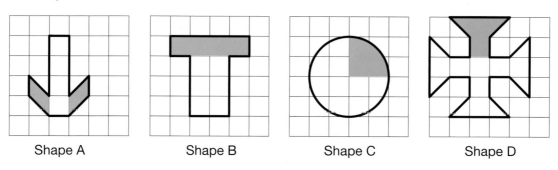

Shape A   Shape B   Shape C   Shape D

a What fraction of shape A is shaded?

b What percentage of shape B is shaded?

c Which of shape C or shape D has the greater percentage shaded?

Explain how you know.

LEVEL 6

3 *1997 Paper 2*

The table shows some information about pupils in a school.

	Left-handed	Right-handed
Girls	32	180
Boys	28	168

There are 408 pupils in the school. What percentage of the pupils are boys?

4 *1998 Paper 2*

The table shows the land area of each of the world's continents

Continent	Land area (in 1000 km²)
Africa	30 264
Antarctica	13 209
Asia	44 250
Europe	9 907
North America	24 398
Oceania	8 534
South America	17 793
World	148 355

a Which continent is approximately 12% of the world's land area?

b What percentage of the world's land area is Antarctica?

5 *1999 Paper 1*

a In a magazine there are three adverts on the same page.
In total, what fraction of the page do the three adverts use?

b An advert costs £10 for each $\frac{1}{32}$ of a page. An advert
uses $\frac{3}{16}$ of a page. How much does the advert cost?

> Advert 1 uses $\frac{1}{4}$ of the page
>
> Advert 2 uses $\frac{1}{8}$ of the page
>
> Advert 3 uses $\frac{1}{16}$ of the page

6 *2001 Paper 1*

On a farm 80 sheep gave birth to lambs. 30% of the sheep gave birth to two lambs.
The rest gave birth to just one lamb.

In total, how many lambs were born?

CHAPTER 5

Algebra **2**

This chapter is going to show you

- how to simplify expressions in algebra
- how to expand brackets
- how to use index notation with algebra

What you should already know

- how to substitute into algebraic expressions
- how to add, subtract and multiply with negative numbers

Algebraic shorthand

In algebra we try not to use the $\times$ sign as it is easily confused with the variable x, so we use shorthand, for example:

$$3 \times m = 3m; \quad a \times b = ab; \quad w \times 7 = 7w; \quad d \times 4c = 4cd; \quad n \times (d + t) = n(d + t)$$

The use of the equals sign

When we use the = sign, each side of the sign must have the same value. The two sides may look different, but will still be equal.

Example 5.1 ▷

Which of the following expressions are equal to each other? Write correct mathematical statements for those that equal each other.

$$a + b \qquad\qquad b - a \qquad\qquad ab \qquad\qquad \frac{b}{a}$$
$$bc$$
$$\frac{a}{b} \qquad\qquad b + a \qquad\qquad a - b$$

We can pick out $a + b$ as being equal to $b + a$ ($a + b = b + a$) and ab as being equal to ba ($ab = ba$). None of the others are the same.

Example 5.2 ▷

Solve the equation $3x + 2 = 23$

We subtract the same value, 2, from both side to keep the sides equal:

$$3x + 2 - 2 = 23 - 2$$

so: $3x = 21$

We now divide both sides by 3, again to keep both sides the equal:

$$\frac{3x}{3} = \frac{21}{3}$$

so: $x = 7$

Example 5.3 ▷

Simplify these expressions:

a $\quad 4a \times b$ **b** $\quad 9p \times 2$ **c** $\quad 3h \times 4i$

Leave out the multiplication sign and write the number to the left of the letters:

a $\quad 4a \times b = 4ab$ **b** $\quad 9p \times 2 = 18p$ **c** $\quad 3h \times 4i = 12hi$

1 Write each of these expressions in as simple a way as possible:

a	$3 \times n$	**b**	$5 \times n$	**c**	$7 \times m$
d	$8 \times t$	**e**	$a \times b$	**f**	$m \times n$
g	$p \times 5$	**h**	$m6$	**i**	$a \times (b + c)$
j	$m \times (p + q)$	**k**	$(a + b) \times c$	**l**	$a \times b \times c$
m	$m \div 3$	**n**	$5 \div n$	**p**	$(a + b) \div c$
q	$7 \div (m + n)$	**r**	$fg2$	**s**	$j5e$
t	$b \times (a + 3)$	**u**	$(5 + g) \div 3$		

2 Simplify the following expressions.

a	$h \times 4p$	**b**	$4s \times t$	**c**	$2m \times 4n$	**d**	$5w \times 5x$
e	$b \times 9c$	**f**	$3b \times 4c \times 2d$	**g**	$4g \times f \times 3a$		

3 Solve the following equations, making correct use of the equals sign.

a	$2x + 1 = 11$	**b**	$4x - 3 = 5$	**c**	$5x + 4 = 19$
d	$2x - 1 = 13$	**e**	$4x + 3 = 9$	**f**	$6x - 3 = 12$
g	$10x + 7 = 12$	**h**	$2x - 5 = 10$	**i**	$3x - 12 = 33$
j	$7x + 3 = 80$	**k**	$5x + 8 = 73$	**l**	$9x - 7 = 65$

4 Find the pairs of expressions in each box that are equal to each other and write them down; the first one is done for you:

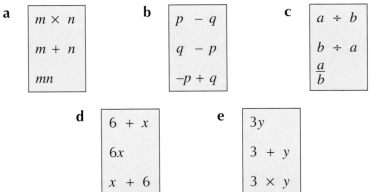

5 Only some of the statements below are true. Write a list of those that are.

a $b + c = d + e$ is the same as $d + e = b + c$

b $a - b = 6$ is the same as $6 = a - b$

c $5x = x + 3$ is the same as $x = 5x + 3$

d $5 - 2x = 8$ is the same as $8 = 2x - 5$

e $ab - bc = T$ is the same as $T = ab - bc$

Show by the use of substitution which of the following are either not true or may be true:

1 $m(b + c) = mb + mc$

2 $(m + n) \times (p + q) = mp + nq$

3 $(m + n) \times (m - n) = (m \times m) - (n \times n)$

4 $a(b + c) + d(b + c) = (a + d) \times (b + c)$

Like terms

5 apples + 3 apples can be simplified to 8 apples. Similarly, we can simplify $5a + 3a$ to $8a$. $5a$ and $3a$ are called **like terms**, which can be combined because they contain exactly the same letters.

5 apples + 3 bananas cannot be simplified. Similarly, $5a + 3b$ cannot be simplified, because $5a$ and $3b$ are **unlike** terms so they can't be combined.

Example 5.4

a $5p - 2p = 3p$

b $5ab + 3ab = 8ab$

c $3x^2 + 6x^2 = 9x^2$

d $7y - 9y = -2y$ (because $7 - 9 = -2$)

e $-3u - 6u = -9u$ (because $-3 - 6 = -9$)

f $5a + 2a + 3b = 7a + 3b$

g $5p - 2p + 7y - 9y = 3p - 2y$

h $8t + 3i - 6t - i = 8t - 6t + 3i - i$
$$= 2t + 2i$$
(put the like terms together before combining)

Exercise 5B

1 Make a list of the terms in each of the following.

a $4a + 2d - 6c$ b $5x - 3 = 7$ c $3x^2 + 4x + 5$ d $9 - 2u - 7$

2 Simplify the following expressions.

a $5h + 6h$

b $4p + p$

c $9u - 3u$

d $3b - 8b$

e $-2j + 7j$

f $-6r - 6r$

g $2k + k + 3k$

h $9y - y$

i $7d - 2d + 5d$

j $10i + 3i - 6i$

k $2b - 5b + 6b$

l $-2b + 5b - 7b$

m $3xy + 6xy$

n $4p^2 + 7p^2$

o $5ab - 10ab$

p $5a^2 + 2a^2 - 3a^2$

q $4fg - 6fg - 8fg$

3 Simplify the following expressions.

a $6h + 2h + 5g$

b $4g - 2g + 8m$

c $8f + 7d + 3d$

d $4x + 5y + 7x$

e $6q + 3r - r$

f $4 + 5s - 3s$

g $c + 2c + 3$

h $12b + 7 + 2b$

i $7w - 7 + 7w$

j $2bf + 4bf + 5g$

k $7d + 5d^2 - 2d^2$

l $6st - 2st + 5t$

m $4s - 7s + 2t$

n $-5h + 2i + 3h$

o $4y - 2w - 7w$

4 Simplify the following expressions.

a $9e + 4e + 7f + 2f$ b $10u - 4u + 9t - 2t$ c $b + 3b + 5d - 2d$

d $4a + 5c + 3a + 2c$ e $f + 2g + 3g + 5f$ f $9h + 4i - 7h + 2i$

g $7p + 8q - 6p - 3q$ h $14j - 5k + 5j + 9k$ i $4u - 5t - 6u + 7t$

j $2s + 5t - 9t + 3s$ k $5p - 2q - 7p + 3q$ l $-2d + 5e - 4d - 9e$

Expanding brackets

When a number multiplies a bracket, it multiplies every term inside the bracket. This is called **multiplying out** or **expanding** the bracket.

Example 5.5

a $3(a + b) = 3a + 3b$

b $4(2s - 3) = 8s - 12$

c $m(2n + 4) = 2mn + 4m$

When a negative number multiplies a bracket, it changes all the signs in the bracket.

Example 5.6

a $-2(x + y) = -2x - 2y$

b $-5(2d - 4e) = -10d + 20e$

c $-(2a + 4b) = -2a - 4b$

d $-(3x - 2) = -3x + 2$

After expanding brackets, it's often possible to simplify the answer.

Example 5.7

a $4m + 2(m - 3n) = 4m + 2m - 6n = 6m - 6n$

b $3(2w + 3v) + 2(4w - v) = 6w + 9v + 8w - 2v = 14w + 7v$

c $4(u - 3t) - 2(4u - t) = 4u - 12t - 8u + 2t = -4u - 10t$

Exercise 5C

1 Expand the following brackets.

a $5(p + q)$ b $9(m - n)$ c $s(t + u)$

d $4(3d + 2)$ e $a(2b + c)$ f $3(5j - 2k)$

g $e(5 + 2f)$ h $10(13 - 5n)$ i $6(4g + 3h)$

j $8(a + b + c)$

2 Expand the following brackets.

a $-(a + b)$ b $-(q - p)$ c $-(3p + 4)$

d $-(7 - 2x)$ e $-3(g + 2)$ f $-2(d - f)$

g $-5(2h + 3i)$ h $-4(6d - 3f)$ i $-3(-2j + k)$

3 Expand and simplify the following expressions.

a $3w + 2(w + x)$ b $7(d + f) - 2d$ c $4h + 5(2h + 3s)$

d $12x + 4(3y + 2x)$ e $2(2m - 3n) - 8n$ f $16p + 3(3q - 4p)$

4 Expand and simplify the following expressions.

a $4(a + b) + 2(a + b)$ b $3(2i + j) + 5(3i + 4j)$

c $6(5p + 2q) + 3(3p + q)$ d $5(d + f) + 3(d - f)$

e $7(2e + t) + 2(e - 3t)$ f $2(3x - 2y) + 6(2x + y)$

g $5(m - x) + 3(2m + x)$ h $7(4u - 3k) + 5(2u - k)$

5 Expand and simplify the following expressions.

a $8h - (3h + 2k)$ b $6v - (t + 2v)$ c $9 - (a + 2)$

d $7p - (3p - 5q)$ e $12 - (3e - 4)$ f $4a - (5b - 6a)$

6 Expand and simplify the following expressions.

a $5(m + n) - (3m + 2n)$ b $8(g + 3h) - 2(2g + h)$

c $7(d + 2e) - 3(2d - 3e)$ d $6(2 - 3x) - 3(2 - 5x)$

Using algebra and shapes

Example 5.8 State **a** the perimeter and **b** the area of the rectangle below:

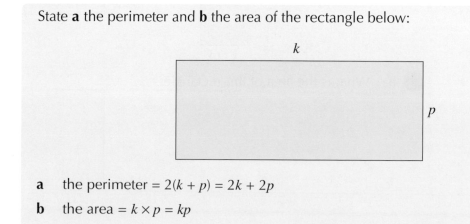

a the perimeter $= 2(k + p) = 2k + 2p$

b the area $= k \times p = kp$

Example 5.9 ▶

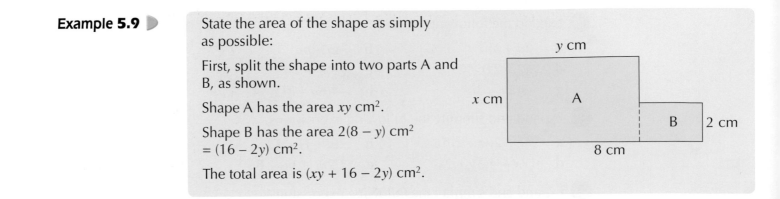

State the area of the shape as simply as possible:

First, split the shape into two parts A and B, as shown.

Shape A has the area xy cm².

Shape B has the area $2(8 - y)$ cm²
$= (16 - 2y)$ cm².

The total area is $(xy + 16 - 2y)$ cm².

Exercise 5D

1 Write down as simply as possible the length of the perimeter of each of these shapes:

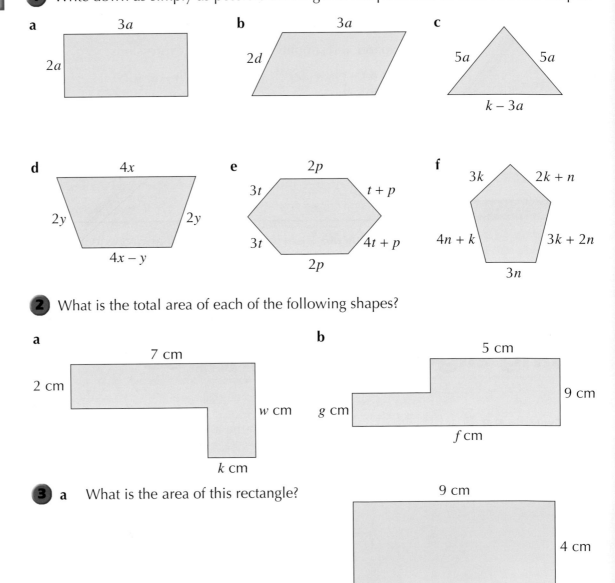

a 3a 2a

b 3a 2d

c 5a 5a k − 3a

d 4x 2y 2y 4x − y

e 2p 3t t + p 3t 4t + p 2p

f 3k 2k + n 4n + k 3k + 2n 3n

2 What is the total area of each of the following shapes?

a 7 cm 2 cm w cm k cm

b 5 cm g cm 9 cm f cm

3 a What is the area of this rectangle?

9 cm 4 cm

The rectangle has been divided into four separate rectangles below:

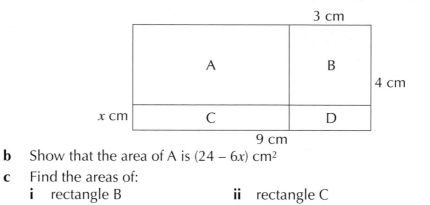

b Show that the area of A is $(24 - 6x)$ cm²

c Find the areas of:
   i rectangle B   **ii** rectangle C   **iii** rectangle D

d Show that when you add up the areas of the four rectangles A, B, C and D, it comes to the same answer that you had in **a**.

4 Write down the area of each smaller rectangle in the larger rectangle:

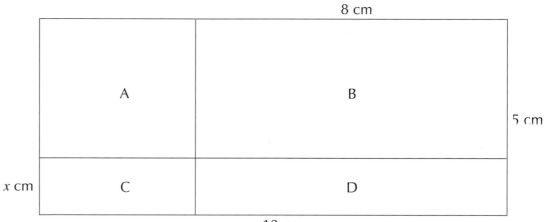

5 The expression in each box is made by adding the expressions in the two boxes it stands on. Copy the diagrams and fill in the missing expressions:

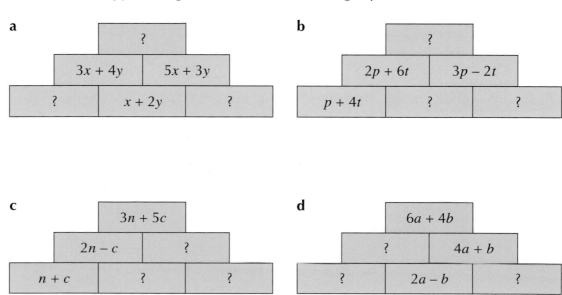

1 Use a spreadsheet to verify that $3a + 3b$ is always the same as $3(a + b)$:

A	B	C	D
put any number in A	put any number in B	put in the formula 3*A1 + 3*B1	put in the formula 3*(A1 + B1)

Copy the formula from C1 and D1 down to about C20 and D20. Put a variety of numbers in each row of columns A and B. Check that for any type of number, negative and decimal, the value in cell C = cell D for each row.

2 Use a spreadsheet to verify that $(a + b) \times (a - b)$ is always the same as $a^2 - b^2$.

Use of index notation with algebra

You can save time by writing $5 \times 5 \times 5$ as 5^3 using index notation.

In the same way, $m \times m \times m$ or mmm can be written briefly as m^3.

Example 5.10

a $x \times x = x^2$

b $4m \times 3m = 12mm = 12m^2$

c $2a \times 3a \times 5a = 30aaa = 30a^3$

Example 5.11

Expand and simplify: **a** $3m(2m - 4n)$ **b** $a(a + 4b) - b(2a - 5b)$.

a $3m(2m - 4n) = 6m^2 - 12mn$

b $a(a + 4b) - b(2a - 5b) = a^2 + 4ab - 2ba + 5b^2$
$$= a^2 + 2ab + 5b^2$$

Exercise 5E

1 Write the following expressions using index form.

a $a \times a \times a \times a \times a$

b $r \times r \times r \times r \times r \times r \times r$

c $b \times b \times b \times b \times b \times b \times b \times b \times b$

d $m \times m \times m \times m \times m \times m \times m \times m \times m \times m \times m \times m \times m$

e $4a \times 3a$

f $p \times 2p$

g $2g \times 3g \times 2g$

h $9k \times 4 \times 2k \times k \times 3k$

2 Write the following expressions as briefly as possible.

a $f + f + f + f + f$

b $w \times w \times w \times w$

c $c + c + c + c + c + c + c$

d $k \times k \times k \times k \times k \times k \times k \times k \times k \times k$

e $D + D + D + D + D + D$

3 Show the difference between $5j$ and j^5.

4 Expand the following brackets.

a $d(d + 1)$ **b** $a(4a - 3)$ **c** $p(4 + p)$

d $w(6 - 3w)$ **e** $f(3f + g)$ **f** $u(2u - 3s)$

g $q(h + 4q)$ **h** $A(9C - 5A)$

5 Expand and simplify the following expressions.

a $4mn + m(2n + 3)$ **b** $i(3i + 7r) - 3ir$

c $3vt + v(5v - 7t)$ **d** $6jk - j(3k + j)$

e $3st - s(2t - 5s)$ **f** $4cq - q(3q + 7c)$

6 Expand and simplify the following expressions.

a $d(d + h) + h(2h + d)$ **b** $m(3m + 7n) + n(2m - 4n)$

c $e(5e + 4f) - f(2e + 3f)$ **d** $y(4x - 2y) + x(7y + 5x)$

e $k(4k - 2t) - t(3k + 7t)$ **f** $j(j + 7r) - r(2r - 9j)$

7 Expand and simplify the following expressions.

a $4d^2 + d(2d - 5)$ **b** $a(a + 1) + a(2a + 3)$

c $t(3t + 5) + t(2t - 3)$ **d** $w(5w + 4) - w(2w + 3)$

e $u(5u - 3) - u(3u - 1)$ **f** $d(2d - 5) - d(7 - 3d)$

8 Use BODMAS to calculate the value of:

a $3(a + 4)$ when   **i** $a = 3$ **ii** $a = 7$ **iii** $a = 10$

b $4b - \dfrac{b}{2}$ when   **i** $b = 6$ **ii** $b = 12$ **iii** $b = 3$

c $(12 - c)^2$ when   **i** $c = 1$ **ii** $c = 7$ **iii** $c = 12$

d $4 + s^2$ when   **i** $s = 2$ **ii** $s = 4$ **iii** $s = 12$

Extension Work

1 Simplify the following expressions.

a $d^3 \times d^2$ **b** $d^5 \times d$ **c** $d^6 \times d^3$ **d** $d \times d^8$

2 **a** Write down a rule for multiplying two powers of the same quantity, as you were doing in Question 1.

  b Copy and complete the following: $d^m \times d^n = d$

3 Use your rule to simplify the following expressions.

a $a^7 \times a^9$ **b** $a^{10}a^6$ **c** $e^{20}e^{25}$ **d** $w^{99}w$ **e** $r^4 r^7 r^5$

4 Simplify the following expressions.

a $5a^7 \times 3a^5$ **b** $j^7 j^7 k^6 k^4$ **c** $8m^6 n^3 \times 3m^9 n^8$ **d** $s^3 t^4 t^7 s^8 t^3$

National Curriculum SATs questions

LEVEL 5

1 *2000 Paper 1*

Write each expression in its simplest form:

a $7 + 2t + 3t$

b $b + 7 + 2b + 10$

c $(3d + 5) + (d - 2)$

d $3m - (-m)$

2 *2002 Paper 1*

A teacher has a large pile of cards.

An expression for the **total** number of cards is $6n + 8$

a The teacher puts the cards in two piles.

The number of cards in the first pile is $2n + 3$

$6n + 8$

$2n + 3$

first pile

?

second pile

Write an expression to show the number of cards in the second pile.

b The teacher puts all the cards together.

Then he uses them to make two **equal piles**.

Write an expression to show the number of cards in one of the piles.

c The teacher puts all the cards together again, then he uses them to make two piles.

23 cards

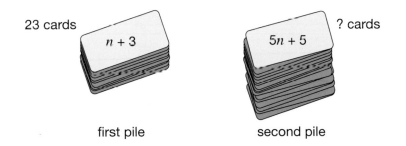

? cards

first pile

second pile

There are **23** cards in the first pile.

How many cards are in the second pile?

Show your working.

LEVEL 6

3 *1999 Paper 2*

    a   Write an expression for each missing length in these rectangles. Write each expression as simply as possible.

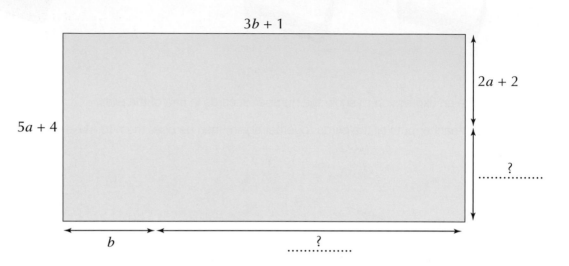

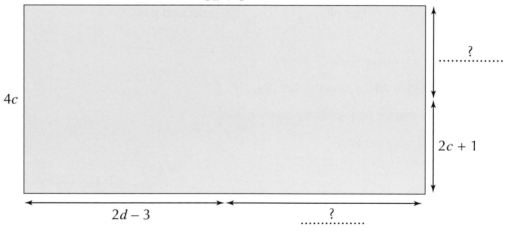

CHAPTER 6 Shape, Space and Measures 2

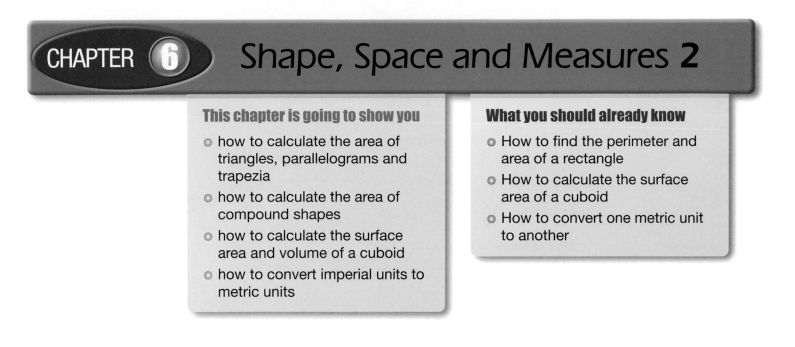

This chapter is going to show you

- how to calculate the area of triangles, parallelograms and trapezia
- how to calculate the area of compound shapes
- how to calculate the surface area and volume of a cuboid
- how to convert imperial units to metric units

What you should already know

- How to find the perimeter and area of a rectangle
- How to calculate the surface area of a cuboid
- How to convert one metric unit to another

Area of a triangle

To find the area of a triangle, we need to know the length of its base and its height. The height of the triangle is sometimes known as its **perpendicular height**. The diagram shows that the area of the triangle is half of the area of a rectangle:

Area 1 = Area 2

and

Area 3 = Area 4

So the area of a triangle is $\frac{1}{2}$ × base × height. The formula for the area of a triangle is given by:

$$A = \tfrac{1}{2} \times b \times h = \tfrac{1}{2}bh = \frac{b \times h}{2}$$

Example 6.1

Calculate the area of this triangle:

$$A = \frac{8 \times 3}{2} = \frac{24}{2} = 12 \text{ cm}^2$$

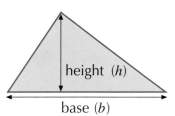

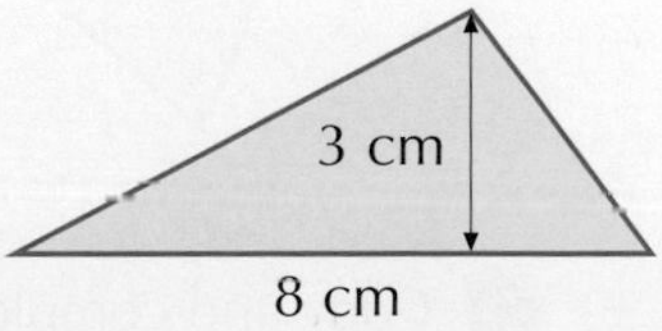

Sometimes the perpendicular height may be shown outside the triangle, as in the example below.

Example 6.2

Calculate the area of this triangle:

$$A = \frac{6 \times 5}{2} = \frac{30}{2} = 15 \text{ cm}^2$$

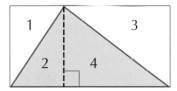

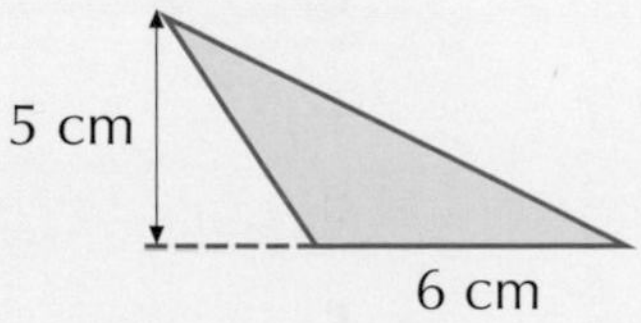

To find the area of a compound shape, made from rectangles and triangles, find the area of each one separately and then add together all the areas to obtain the total area of the shape.

Example 6.3 ▶

Calculate the area of this shape:

Divide the shape into a rectangle A and a triangle B:

Area of A = 8 × 4 = 32 cm²

Area of B = $\frac{6 \times 8}{2} = \frac{48}{2}$ = 24 cm²

Area of shape = 32 + 24 = 56 cm²

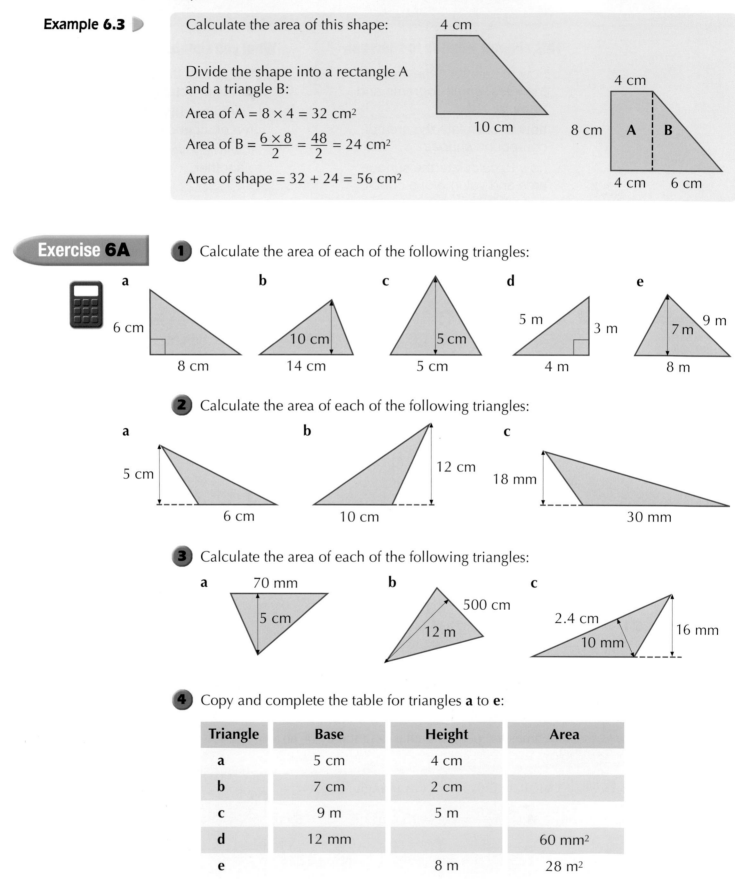

Exercise 6A

1 Calculate the area of each of the following triangles:

a 6 cm, 8 cm
b 10 cm, 14 cm
c 5 cm, 5 cm
d 5 m, 3 m, 4 m
e 9 m, 7 m, 8 m

2 Calculate the area of each of the following triangles:

a 5 cm, 6 cm
b 12 cm, 10 cm
c 18 mm, 30 mm

3 Calculate the area of each of the following triangles:

a 70 mm, 5 cm
b 500 cm, 12 m
c 2.4 cm, 10 mm, 16 mm

4 Copy and complete the table for triangles **a** to **e**:

Triangle	Base	Height	Area
a	5 cm	4 cm	
b	7 cm	2 cm	
c	9 m	5 m	
d	12 mm		60 mm²
e		8 m	28 m²

5 On centimetre-squared paper, draw axes for x and y from 0 to 6 for each of the following questions, and then plot the coordinates and find the area of each triangle:

  a △ABC with A(2, 0), B(5, 0) and C(4, 4).

  b △DEF with D(1, 1), E(6, 1) and F(3, 5).

  c △PQR with P(2, 1), Q(2, 5) and R(5, 3).

  d △XYZ with X(0, 5), Y(6, 5) and Z(4, 1).

6 Calculate the area of each compound shape below:

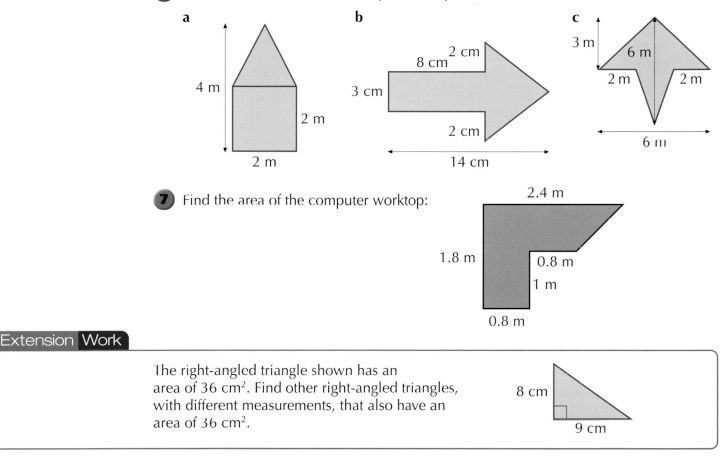

a

4 m
2 m
2 m

b

8 cm
2 cm
3 cm
2 cm
14 cm

c

3 m
6 m
2 m
2 m
6 m

7 Find the area of the computer worktop:

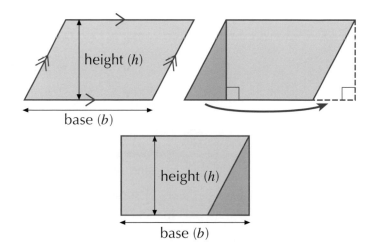

2.4 m
1.8 m
0.8 m
1 m
0.8 m

Extension Work

The right-angled triangle shown has an area of 36 cm². Find other right-angled triangles, with different measurements, that also have an area of 36 cm².

8 cm

9 cm

Area of a parallelogram

To find the area of a parallelogram, we need to know the length of its base and its height. The height of the parallelogram is sometimes known as its **perpendicular height**. The diagrams show that the parallelogram has the same area as that of a rectangle with the same base and height. So the area of a parallelogram is base × height.

height (h)
base (b)

height (h)
base (b)

The formula for the area of a parallelogram is given by:

$A = b \times h = bh$

height (h)
base (b)

Example 6.4 ▷ Calculate the area of this parallelogram:

$A = 6 \times 10 = 60$ cm²

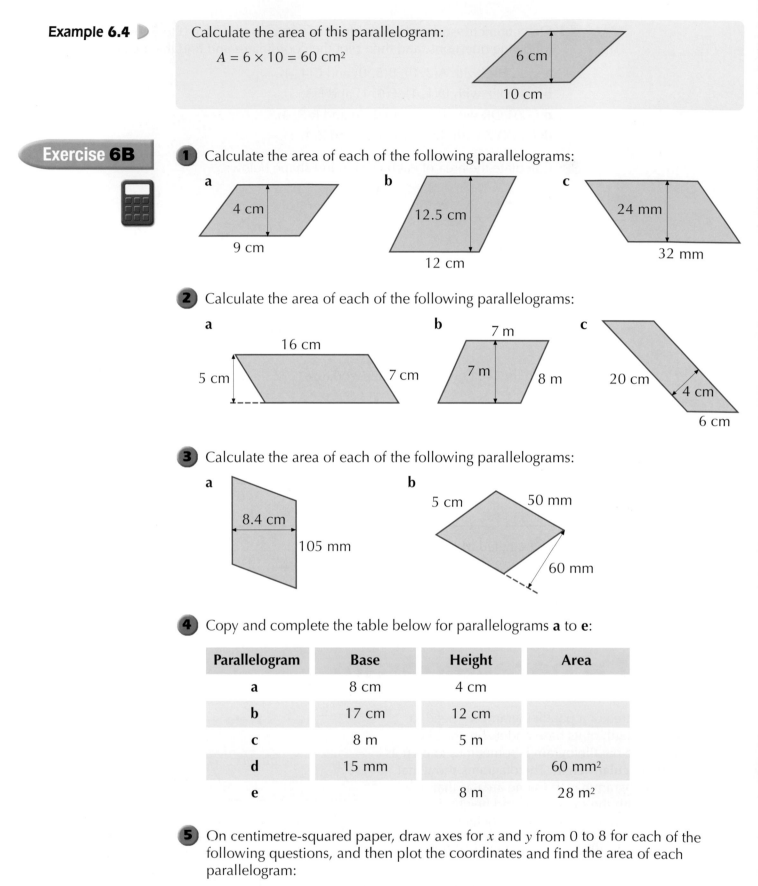

Exercise 6B

1 Calculate the area of each of the following parallelograms:

a 4 cm 9 cm

b 12.5 cm 12 cm

c 24 mm 32 mm

2 Calculate the area of each of the following parallelograms:

a 16 cm 5 cm 7 cm

b 7 m 7 m 8 m

c 20 cm 4 cm 6 cm

3 Calculate the area of each of the following parallelograms:

a 8.4 cm 105 mm

b 5 cm 50 mm 60 mm

4 Copy and complete the table below for parallelograms **a** to **e**:

Parallelogram	Base	Height	Area
a	8 cm	4 cm	
b	17 cm	12 cm	
c	8 m	5 m	
d	15 mm		60 mm²
e		8 m	28 m²

5 On centimetre-squared paper, draw axes for x and y from 0 to 8 for each of the following questions, and then plot the coordinates and find the area of each parallelogram:

a Parallelogram ABCD: A(2, 0), B(6, 0), C(8, 5) and D(4, 5).

b Parallelogram EFGH: E(1, 2), F(4, 2), G(7, 7) and H(4, 7).

c Parallelogram PQRS: P(1, 8), Q(7, 5), R(7, 1) and S(1, 4).

6 The area of the parallelogram is 27 cm². Calculate the perpendicular height of the parallelogram.

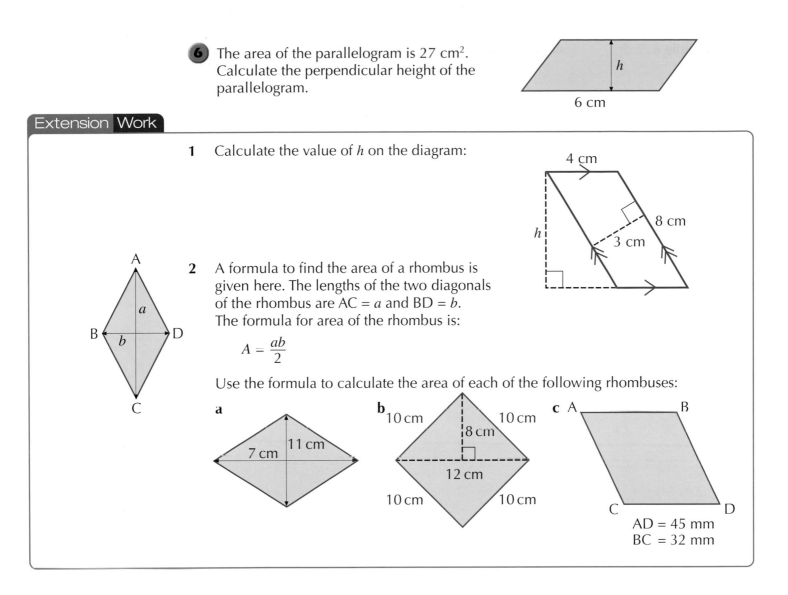

1 Calculate the value of h on the diagram:

2 A formula to find the area of a rhombus is given here. The lengths of the two diagonals of the rhombus are AC = a and BD = b. The formula for area of the rhombus is:

$$A = \frac{ab}{2}$$

Use the formula to calculate the area of each of the following rhombuses:

a

b 10 cm, 8 cm, 10 cm, 12 cm, 10 cm, 10 cm

c A B C D
AD = 45 mm
BC = 32 mm

Area of a trapezium

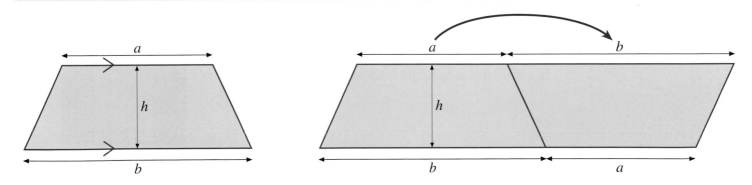

To find the area of a trapezium, we need to know the length of its two parallel sides, a and b, and the perpendicular height, h, between the parallel sides. The diagram shows how two equivalent trapezia fit together to form a parallelogram. So the area of a trapezium is $\frac{1}{2}$ × the sum of the lengths of the parallel sides × the height. The formula for the area of a trapezium is therefore given by:

$$A = \tfrac{1}{2} \times (a + b) \times h = \tfrac{1}{2}(a + b)h = \frac{(a + b)h}{2}$$

Example 6.5 ▷ Calculate the area of this trapezium:

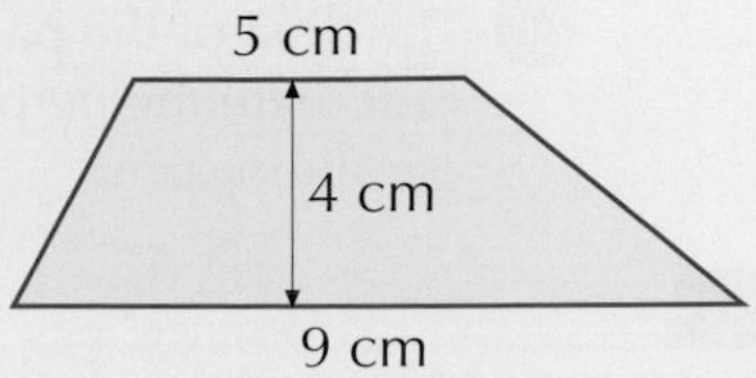

$A = \frac{1}{2} \times (9 + 5) \times 4$

$= \frac{14 \times 4}{2}$

$= 28 \text{ cm}^2$

5 cm

4 cm

9 cm

Exercise 6C

1 Calculate the area of each of the following trapezia:

a
2 cm
5 cm
12 cm

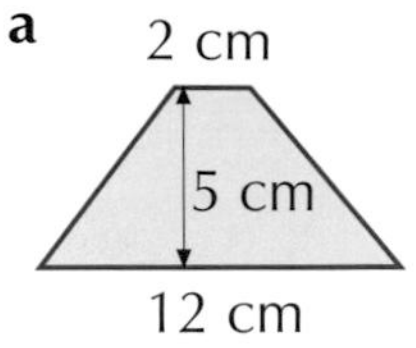

b
4 cm
8 cm
10 cm

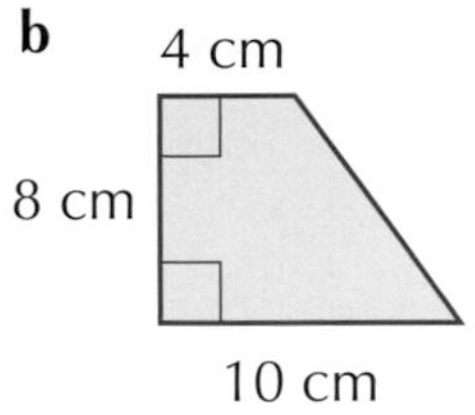

c
5 m
2 m
3 m

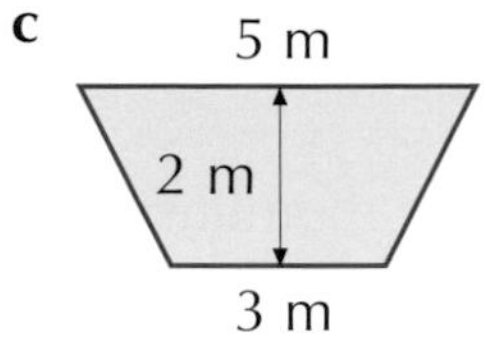

d
9 m
5 m
5 m

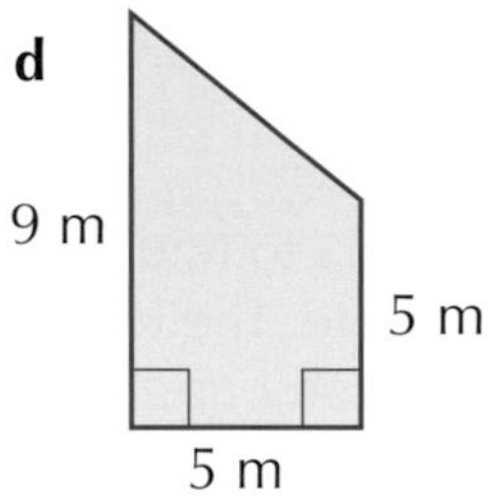

e
7 mm
16 mm
13 mm

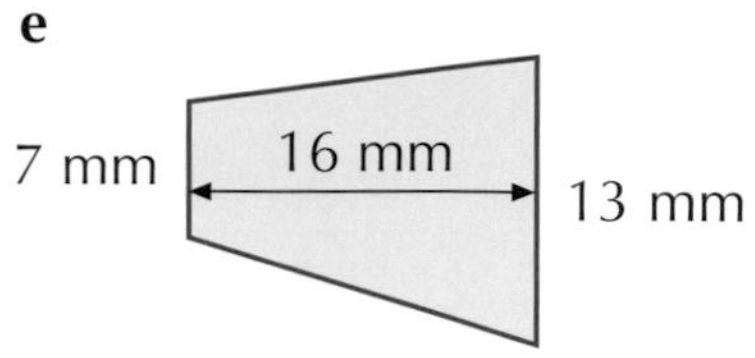

2 Copy and complete the table below for trapezia **a** to **f**:

Trapezium	Length a	Length b	Height h	Area A
a	4 cm	6 cm	3 cm	
b	10 cm	12 cm	6 cm	
c	9 m	3 m	5 m	
d	5 cm	5 cm		20 cm²
e	8 cm	12 cm		100 cm²
f	6 m		4 m	32 m²

3 The diagram shows the end wall of a garden shed. The shaded area is the door.

   a   Find the area of the door.

   b   Find the area of the brick wall.

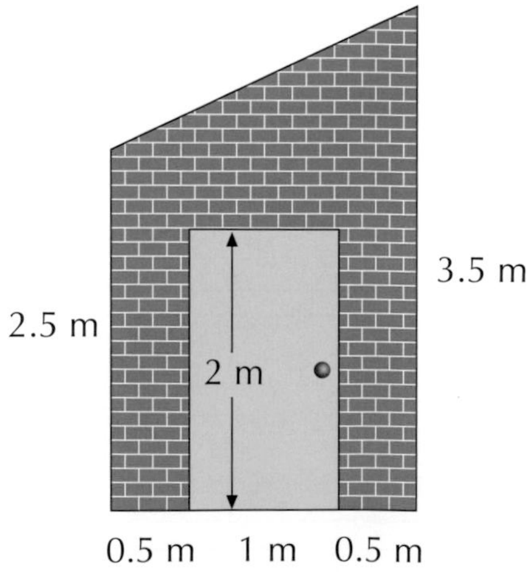

3.5 m

2.5 m

2 m

0.5 m   1 m   0.5 m

4 The side of a swimming pool is a trapezium, as shown in the diagram below. Calculate its area.

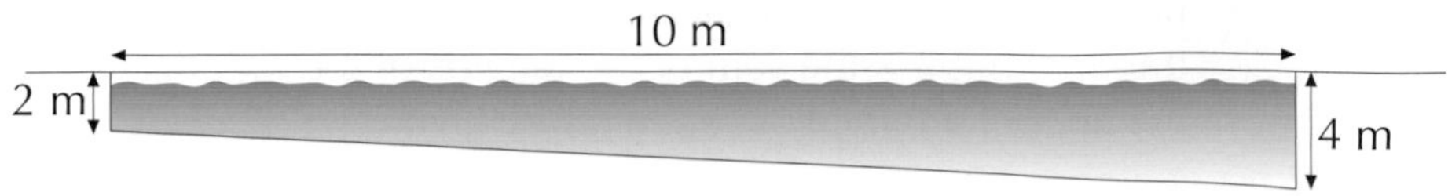

10 m

2 m

4 m

5 The diagram shows the measurements of a sauce bottle label. Calculate its area.

25 mm

52 mm

Tomato

SAUCE

20 mm

30 mm

6 Find the solid area of this mathematical stencil, which has the shapes cut out.

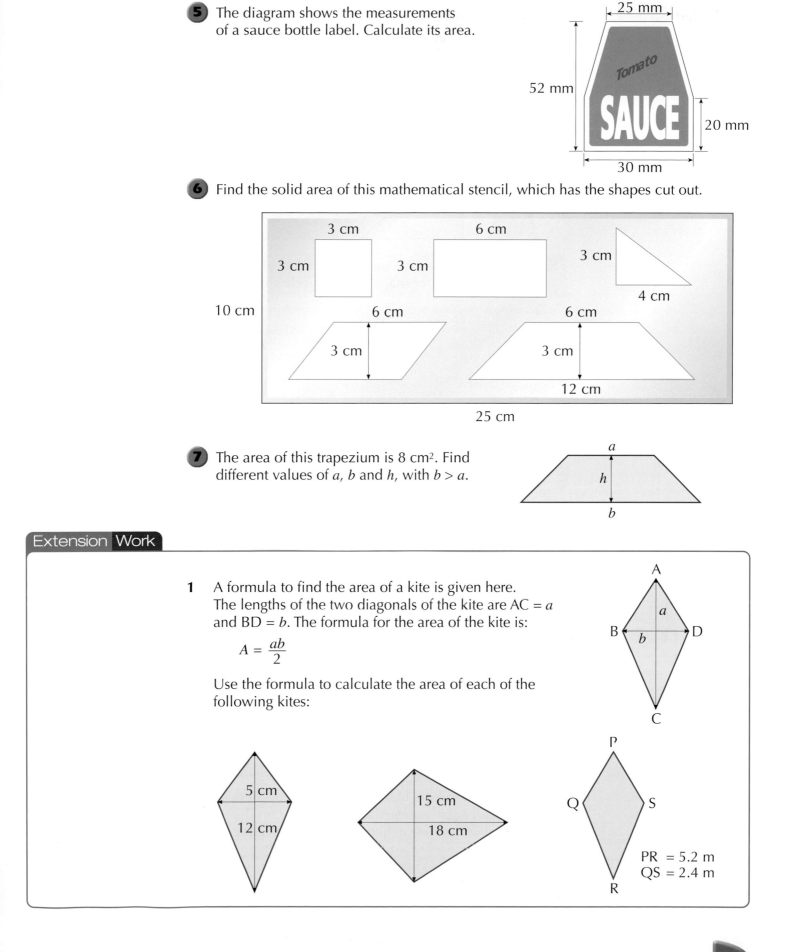

3 cm

3 cm

6 cm

3 cm

3 cm

4 cm

10 cm

6 cm

3 cm

6 cm

3 cm

12 cm

25 cm

7 The area of this trapezium is 8 cm². Find different values of *a*, *b* and *h*, with *b* > *a*.

a

h

b

Extension Work

1 A formula to find the area of a kite is given here. The lengths of the two diagonals of the kite are AC = *a* and BD = *b*. The formula for the area of the kite is:

$$A = \frac{ab}{2}$$

Use the formula to calculate the area of each of the following kites:

A

a

B

b

D

C

5 cm

12 cm

15 cm

18 cm

P

Q

S

R

PR = 5.2 m
QS = 2.4 m

2   The shapes below are drawn on a 1 cm grid of dots.

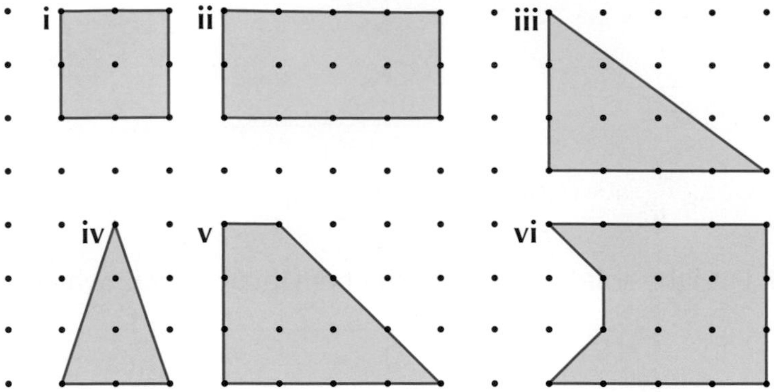

Shape	Number of dots on perimeter of shape	Number of dots inside shape	Area of shape (cm²)
i			
ii			
iii			
iv			
v			
vi			

a   Copy and complete the table for each shape.

b   Find a formula that connects the number of dots on the perimeter P, the number of dots inside I and the area A of each shape.

c   Check your formula by drawing different shapes on a 1 cm grid of dots.

Volume of a cuboid

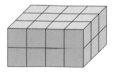

Volume is the amount of space inside a three-dimensional (3-D) shape.

The diagram shows a cuboid that measures 4 cm by 3 cm by 2 cm. The cuboid is made up of cubes of edge length 1 cm. The top layer consists of 12 cubes and, since there are two layers, altogether the cuboid has 24 cubes. The volume of the cuboid is therefore found by calculating $4 \times 3 \times 2 = 24$ cubes.

The volume of a cuboid is found by multiplying its length by its width by its height:

Volume of a cuboid = length × width × height

$$V = l \times w \times h = lwh$$

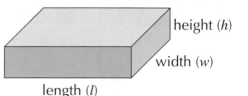

The metric units of volume in common use are the:
- cubic millimetre (mm³)
- cubic centimetre (cm³)
- cubic metre (m³)

The **capacity** of a 3-D shape is the volume of liquid or gas it can hold. The metric unit of capacity is the litre (l) with:
- 100 centilitres (cl) = 1 litre
- 1000 millilitres (ml) = 1 litre

The following metric conversions between capacity and volume should be learnt:
- 1 l = 1000 cm³
- 1 ml = 1 cm³
- 1000 l = 1 m³

Example 6.6 ▷ Calculate the total surface area and volume of the following cuboid.

The formula for the total surface area S of a cuboid is:

$$S = 2lw + 2lh + 2wh$$
$$= (2 \times 5 \times 4) + (2 \times 5 \times 3) + (2 \times 4 \times 3)$$
$$= 40 + 30 + 24$$
$$= 94 \text{ cm}^2$$

The formula for the volume of a cuboid is:

$$V = lwh$$
$$= 5 \times 4 \times 3$$
$$= 60 \text{ cm}^3$$

Example 6.7 ▷ Calculate the volume of the tank shown and then work out the capacity of the tank in litres.

$$V = 50 \times 30 \times 10 = 15\,000 \text{ cm}^3$$

Since 1000 cm³ = 1 l, the capacity of the tank = 15 000 ÷ 1000 = 15 l.

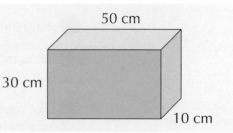

Example 6.8 ▷ Calculate the volume of the shape shown.

The shape is made up of two cuboids with measurements 7 m by 3 m by 2 m and 2 m by 3 m by 6 m. So the volume of the shape is given by:

$$V = (7 \times 3 \times 2) + (2 \times 3 \times 6)$$
$$= 42 + 36$$
$$= 78 \text{ m}^3$$

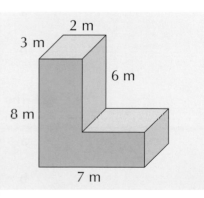

1 Find **i** the surface area and **ii** the volume of each of the following cuboids:

a

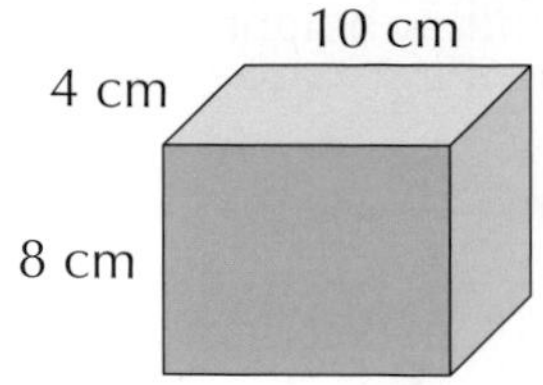

10 cm
4 cm
8 cm

b

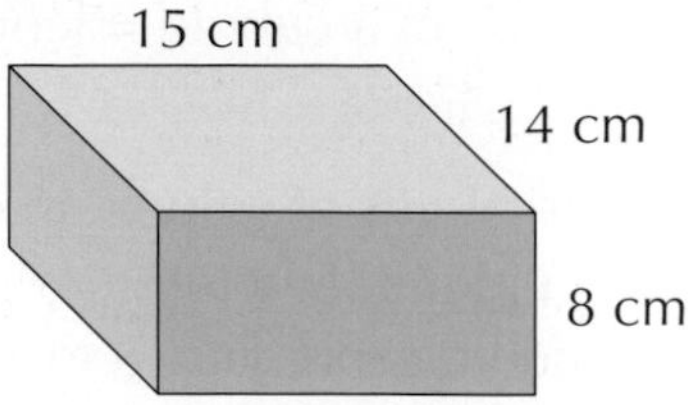

15 cm
14 cm
8 cm

c

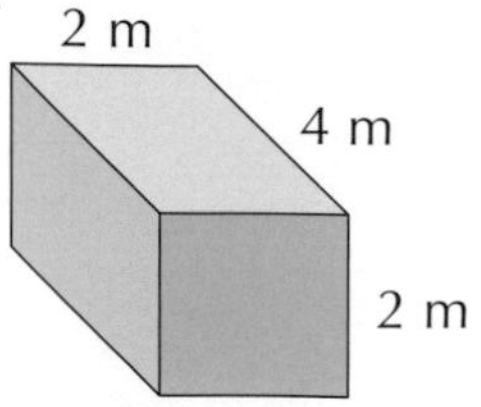

2 m
4 m
2 m

2 Find the capacity, in litres, of each of the following cuboid containers:

a

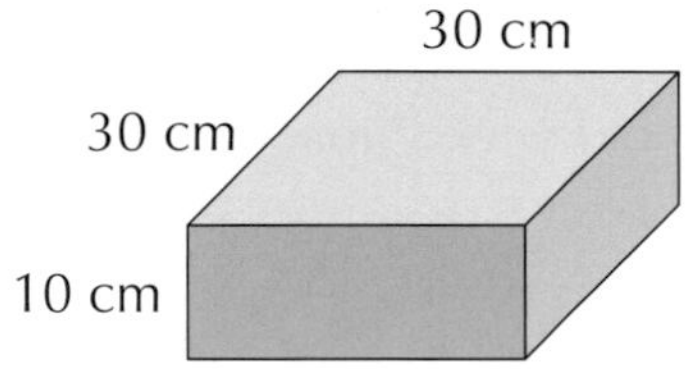

30 cm
30 cm
10 cm

b

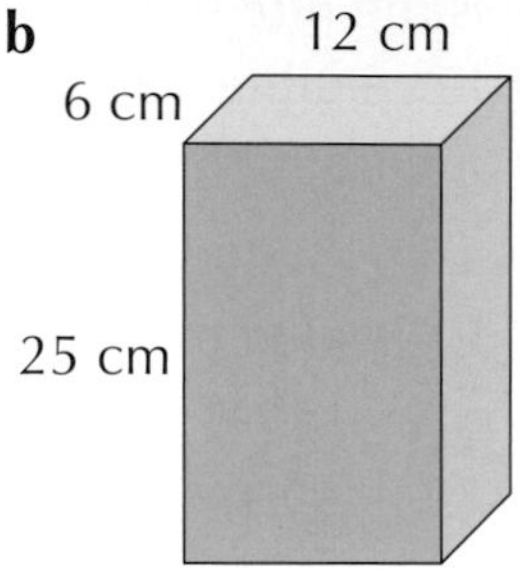

12 cm
6 cm
25 cm

c

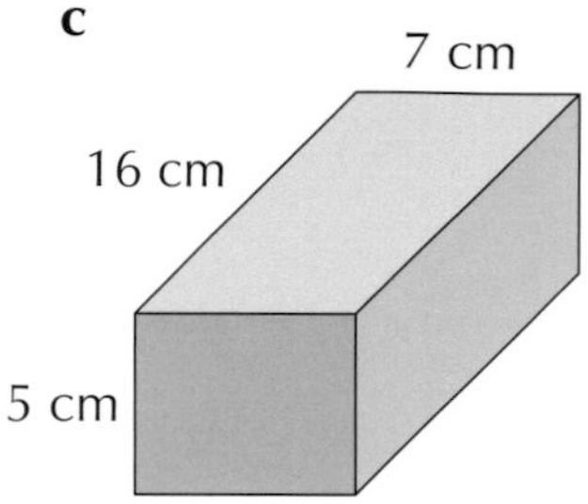

7 cm
16 cm
5 cm

3 Copy and complete the table of cuboids **a** to **e**.

	Length	Width	Height	Volume
a	6 cm	4 cm	1 cm	
b	3.2 m	2.4 m	0.5 m	
c	8 cm	5 cm		120 cm³
d	20 mm	16 mm		960 mm³
e	40 m	5 m		400 m³

4 Calculate the volume for each of the cubes with the following edge lengths:

a 2 cm   **b** 5 cm   **c** 12 cm

5 Find the volume of a hall that is 30 m long, 20 m wide and 10 m high.

6 How many packets of sweets that each measure 8 cm by 5 cm by 2 cm can be packed into a cardboard box that measures 32 cm by 20 cm by 12 cm?

7 The diagram shows the dimensions of a swimming pool:

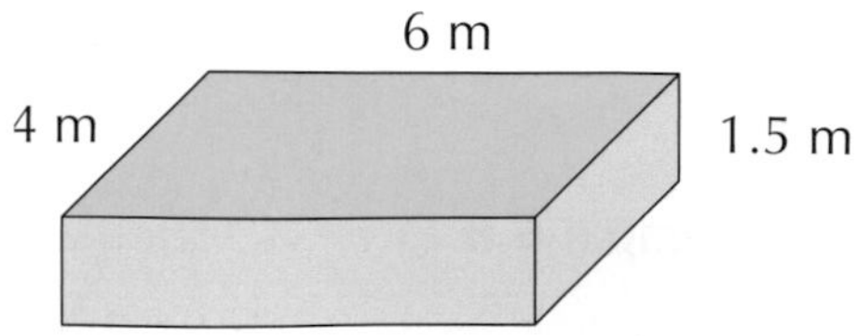

6 m
4 m
1.5 m

a Calculate the volume of the pool, giving the answer in cubic metres.

b How many litres of water does the pool hold when it is full?

8 The diagram shows the dimensions of a rectangular carton of orange juice:

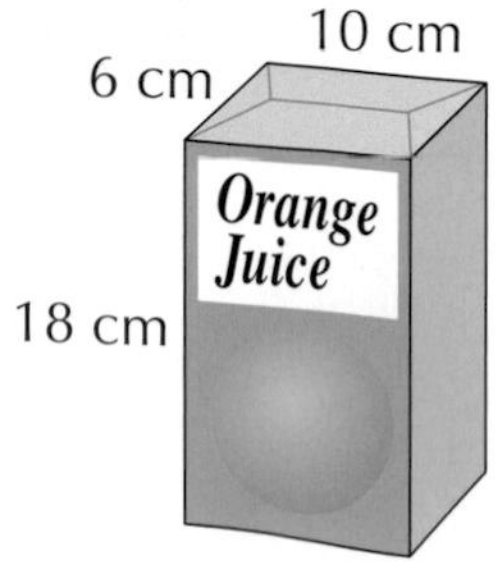

10 cm
6 cm
Orange Juice
18 cm

a Calculate the volume of the carton, giving your answer in cubic centimetres.

b How many glasses can be filled with orange juice from four full cartons, if each glass holds 240 ml?

9 a Find the volume of this block of wood, giving your answer in cubic centimetres:

b Calculate the mass of the block if 1 cm³ of the wood has a mass of 0.7 g.

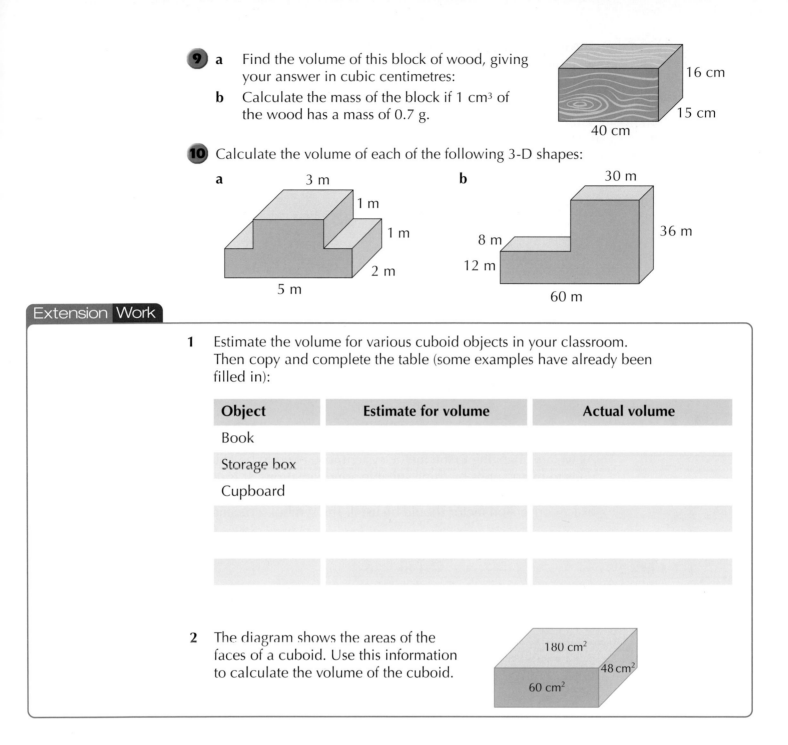

16 cm

15 cm

40 cm

10 Calculate the volume of each of the following 3-D shapes:

a

3 m

1 m

1 m

2 m

5 m

b

30 m

36 m

8 m

12 m

60 m

Extension Work

1 Estimate the volume for various cuboid objects in your classroom. Then copy and complete the table (some examples have already been filled in):

Object	Estimate for volume	Actual volume
Book		
Storage box		
Cupboard		

2 The diagram shows the areas of the faces of a cuboid. Use this information to calculate the volume of the cuboid.

180 cm²

48 cm²

60 cm²

Imperial units

I need to order 3 pints of milk

The distance to London is 256 miles

My height is 5' 7"

The recipe requires ½ lb of butter

In Britain we are gradually changing to the metric system of units, but people still often prefer to use the Imperial system of units in certain cases, as the examples show.

The following Imperial units are still commonly used and it is a good idea to be familiar with them:

Imperial units of length	Imperial units of mass	Imperial units of capacity
12 inches (in) = 1 foot (ft) 3 feet = 1 yard (yd) 1760 yards = 1 mile	16 ounces (oz) = 1 pound (lb) 14 pounds = 1 stone (st) 2240 pounds = 1 ton	8 pints (pt) = 1 gallon (gall)

Example 6.9 ▷ Express 5 ft 6 in in inches:

5 ft = 5 × 12 = 60 in

So, 5 ft 6in = 60 + 6 = 66 in

Example 6.10 ▷ Express 100 lb in stones and pounds:

100 lb ÷ 14 = 7 stone with 2 pounds left over.

So 100 lb = 7 st 2 lb

(Note that if a calculator is used, the answer will be a decimal.)

Rough metric equivalents of Imperial units

As we are changing to the metric system, you need to be able to convert from Imperial units to metric units by using suitable approximations. It is useful to know the following rough metric equivalents of Imperial units, although if better accuracy is required the exact conversion factor should be used. The symbol ≈ means 'is approximately equal to'.

Units of length	Units of mass	Units of capacity
1 in ≈ 2.5 cm 1 yard ≈ 1 metre 5 miles ≈ 8 km	1 oz ≈ 30 g 1 lb ≈ 500 g	$1\frac{3}{4}$ pints ≈ 1 l 1 gallon ≈ 4.5 l

Example 6.11 ▷ Approximately how many kilometres are there in 20 miles?

5 miles ≈ 8 km

So 20 miles ≈ 4 × 8 ≈ 32 km

Example 6.12 ▷ Approximately how many gallons are there in 18 litres?

1 gallon ≈ 4.5 l

So 18 l ≈ 18 ÷ 4.5 ≈ 4 gallons

Exercise 6E

1   Express each of the following in the units given in brackets:

    a   6 ft 2 in (in)   **b**   22 yd (ft)   **c**   2 lb 10 oz (oz)

    d   6 st 5 lb (lb)   **e** $3\frac{1}{2}$ gallons (pints)

2 Express each of the following in the units given in brackets:

    a   30 in (ft and in)   **b**   20 ft (yd and ft)   **c**   72 oz (lb and oz)

    d   35 lb (st and lb)   **e**   35 pints (gallons and pints)

3 How many inches are there in:

    a   a yard   **b**   a mile?

4 How many ounces are there in:

    a   a stone   **b**   a ton?

5 Convert each of the following Imperial quantities into the metric quantity given in brackets:

    a   6 in (cm)   **b**   10 yd (m)   **c**   25 miles (km)

    d   8 oz (g)   **e** $1\frac{1}{2}$ lb (g)   **f**   7 pints (l)

    g   8 gallons (l)

6 Convert each of the following metric quantities into the Imperial quantity given in brackets:

    a   30 cm (in)   **b**   200 m (ft)   **c**   80 km (miles)

    d   150 g (oz)   **e**   3 kg (lb)   **f**   6 l (pints)

    g   54 l (gallons)

7 Pièrre is on holiday in England and he sees this sign near to his hotel. Approximately how many metres is it from his hotel to the beach?

> **To the beach** ➡ $\frac{1}{2}$ mile

8 Mike is travelling on a German autobahn and he sees this road sign. He knows that it means that the speed limit is 120 kilometres per hour. What is the approximate speed limit in miles per hour?

120

9 Steve needs 6 gallons of petrol to fill the tank of his car. The pump only dispenses petrol in litres. Approximately how many litres of petrol does he need?

10 A metric tonne is 1000 kg. Approximately how many pounds is this?

11 Anne's height is 5 ft 6 in. She is filling in an application form for a passport and needs to know her height in metres. What height should she enter on the form?

1 Working in pairs or groups, draw a table to show each person's height and weight in Imperial and in metric units.

2 Other Imperial units are less common, but are still used in Britain. For example:
   - furlongs to measure distance in horse racing
   - fathoms to measure the depth of sea water
   - nautical miles to measure distance at sea.

   Use reference material or the Internet to find metric approximations for these units. Can you find other Imperial units for measuring length, mass and capacity that are still in use?

3 How long is 1 million seconds? Give your answer in days, hours, minutes and seconds.

What you need to know for level 5

- How to convert one metric unit to another
- How to convert Imperial units into metric units using rough equivalents

What you need to know for level 6

- How to use the appropriate formulae to find the area of triangles, parallelograms and trapezia
- How to find the volume of a cuboid

National Curriculum SATs questions

LEVEL 5

1 *2000 Paper 2*

   How many kilometres are there in 5 miles?

   Copy and complete the missing part of the sign.

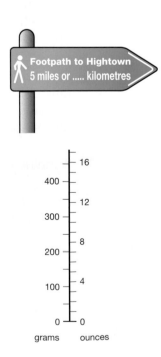

2 *2002 Paper 1*

   A scale measures in grams and in ounces.

   Use the scale to answer these questions:

   a About how many ounces is 400 grams?

   b About how many grams is 8 ounces?

   c About how many ounces is 1 kilogram? Explain your answer.

LEVEL 6

3 *1998 Paper 1*

Each shape in this question has an area of 10 cm². No diagram is drawn to scale.

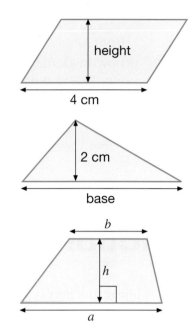

a Calculate the height of this parallelogram, which has an area of 10 cm².

b Calculate the length of the base of this triangle, which has an area of 10 cm².

c What might be the values of h, a and b in this trapezium, which has an area of 10 cm²? (a is greater than b.)

What else might the values of h, a and b be?

4 *2002 Paper 2*

The drawing shows two cuboids that have the same volume:

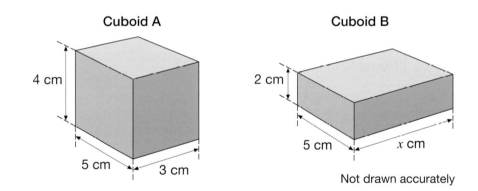

Not drawn accurately

a What is the volume of cuboid A?

Remember to state your units.

b Work out the value of the length marked x in Cuboid B.

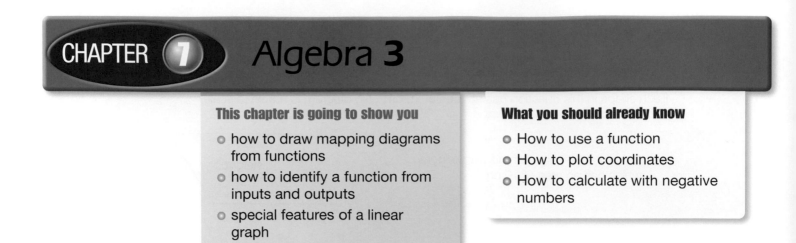

CHAPTER 7 — Algebra 3

This chapter is going to show you

- how to draw mapping diagrams from functions
- how to identify a function from inputs and outputs
- special features of a linear graph

What you should already know

- How to use a function
- How to plot coordinates
- How to calculate with negative numbers

Linear functions

A linear function is a simple rule that involves any of the following:

| addition | subtraction | multiplication | division |

Mapping diagrams can illustrate these functions as shown in Example 7.1.

Example 7.1 ▷ Draw a mapping diagram to illustrate:

$x \rightarrow 2x + 3$

We draw two number lines; usually the top one is for the starting points and the bottom one shows where the numbers map to with the function (see opposite page). The starting number line is often from −2 to 5. We can see that if:

$x \rightarrow 2x + 3$

then:

$-2 \rightarrow -1$

$-1 \rightarrow 1$

$\;\;0 \rightarrow 3$

$\;\;1 \rightarrow 5$

We illustrate the function by drawing arrows between the two number lines to show where each number maps to:

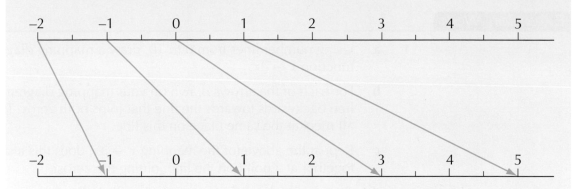

The illustration shows, of course, only part of a very long pair of number lines that contain hundreds of numbers. We only draw this part to illustrate what the pattern looks like.

1 **a** Copy the mapping diagram for the function $x \rightarrow x + 3$:

b Complete the mapping diagram for all the integer values from –2 to 2.

c Complete the mapping diagram for the values:

   i 1.5   **ii** 0.5   **iii** –0.5   **iv** –1.5

2 **a** Using two number lines from –5 to 10, draw mapping diagrams to illustrate the functions:

   i $x \rightarrow x + 2$ **ii** $x \rightarrow 2x + 1$ **iii** $x \rightarrow x - 2$ **iv** $x \rightarrow 2x - 1$

b In each of your mapping diagrams from **2a**, draw the lines from –1.5, 0.5 and 1.5.

3 **a** Using number lines from –5 to 15, draw mapping diagrams to illustrate the functions:

   i $x \rightarrow 3x + 1$ **ii** $x \rightarrow 4x - 1$ **iii** $x \rightarrow 2x + 5$ **iv** $x \rightarrow 3x - 5$

b In each of your mapping diagrams from **3a**, draw the lines from –0.5, 1.5 and 2.5.

4 Write down the similarity between all the mapping diagrams of functions like:

$$x \rightarrow x + 2 \qquad x \rightarrow x + 1 \qquad x \rightarrow x + 5 \qquad x \rightarrow x + 7$$

1 a Using number lines from 0 to 10, draw a mapping diagram of the function $x \rightarrow 2x$.

b For each of the arrows drawn on your mapping diagram, extend the line backwards towards the line that joins both zeros. They should all meet at the same place on this line.

c Repeat the above for the mapping $x \rightarrow 3x$; does this also join together at a point on the line joining the zeros?

d Can you explain why this works for all similar functions?

Finding a function from its inputs and outputs

Any function will have a particular set of outputs for particular set of inputs. If we can identify some outputs for particular inputs, then we can identify the function.

Example 7.2

State the function that maps the inputs {−1, 0, 1, 2, 3} to {−1, 3, 7, 11, 15}.

Notice that for each integer increase in the inputs, the outputs **increase by 4**, which suggests that part of the function is:

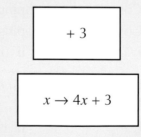

The input **0 maps to 3**, hence the function uses:

+ 3

This leads to the function:

$x \rightarrow 4x + 3$

A quick check that this does map 1 to 7 and 2 to 11 confirms the function is correct.

Exercise 7B

1 State the function that maps the following inputs with their respective outputs:

a {−1, 0, 1, 2, 3} ⟶ {4, 5, 6, 7, 8}

b {−1, 0, 1, 2, 3} ⟶ {−2, −1, 0, 1, 2}

c {−1, 0, 1, 2, 3} ⟶ {−1, 1, 3, 5, 7}

d {−1, 0, 1, 2, 3} ⟶ {3, 5, 7, 9, 11}

e {−1, 0, 1, 2, 3} ⟶ {2, 5, 8, 11, 14}

2 What are the functions that generate the following mixed outputs from the given mixed inputs? (*Hint:* Put the numbers in sequence first.)

a {2, 5, 3, 0, 6, 4} ⟶ {6, 8, 9, 3, 7, 5}
b {5, 9, 6, 4, 10, 8} ⟶ {15, 17, 12, 16, 11, 13}
c {5, 1, 8, 4, 0, 6} ⟶ {5, 13, 15, 3, 19, 11}
d {3, 1, 7, 5, 8, 2} ⟶ {9, 1, 13, 5, 15, 3}
e {9, 5, 10, 6, 3, 7} ⟶ {16, 10, 28, 19, 31, 22}

3 This question looks at using the simple functions:

| + 2 | | – 3 | | × 5 |

By using any two, you can create six different combined functions, such as:

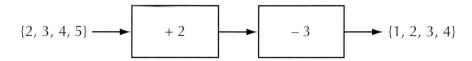

{2, 3, 4, 5} ⟶ | + 2 | ⟶ | – 3 | ⟶ {1, 2, 3, 4}

Draw a diagram like the one above for the other five possible combined functions.

Graphs from functions

There are different ways to write functions down. For example, the function:

$x \rightarrow 4x + 3$

can also be written as:

$y = 4x + 3$

with the inputs as x and the outputs as y.

This latter way of writing functions is simpler when it comes to drawing graphs.

Every function has a graph associated with it, which we find by finding ordered pairs, or coordinates, from the function, and plotting them. Every graph of a linear function is a straight line.

Example 7.3 ▷ Draw a graph of the function:

$y = 3x + 1$

First, we draw up a table of simple values for x:

x		−2	−1	0	1	2	3
$y = 3x + 1$		−5	−2	1	4	7	10

Then we plot each point on a grid, and join up all the points.

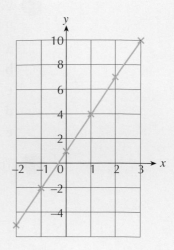

Notice that the line we have drawn is actually hundreds of other coordinates too – *all* of these obey the same rule of the function, that is $y = 3x + 1$. Choose any points on the line that have not been plotted and show that this is true.

Exercise 7C

1 a Complete the table below for the function $y = x + 3$:

x	−2	−1	0	1	2	3
$y = x + 3$			3			

    b Draw a grid with its x-axis from −2 to 3 and y-axis from −1 to 7.

    c Use the table to help draw, on the grid, the graph of the function $y = x + 3$.

2 a Complete the table below for the function $y = x − 2$:

x	−2	−1	0	1	2	3
$y = x − 2$			−2			

    b Draw a grid with its x-axis from −2 to 3 and y-axis from −4 to 2.

    c Use the table to help draw, on the grid, the graph of the function $y = x − 2$.

3 a Complete the table below for the function $y = 4x + 1$:

x	−2	−1	0	1	2	3
$y = 4x + 1$			1			

    b Draw a grid with its x-axis from −2 to 3 and y-axis from −7 to 13.

    c Use the table to help draw, on the grid, the graph of the function $y = 4x + 1$.

4 a Complete the table below for the function $y = 4x − 1$:

x	−2	−1	0	1	2	3
$y = 4x − 1$			−1			

    b Draw a grid with its x-axis from −2 to 3 and y-axis from −9 to 11.

    c Use the table to help draw, on the grid, the graph of the function $y = 4x − 1$.

5 **a** Complete the table below for the functions shown:

x	-2	-1	0	1	2	3
$y = 2x + 5$	1					11
$y = 2x + 3$		1			7	
$y = 2x + 1$			1	3		
$y = 2x - 1$			-1	1		
$y = 2x - 3$		-5			1	

b Draw a grid with its x-axis from -2 to 3 and y-axis from -7 to 11.

c Draw the graph for each function in the table above.

d What two properties do you notice about each line?

e Use the properties you have noticed to draw the graphs of the functions:
  i $y = 2x + 2.5$ **ii** $y = 2x - 1.5$

6 **a** Complete the table below for the functions shown:

x	-2	-1	0	1	2	3
$y = 3x + 4$	-2					13
$y = 3x + 2$		-1			8	
$y = 3x$			0	3		
$y = 3x - 2$			-2	1		
$y = 3x - 4$		-7			2	

b Draw a grid with its x-axis from -2 to 3 and y-axis from -10 to 13.

c Draw the graph for each function in the table above.

d What two properties do you notice about each line?

e Use the properties you have noticed to draw the graphs of the functions:
  i $y = 3x + 2.5$ **ii** $y = 3x - 2.5$

Extension Work

Draw the graphs of:

$y = 0.5x - 2$ and $y = 0.5x + 2$.

Now draw, without any further calculations, the graphs of:

$y = 0.5x - 0.75$ and $y = 0.5x + 1.3$

Gradient of a straight line (steepness)

The gradient of a straight line is:

the increase in the y ordinate for an increase of 1 in the x ordinate

Examples of gradients:

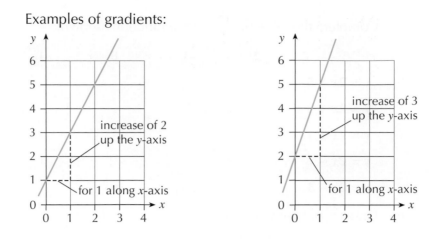

For any linear equation of the form $y = mx + c$, you might have found out the following from the previous exercise:

$y = mx + c$

The m is the same as the gradient of the line (steepness).

The c is the number on the y-axis where the line cuts through.

Example 7.4

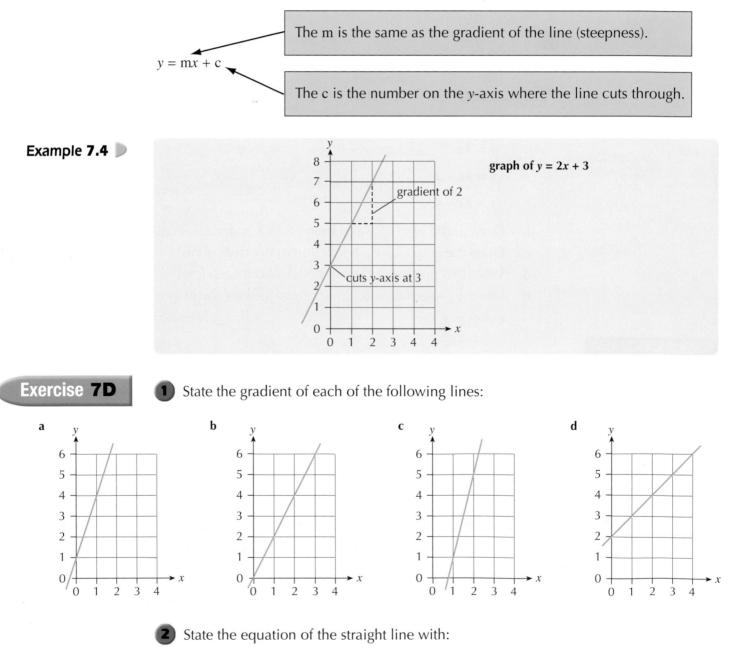

graph of $y = 2x + 3$

gradient of 2

cuts y-axis at 3

1 State the gradient of each of the following lines:

a

b

c

d

2 State the equation of the straight line with:

    a   A gradient of 3 passing through the y-axis at (0, 5).

    b   A gradient of 2 passing through the y-axis at (0, 7).

    c   A gradient of 1 passing through the y-axis at (0, 4).

    d   A gradient of 7 passing through the y-axis at (0, 15).

3 State the equations of the lines in each of the following diagrams:

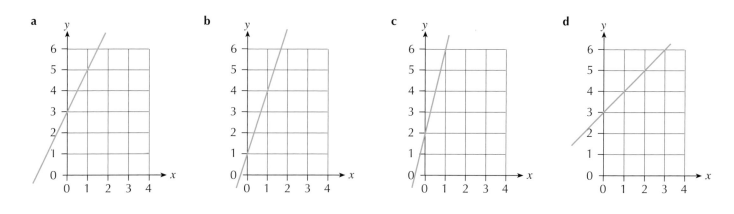

4 a By drawing suitable straight lines, find five functions with graphs that pass through the point (2, 8).

   b By drawing suitable straight lines, find five functions with graphs that pass through the point (3, 7).

5 Write down three functions with graphs that pass through the point (−2, 3).

Real-life graphs

Graphs are all around us; they are found in newspapers, adverts, on TV, and so on.

Most of these graphs show a relationship between what is given on one axis and what is given on the other.

A distance-time graph can be used to describe a journey:

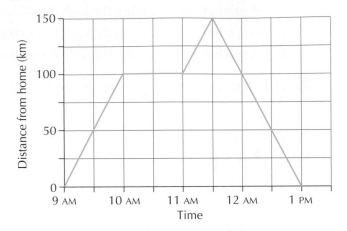

When you draw graphs from data such as time and distance, you need to find key coordinates to plot to identify the line or lines that make up the graph. The axes need to be labelled, and to be accurate.

Example 7.5 ▷ I set off from home to pick up a dog from the vet. I travelled $1\frac{1}{2}$ hours at an average speed of 60 km/hour. It took me 30 minutes to get the dog settled into my car. I then travelled back home at an average speed of 40 km/hour as I didn't want to jolt the dog. Draw a distance–time graph of the journey.

The key coordinates (time, distance from home) are:

• the start from home at (0, 0)

• arrive at the vets at $(1\frac{1}{2}, 90)$

• set off from the vet at (2, 90)

• arrive back home at $(4\frac{1}{4}, 0)$

(Note $90 \div 40 = 2\frac{1}{4}$ hours for the return journey.)

Then plot the points and draw the graph:

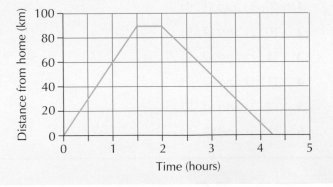

1 a Draw a grid with the following scale:
horizontal, time, showing 0 to 5 hours, with 1 cm to 30 minutes;
vertical, distance from home, showing 0 to 100 km, 1 cm to 20 km.

b Draw on the grid the travel graph that shows the following:
I travelled from home to Manchester Airport, at an average speed of 50 km/hour. It took me 2 hours. I stopped there for 30 minutes, and picked up Auntie Freda. I brought her straight back home, driving this time at an average of 40 km/hour.

c I set off to the airport at 9AM. Use the graph to determine what time I arrived back home.

2 **a** Draw a grid with the following scale:
horizontal, time showing 0 to 2 hours, 1 cm to 20 minutes;
vertical, distance from home, showing 0 to 60 km, 1 cm to 10 km.

b Draw on the grid the travel graph showing the following:
Elise travelled to meet Ken who was 60 km away. She left home at 11.00AM and travelled the first 40 km in 1 hour. She stopped for 30 minutes to buy a present, and then completed her journey in 20 minutes.

c What was Elise's average speed over the last 20 minutes?

3 **a** Draw a grid with the following scale;:
horizontal, time showing 0 to 60 minutes, 1 cm to 5 minutes;
vertical, depth showing 0 to 200 cm, 2 cm to 50 cm.

b A swimming pool, 2 m deep, was filled with water from a hose. The pool was empty at the start and the depth of water in the pool increased at the rate of 4 cm/minute. Complete the table below, showing the depth of water after various times.

Time (minutes)	0	10	25	40	50
Depth (cm)					

c Draw a graph to show the increase in depth of water against time.

4 Draw a graph for the depth of water in the same swimming pool if the water was poured in with a different hose that filled the pool quicker, at the rate of 5 cm/minute.

5 A different swimming pool that contained water was emptied by a pump at the rate of 30 gallons/minute. It took 3 hours for the pool to be emptied.

a Complete the following table that shows how much water is in the pool:

Time (minutes)	0	30	60	90	120	150	180
Water left (gallons)	5400						

b Draw a graph to show the amount of water left in the pool against time.

Extension Work

At 11AM, Billy and Leon set off towards each other from different places 32 km apart. Billy cycled at 20 km/h and Leon walked at 5 km/h.

Draw distance–time graphs of their journeys on the same grid to find out:

1 The time at which they meet.

2 When they are 12 km apart.

What you need to know for level 5

- How to use and interpret coordinates in all four quadrants
- How to generate coordinates from a linear function
- How to plot graphs from linear functions

What you need to know for level 6

- How to plot negative coordinates
- How to interpret the general features of linear graphs

National Curriculum SATs questions

LEVEL 5

1 *2000 Paper 2*

The graph shows my journey in a lift.
I got in the lift at floor number 10.

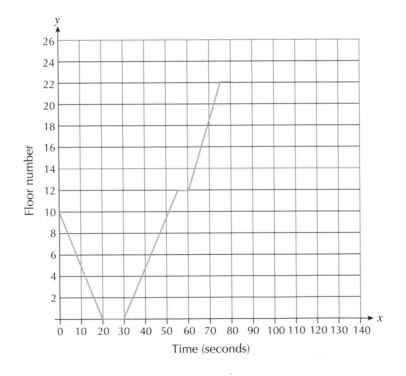

a The lift stopped at two different floors before I got to floor number 22.

b For how long was I in the lift while it was moving?

c After I got out of the lift at floor number 22, the lift went directly to the ground floor.

It took 45 seconds.

On a copy of the graph, show the journey of the lift from floor 22 to the ground floor.

LEVEL 6

2   *2002 Paper 2*

I went for a walk.

The distance–time graph shows information about my walk.

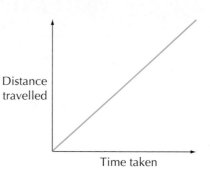

Distance travelled

Time taken

Write out the statement below that describes my walk:

I was walking faster and faster.

I was walking slower and slower.

I was walking north-east.

I was walking at a steady speed.

I was walking uphill.

3   *2002 Paper 1*

The graph shows a straight line. The equation of the line is $y = 3x$.

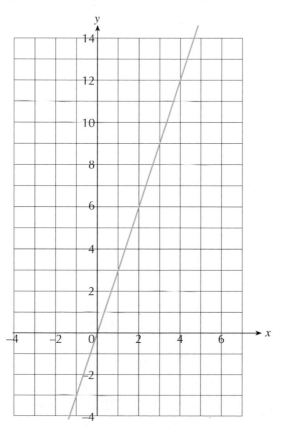

Does the point (25, 75) lie on the straight line $y = 3x$?

Explain how you know.

This chapter is going to show you

- how to multiply and divide by powers of 10
- how to round numbers to one or two decimal places
- how to check calculations by approximations
- how to use a calculator efficiently

What you should already know

- How to multiply and divide by 10, 100 and 1000
- How to round to the nearest 10, 100 and 1000
- How to use brackets and memory keys on a calculator
- How to use standard column methods for the four operations

Rounding

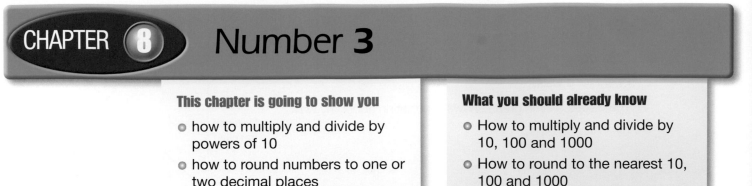

The nearest star, Proxima Centauri, is 40 653 234 200 000 kilometres from earth. An atom is 0.000 000 0001 metres wide. When dealing with very large and very small numbers it is easier to round them and work with powers of 10. You will meet this later when you do work on Standard Form. In this section you will round numbers, and multiply and divide by powers of 10.

Example 8.1 ▷

Multiply:

a 0.937   **b** 2.363   **c** 0.002 81

by **i** 10   **ii** 10^2 **iii** 10^4.

a   **i** $0.937 \times 10 = 9.37$ **ii** $0.937 \times 10^2 = 93.7$ **iii** $0.937 \times 10^4 = 9370$

b   **i** $2.363 \times 10 = 23.63$ **ii** $2.363 \times 10^2 = 236.3$ **iii** $2.363 \times 10^4 = 23630$

c   **i** $0.00281 \times 10 = 0.0281$ **ii** $0.00281 \times 10^2 = 0.281$ **iii** $0.00281 \times 10^4 = 28.1$

Example 8.2 ▷

Multiply and divide:

a 6   **b** 50   **c** 7.8

by **i** 0.1   **ii** 0.01

a   **i** $6 \times 0.1 = 0.6, 6 \div 0.1 = 60$ **ii** $6 \times 0.01 = 0.06, 6 \div 0.01 = 600$

b   **i** $50 \times 0.1 = 5, 50 \div 0.1 = 500$ **ii** $50 \times 0.01 = 0.5, 50 \div 0.01 = 5000$

c   **i** $7.8 \times 0.1 = 0.78, 7.8 \div 0.1 = 78$ **ii** $7.8 \times 0.01 = 0.078, 7.8 \div 0.01 = 780$

Exercise 8A

1   Round these numbers to   **i** one decimal place and   **ii** two decimal places:

   a 4.722   **b** 3.097   **c** 2.634   **d** 1.932   **e** 0.784

   f 0.992   **g** 3.999   **h** 2.604   **i** 3.185   **j** 3.475

2 Multiply these numbers by **i** 10 and **ii** 10^2:

    a   5.3   **b**   0.79   **c**   24   **d**   5.063   **e**   0.003

3 Divide these numbers by **i** 10 and **ii** 10^3:

    a   83   **b**   4.1   **c**   457   **d**   6.04   **e**   34 781

4 Write down the answers to:

a 3.1×10	**b** 6.78×10^2	**c** 0.56×10^3	**d** $34 \div 10^3$
e $823 \div 10^2$	**f** $9.06 \div 10^3$	**g** 57.89×10^2	**h** $57.89 \div 10^2$
i 0.038×10^3	**j** $0.038 \div 10$	**k** 0.05×10^5	**l** $543 \div 10^5$

5 This grid represents a 1 cm × 1 cm square that has been split into 100 equal smaller squares. Give all your answers to the questions below in centimetres.

    a   What is the area of each small square?

    b   How many small squares are there inside rectangle A, and what is its area?

    c   Use your answer to **b** to write down the answer to 0.3×0.5.

    d   Rectangle B has an area of 0.3 cm^2. Use this fact and the diagram to write down the answer to $0.3 \div 0.6$.

6 Multiply these numbers by **i** 0.1 and **ii** 0.01:

    a   4.5   **b**   56.2   **c**   0.04   **d**   400   **e**   0.7

7 Divide these numbers by **i** 0.1 and **ii** 0.01:

    a   6.3   **b**   300   **c**   7   **d**   81.3   **e**   29

Extension Work

1   Write down the answers to:

    a 5×10 **b** 70×10 **c** 0.8×10 **d** 6.3×10

2   Write down the answers to:

    a $5 \div 10$ **b** $70 \div 10$ **c** $0.8 \div 10$ **d** $6.3 \div 10$

3   Write down the answers to:

    a $5 \div 0.1$ **b** $70 \div 0.1$ **c** $0.8 \div 0.1$ **d** $6.3 \div 0.1$

4   Write down the answers to:

    a 5×0.1 **b** 70×0.1 **c** 0.8×0.1 **d** 6.3×0.1

5   Explain the connection between the answers to the above problems, particularly the connection between multiplying by 10 and dividing by 0.1

6   What is a quick way to calculate $73 \div 0.01$?

Powers of 10

Example 8.3 ▷

	10^6	10^5	10^4	10^3	10^2	10	1
a	6	0	5	8	7	0	2
b	1	7	0	0	0	5	6

Write down the two numbers shown in the diagram on the left in words. Consider the numbers in blocks of three digits, that is:

6   058   702

1   700   056

a 6 058 702 = Six million, fifty-eight thousand, seven hundred and two

b 1 700 056 = One million, seven-hundred thousand, and fifty six.

Example 8.4 ▷ The United Kingdom is said to have a population of 55 million. What is the largest and smallest population this could mean?

As the population is given to the nearest million, the actual population could be as much as half a million either way, so the population is between $54\frac{1}{2}$ million and $55\frac{1}{2}$ million or 54 500 000 and 55 500 000.

Example 8.5 ▷ **a** The bar chart shows the annual profits for a large company over the previous five years. Estimate the income each year.

b The company chairman says, 'Income in 2002 was nearly 50 million pounds.' Is the chairman correct?

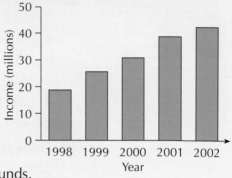

a In 1998 the profits were about 19 million pounds.
In 1999 they were about 25 million pounds.
In 2000 they were about 31 million pounds.
In 2001 they were about 39 million pounds.
In 2002 they were about 43 million pounds.

b The chairman is wrong, as in 2002 the income is nearer 40 million pounds.

Exercise 8B

1 Write the following numbers in words:

    a 3 452 763   **b** 2 047 809   **c** 12 008 907   **d** 3 006 098

2 Write the following numbers using figures:

    a Four million, forty-three thousand, two hundred and seven

    b Nineteen million, five hundred and two thousand and thirty seven

    c One million, three hundred and two thousand and seven

3 The bar chart shows the population of some countries in the European Community. Estimate the population of each country.

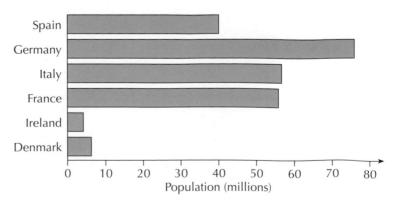

4 Round off the following numbers to **i** the nearest ten thousand, **ii** the nearest hundred thousand and **iii** the nearest million:

    a 3 547 812   **b** 9 722 106   **c** 3 042 309   **d** 15 698 999

5 The diagram shows a calculator display.   `6.4`³

This means $6.4 \times 10^3 = 6.4 \times 1000 = 6400$

What numbers do the following calculator displays show?

    a `2.4`⁰⁴   **b** `3.6`⁰⁵   **c** `7.8`⁰³   **d** `8.2`⁰⁶

6 There are 2 452 800 people out of work. The government says, 'Unemployment is just over two million.' The opposition says, 'Unemployment is still nearly three million.' Who is correct and why?

7 There are 8 million people living in London. What are the highest and lowest figures that the population of London could be?

Extension Work

Standard Form is a way of writing large numbers in a more manageable form.
For example, 3.1×10^6 means $3.1 \times 1\,000\,000 = 3\,100\,000$, and
$4.54 \times 10^9 = 4\,540\,000\,000$.
Write these Standard Form numbers out in full:

    a 2.9×10^7 **b** 3.56×10^5 **c** 1.17×10^8 **d** 2.2×10^6

    e 9.5×10^8 **f** 8.3×10^6 **g** 2.31×10^{10} **h** 5.04×10^5

Estimations

Example 8.6

Estimate the answers to:

    a 12% of 923   **b** $\dfrac{11.2 + 53.6}{18.7 - 9.6}$ **c** $324 \div 59$

    a Round to 10% of 900 = 90

    b Round to $\dfrac{10 + 50}{20 - 10} = \dfrac{60}{10} = 6$

    c Round to $300 \div 60 - 5$

Example 8.7

Choose the answer given within brackets that is most appropriate for the calculation (give a reason for your choice):

    a $\sqrt{18}$ (4.24, 5.24, 6.24)   **b** $6 \div 0.7$ (5.8, 8.6, 65)

    c 29×45 (905, 1250, 1305)

    a $\sqrt{18}$ must be between $\sqrt{16}$ and $\sqrt{25}$, so 4.24 is the best choice.

    b $6 \div 0.7$ must be bigger than 6, but not as large as 65, so 8.6 is the best choice.

    c The answer is bigger than $30 \times 40 \approx 1200$, but must end in $9 \times 5 = ?5$, so 1305 is the best answer.

1 Estimate the value the arrow is pointing at in each of these:

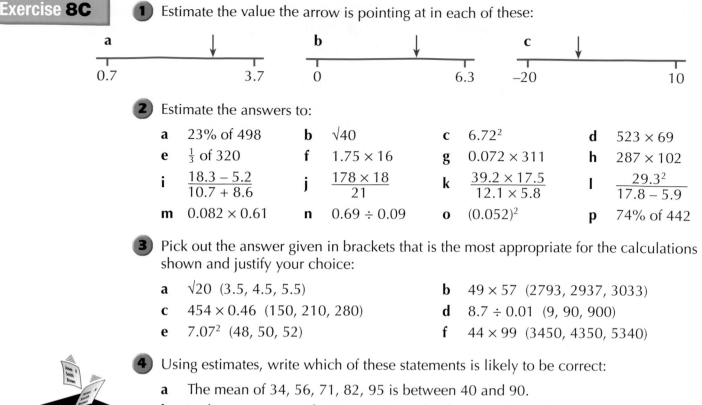

2 Estimate the answers to:

a	23% of 498	**b**	$\sqrt{40}$	**c**	6.72^2	**d**	523×69
e	$\frac{1}{3}$ of 320	**f**	1.75×16	**g**	0.072×311	**h**	287×102
i	$\dfrac{18.3 - 5.2}{10.7 + 8.6}$	**j**	$\dfrac{178 \times 18}{21}$	**k**	$\dfrac{39.2 \times 17.5}{12.1 \times 5.8}$	**l**	$\dfrac{29.3^2}{17.8 - 5.9}$
m	0.082×0.61	**n**	$0.69 \div 0.09$	**o**	$(0.052)^2$	**p**	74% of 442

3 Pick out the answer given in brackets that is the most appropriate for the calculations shown and justify your choice:

a $\sqrt{20}$ (3.5, 4.5, 5.5)   **b** 49×57 (2793, 2937, 3033)

c 454×0.46 (150, 210, 280)   **d** $8.7 \div 0.01$ (9, 90, 900)

e 7.07^2 (48, 50, 52)   **f** 44×99 (3450, 4350, 5340)

4 Using estimates, write which of these statements is likely to be correct:

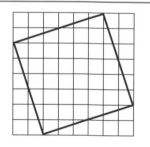

a The mean of 34, 56, 71, 82, 95 is between 40 and 90.

b In the most recent election 46% voted Labour, 37% voted Conservative and 16% voted for other parties (46% + 37% + 16% = 99%).

c $(5.2915)^2 = 38$ **d** $7 \times \frac{23}{5} = 23.2$

e Eight packets of crisps at 47p per packet costs £4.14.

Extension Work

Without working out areas or counting squares, explain why the area of the square shown must be between 36 and 64 grid squares.

a Now calculate the area of the square.

b Using an 8 × 8 grid draw a square with an area of exactly 50 grid squares.

Adding and subtracting decimals

Example 8.8

Work out:

a $64.062 + 178.9 + 98.27$ **b** $20 - 8.72 - 6.5$

The numbers need to be lined up in columns with the decimal point in line. Blank places can be filled with zeros if needed. Part **b** needs to be done in two stages.

a
```
   64.062
  178.900
+  98.270
  341.232
    21 1
```

b
```
  ¹9⁹9¹
  20.00        ⁰¹
- 8.72        11.28
  11.28      - 6.50
              4.78
```

Example 8.9 ▶

In a Science lesson a student adds 0.45 kg of water and 0.72 kg of salt to a beaker that weighs 0.092 kg. He then pours out 0.6 kg of the mixture. What is the total mass of the beaker and mixture remaining?

This has to be set up as an addition and subtraction problem, that is:
0.092 + 0.45 + 0.72 − 0.6

The problem has to be done in two stages:

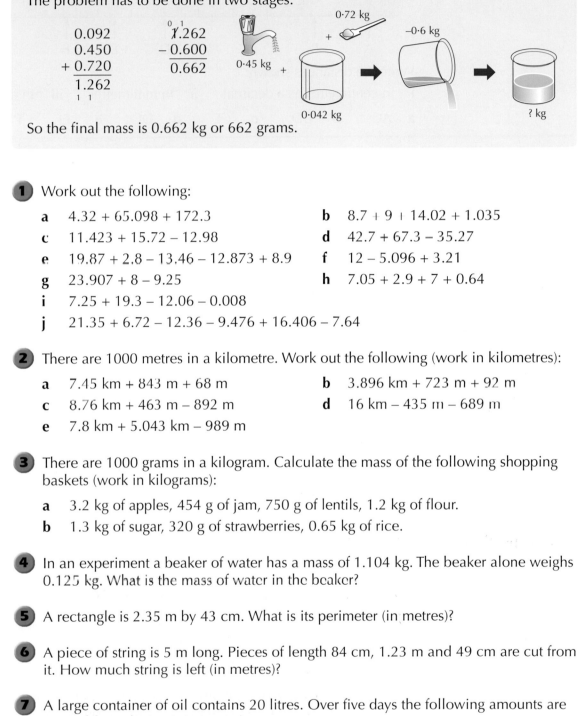

So the final mass is 0.662 kg or 662 grams.

Exercise 8D

1 Work out the following:

   a   4.32 + 65.098 + 172.3   **b**   8.7 + 9 + 14.02 + 1.035

   c   11.423 + 15.72 − 12.98   **d**   42.7 + 67.3 − 35.27

   e   19.87 + 2.8 − 13.46 − 12.873 + 8.9   **f**   12 − 5.096 + 3.21

   g   23.907 + 8 − 9.25   **h**   7.05 + 2.9 + 7 + 0.64

   i   7.25 + 19.3 − 12.06 − 0.008

   j   21.35 + 6.72 − 12.36 − 9.476 + 16.406 − 7.64

2 There are 1000 metres in a kilometre. Work out the following (work in kilometres):

   a   7.45 km + 843 m + 68 m   **b**   3.896 km + 723 m + 92 m

   c   8.76 km + 463 m − 892 m   **d**   16 km − 435 m − 689 m

   e   7.8 km + 5.043 km − 989 m

3 There are 1000 grams in a kilogram. Calculate the mass of the following shopping baskets (work in kilograms):

   a   3.2 kg of apples, 454 g of jam, 750 g of lentils, 1.2 kg of flour.

   b   1.3 kg of sugar, 320 g of strawberries, 0.65 kg of rice.

4 In an experiment a beaker of water has a mass of 1.104 kg. The beaker alone weighs 0.125 kg. What is the mass of water in the beaker?

5 A rectangle is 2.35 m by 43 cm. What is its perimeter (in metres)?

6 A piece of string is 5 m long. Pieces of length 84 cm, 1.23 m and 49 cm are cut from it. How much string is left (in metres)?

7 A large container of oil contains 20 litres. Over five days the following amounts are poured from the container:

      2.34 l, 1.07 l, 0.94 l, 3.47 l, 1.2 l

How much oil is left in the container?

Much as fractions and decimals show the same thing, centimetres and millimetres both show lengths. The first length shown on the rule below, AB, can be given as 1.6 cm, 16 mm or $1\frac{3}{5}$ cm.

cm 0 1 2 3 4 5 6 7 8 9 10 11 12

A   B   C   D E F   G

Write the distances shown:

i in centimetres as a decimal   **ii** in millimetres   **iii** in centimetres as a fraction

a AC   **b** BD   **c** CE   **d** DE   **e** EF   **f** EG

Efficient calculations

It is important that you know how to use your calculator. You should be able to use the basic functions ($\times$, $\div$, $+$, $-$) and the square, square root and brackets keys. You have also met the memory and sign-change keys. This exercise introduces the fraction and power keys.

Example 8.10

Use a calculator to work out:

a $(1\frac{3}{10} - \frac{4}{5}) \times \frac{3}{4}$ **b** $\dfrac{1\frac{2}{5} + 1\frac{1}{4}}{2\frac{1}{2} - 1\frac{7}{8}}$

a Using the fraction button $a\frac{b}{c}$, type in the calculation as:

(1 $a\frac{b}{c}$ 3 $a\frac{b}{c}$ 1 0 − 4 $a\frac{b}{c}$ 5) × 3 $a\frac{b}{c}$ 4 =

The display should show   **3⌐8** , which represents the fraction $\frac{3}{8}$. Note that the way this is keyed in may be different on your calculator.

b Using brackets and the fraction buttons gives an answer of $4\frac{6}{25}$.

(Shown in some displays as **4⌐6⌐25** .)

Example 8.11

Use a calculator to work out:

a 5^6 **b** $\sqrt[3]{729}$ **c** $\sqrt{19.5^2 - 7.5^2}$

a Using the power button, which may look like x^y , the answer should be 15 625.

b This can be keyed in as 7 2 9 $\sqrt[3]{}$ = or $\sqrt[3]{}$ 7 2 9 =

or 7 2 9 x^y (1 $a\frac{b}{c}$ 3) =

The answer is 9. Make sure you can use your calculator to find this answer.

c Using the square root, bracket and square keys the answer should be 18. For example, the following are two ways to key the problem in to the calculator:

$\sqrt{}$ (1 9 . 5 x^2 − 7 . 5 x^2) =

or (1 9 . 5 x^2 − 7 . 5 x^2) $\sqrt{}$ =

1 Use the bracket and/or memory keys on your calculator to work out each of these:

a $\dfrac{38.7 - 23.1}{3.82 + 1.38}$

b $\sqrt{4.1^2 - 0.9^2}$

c $9.75 \div (3.2 - 1.7)$

2 Use the fraction key on your calculator to work out each of these (give your answer as a mixed number or a fraction in its simplest form):

a $\frac{1}{8} + \frac{3}{5} + \frac{3}{16}$

b $1\frac{2}{3} + 2\frac{2}{9} - \frac{5}{6}$

c $\frac{3}{8} \times \frac{4}{15} \div \frac{4}{5}$

d $(2\frac{1}{5} + 3\frac{3}{4}) \times 2\frac{1}{7}$

e $\dfrac{2\frac{1}{4} - 1\frac{2}{7}}{1\frac{1}{2} + 1\frac{1}{14}}$

f $\dfrac{4\frac{3}{5} - 3\frac{2}{3}}{3\frac{3}{8} - 1\frac{4}{5}}$

g $(1\frac{3}{4})^2$

h $\sqrt{3\frac{11}{16} - 1\frac{7}{16}}$

i $(2\frac{2}{3} + 1\frac{1}{8}) \div \frac{7}{8}$

3 Use the power, cube and cube root keys on your calculator to work out each of these (round your answers to one decimal point if necessary):

a 4^6

b 2.3^3

c $\sqrt[3]{1331}$

d $\sqrt{3^4 + 4^3}$

e 2^{10}

f $4 \times (5.78)^3$

g 3×7.2^2

h $(3 \times 7.2)^2$

i $\sqrt{8.9^2 - 3.1^2}$

4 A time given in hours and minutes can be put into a calculator as a fraction. For example, 3 hours and 25 minutes is $3\frac{25}{60}$, which is entered as 3 $\boxed{a\frac{b}{c}}$ 25 $\boxed{a\frac{b}{c}}$ 60. Using the fraction button on your calculator and remembering that $\frac{1}{3}$ hour = 20 minutes, $\frac{1}{5}$ hour = 12 minutes, and so on, do the following time problems (give your answers in hours and minutes):

a Add 2 hours and 25 minutes to 3 hours and 55 minutes.

b Subtract 1 hour 48 minutes from 3 hours 24 minutes.

c Multiply 1 hour 32 minutes by 5.

5 Most square and cube roots cannot be given as an exact value, so we have to approximate them. The following are a selection of square and cube roots of whole numbers. Unfortunately, you do not know if the number is a square root or a cube root. Use your calculator to find out if it is a square root or a cube root and the number for which it is either of these (**a** and **b** are done for you below):

a 1.41421   **b** 2.15443   **c** 3.41995   **d** 2.23607
e 4.47214   **f** 1.44225   **g** 2.28943   **h** 5.47723

a $1.41421^2 = 1.999396$, so $\sqrt{2} \approx 1.41421$

b $2.15443^3 = 9.9995$, so $\sqrt[3]{10} \approx 2.15443$

Extension Work

On your calculator you may have a key or a function above a key marked $\boxed{x!}$.

Find out what this key does. For example, on some calculators you can key:

3 $\boxed{x!}$ and the display shows 6, and you can key:

7 $\boxed{x!}$ which gives a display of 5040.

Similarly, investigate what the key marked $\boxed{1/x}$ or $\boxed{x^{-1}}$ does.

Multiplying and dividing decimals

Example 8.12 ▷ Work out:

a 8.6×6.5 **b** 1.43×3.4

a   Firstly, estimate the answer, that is $9 \times 6 = 54$. This problem is done using a box method, breaking the two numbers into their whole number and fractions. Each are multiplied together and the totals added:

×	8	0.6
6	48	3.6
0.5	4	0.3

Sum of multiplications

$$\begin{array}{r} 48 \\ 4 \\ 3.6 \\ 0.3 \\ \hline 55.9 \end{array}$$

The answer is 55.9.

b   Firstly, estimate the answer, that is $1.5 \times 3 = 4.5$, to show where the decimal point will be. This problem is then done using standard column methods without decimal points:

$$\begin{array}{r} 143 \\ \times 34 \\ \hline 572 \\ 4290 \\ \hline 4862 \end{array}$$

The position of the decimal point is shown by the estimate, and so the answer is 4.862.

Note that the number of decimal points in the answer is the same as in the original problem, that is $1.\underline{43} \times 3.\underline{4} = 4.\underline{862}$

Example 8.13 ▷ Work out:

a $76.8 \div 16$ **b** $156 \div 2.4$

a   Firstly, estimate the answer, that is $80 \div 16 = 5$.
Now consider the problem as $768 \div 16$:

$$\begin{array}{rl} 768 & \\ - 640 & (40 \times 16) \\ \hline 128 & \\ 64 & (4 \times 16) \\ \hline 64 & \\ 64 & (4 \times 16) \\ \hline 0 & (48 \times 16) \end{array}$$

The position of the decimal point is shown by the estimate, and so the answer is 4.8.

b   Firstly, estimate the answer, that is $150 \div 3 = 50$.
Now consider the problem as $1560 \div 24$:

$$\begin{array}{rl} 1560 & \\ - 960 & (40 \times 24) \\ \hline 600 & \\ - 480 & (20 \times 24) \\ \hline 120 & \\ 120 & (5 \times 24) \\ \hline 0 & (65 \times 24) \end{array}$$

The position of the decimal point is shown by the estimate, and so the answer is 65.

As you become used to this method of division, you can start to take away longer 'chunks' each time. For example, in **b** you could take away 60×24 instead of 40×24 and then 20×24. This will improve your mental multiplication too!

1 Without using a calculator, and using any other method you are happy with, work out:

a	6.3×9.4	**b**	5.8×4.5	**c**	2.7×2.7	**d**	1.4×12.6
e	0.78×2.5	**f**	1.26×3.5	**g**	2.58×6.5	**h**	0.74×0.22

2 Without using a calculator, and using any other method you are happy with, work out:

a	$78.4 \div 14$	**b**	$7.92 \div 22$	**c**	$24 \div 3.2$	**d**	$12.6 \div 3.6$
e	$143 \div 5.5$	**f**	$289 \div 3.4$	**g**	$57 \div 3.8$	**h**	$10.8 \div 0.24$

3 Roller ball pens cost £1.23 each. How much will 72 pens cost?

4 Number fans cost 65p each. How many can be bought for £78?

Extension Work

The box method can be used to do quite complicated decimal multiplications. For example, 2.56×4.862 can be worked out as follows:

×	**4**	**0.8**	**0.06**	**0.002**	**Sum of row**
2	8	1.6	0.12	0.004	9.724
0.5	2	0.4	0.03	0.001	2.431
0.06	0.24	0.048	0.0036	0.00012	0.29172
				Total	12.44672

Use the box method to calculate 1.47×2.429.

Check your answer with a calculator.

What you need to know for level 5

- How to round numbers to one decimal place
- How to use the bracket, square, square root and sign-change keys on your calculator
- How to make estimations of calculations

What you need to know for level 6

- How to deal with addition and subtraction of integers and decimals up to two decimal places
- How to round numbers to any power of 10 and to two decimal places

National Curriculum SATs questions

LEVEL 5

1 *2001 Paper 1*

   a A football club is planning a trip. The club hires 234 coaches. Each coach holds 52 passengers. How many passengers is that altogether?

   b The club wants to put one first aid kit into each of the 234 coaches. The first aid kits are sold in boxes of 18. How many boxes does the club need?

2 *2002 Paper 1*

   a Peter's height is 0.9 m. Lucy is 0.3 m taller than Peter. What is Lucy's height?

   b Lee's height is 1.45 m. Misha is 0.3 m shorter than Lee. What is Misha's height?

   c Zita's height is 1.7 m. What is Zita's height in centimetres?

LEVEL 6

3 *1998 Paper 1*

Each of these calculations has the same answer (60). Copy the diagram below and fill in each gap with a number:

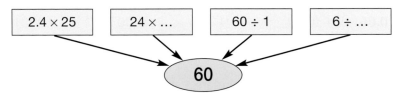

4 *2002 Paper 1*

   a The number 6 is halfway between 4.5 and 7.5. What are the missing numbers below?

      The number 6 is halfway between 2.8 and …

      The number 6 is halfway between −12 and …

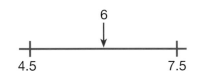

   b Work out the number that is halfway between 27×38 and 33×38.

5 *2002 Paper 2*

A company sells and processes films of two different sizes. The tables show how much the company charges:

I want to take 360 photos. I need to buy the film, pay for the film to be printed and pay for the postage.

   a Is it cheaper to use all films of 24 photos or all films of 36 photos?

   b How much cheaper is it?

Film size: 24 photos	
Cost of each film	£2.15
Postage	Free
Cost to print film	£0.99
Postage of each film	60p

Film size: 36 photos	
Cost of each film	£2.65
Postage	Free
Cost to print film	£2.89
Postage of each film	60p

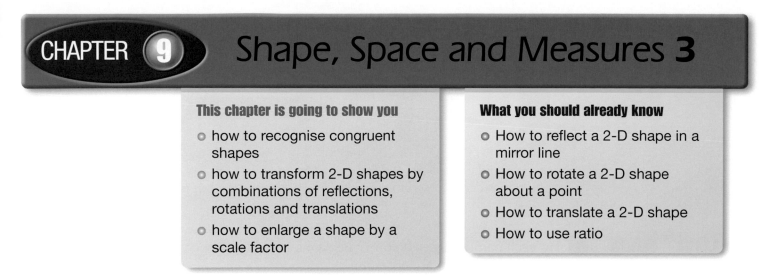
This chapter is going to show you

- how to recognise congruent shapes
- how to transform 2-D shapes by combinations of reflections, rotations and translations
- how to enlarge a shape by a scale factor

What you should already know

- How to reflect a 2-D shape in a mirror line
- How to rotate a 2-D shape about a point
- How to translate a 2-D shape
- How to use ratio

Congruent shapes

All the triangles on the grid below are reflections, rotations or translations of Triangle A. What do you notice about them?

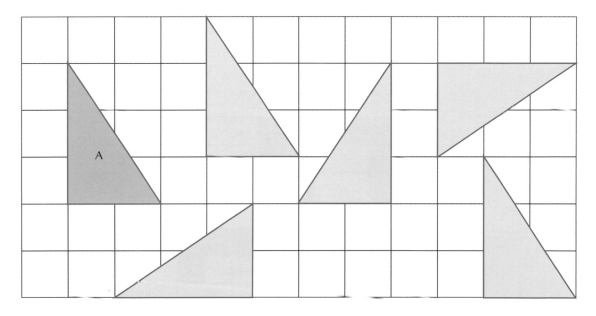

You should remember that the image triangles are exactly the same shape and size as the object Triangle A.

Two shapes are said to be **congruent** if they are exactly the same shape and size. Reflections, rotations and translations all produce images that are congruent to the original object. For shapes that are congruent, all the corresponding sides and angles are equal.

Example 9.1 ▷ Which two shapes below are congruent?

Shapes **b** and **d** are exactly the same shape and size, so **b** and **d** are congruent.
Tracing paper can be used to check that two shapes are congruent.

Exercise 9A

① For each pair of shapes below, state whether they are congruent or not (use tracing paper to help if you are not sure):

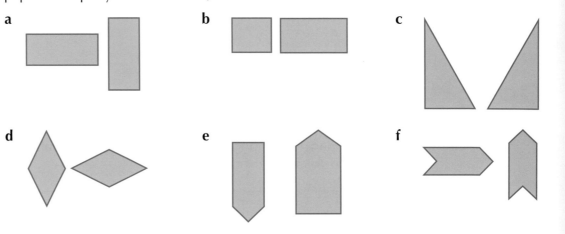

② Which pairs of shapes on the grid below are congruent?

3 Which of the shapes below are congruent?

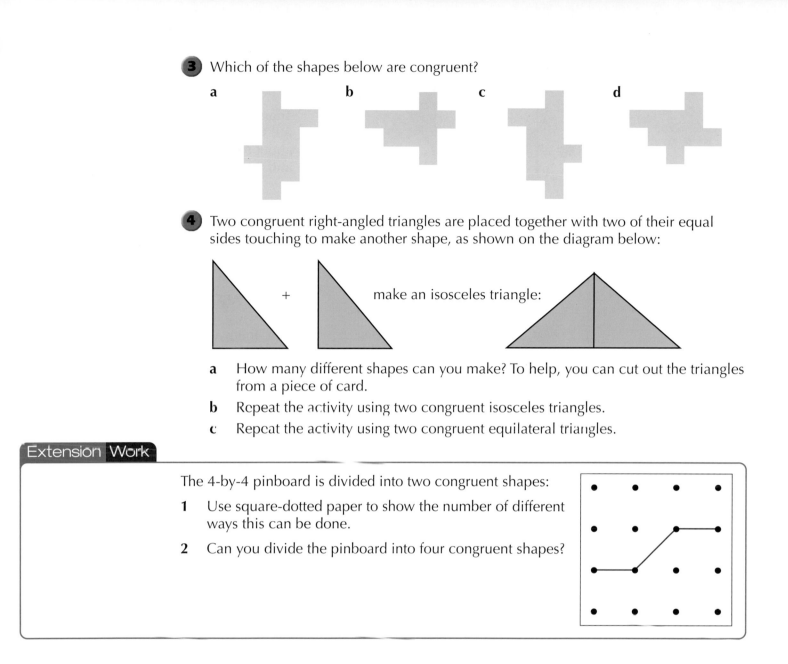

a   b   c   d

4 Two congruent right-angled triangles are placed together with two of their equal sides touching to make another shape, as shown on the diagram below:

+   make an isosceles triangle:

   a   How many different shapes can you make? To help, you can cut out the triangles from a piece of card.

   b   Repeat the activity using two congruent isosceles triangles.

   c   Repeat the activity using two congruent equilateral triangles.

Extension Work

The 4-by-4 pinboard is divided into two congruent shapes:

1   Use square-dotted paper to show the number of different ways this can be done.

2   Can you divide the pinboard into four congruent shapes?

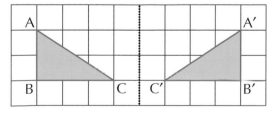

Combinations of transformations

The three single transformations you have met so far and the notation that we use to explain these transformations are shown below.

Reflections   Mirror line

Triangle ABC is mapped onto triangle A'B'C' by a reflection in the mirror line. The object and the image are congruent.

Rotations

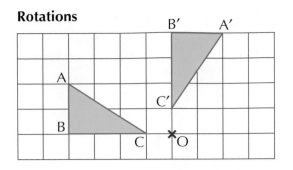

Triangle ABC is mapped onto triangle A′B′C′ by a rotation of 90° clockwise about the centre of rotation O. The object and the image are congruent.

Translations

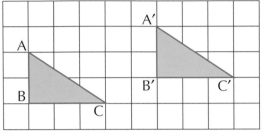

Triangle ABC is mapped onto triangle A′B′C′ by a translation of five units to the right, followed by one unit up. The object and the image are congruent.

The example below shows how a shape can be transformed by a combination of two of the above transformations.

Example 9.2 ▷

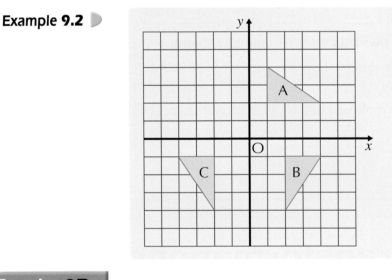

Triangle A is mapped onto triangle C after two combined transformations. Firstly, a rotation of 90° clockwise about the origin O maps A onto B, and secondly a reflection in the y-axis maps B onto C. So Triangle A is mapped onto Triangle C after a rotation of 90° clockwise about the origin O followed by a reflection in the y-axis.

Exercise 9B

Tracing paper and a mirror will be useful for this exercise.

1 Copy the diagram below onto squared paper:

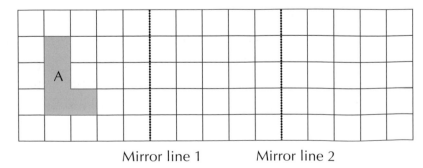

Mirror line 1   Mirror line 2

a   Reflect shape A in mirror line 1 to give shape B.

b   Reflect shape B in mirror line 2 to give shape C.

c   Describe the single transformation that maps shape A onto shape C.

2   Copy the diagram below onto squared paper:

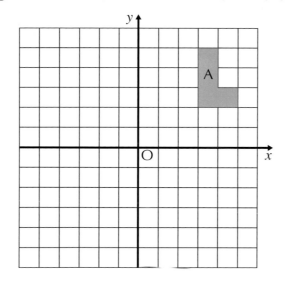

a   Reflect shape A in the *x*-axis to give shape B.

b   Reflect shape B in the *y*-axis to give shape C.

c   Describe the single transformation that maps shape A onto shape C.

3   Copy the diagram below onto squared paper:

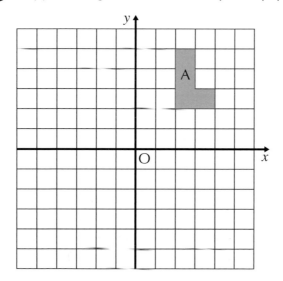

a   Rotate shape A 90° clockwise about the origin O to give shape B.

b   Rotate shape B 90° clockwise about the origin O to give shape C.

c   Describe the single transformation that maps shape A onto shape C.

Copy the diagram below onto squared paper:

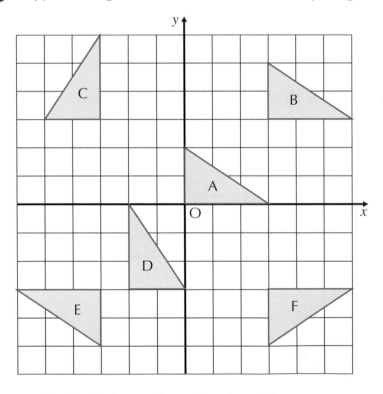

a Translate shape A three units to the right, followed by two units up, to give shape B.

b Translate shape B four units to the right, followed by 1 unit down, to give shape C.

c Describe the single transformation that maps shape A onto shape C.

5 Copy the triangles A, B, C, D, E and F onto a square grid, as shown:

a Find a single transformation that will map:

    i A onto B   **ii** E onto F   **iii** B onto E   **iv** C onto B

b Find a combination of two transformations that will map:

    i A onto C   **ii** B onto F   **iii** F onto D   **iv** B onto E

c Find other examples of combined transformations for different pairs of triangles.

6 On squared paper, show how repeated reflections of a rectangle generate a tessellating pattern.

1 Copy the congruent 'T' shapes A, B, C and D onto a square grid, as shown.

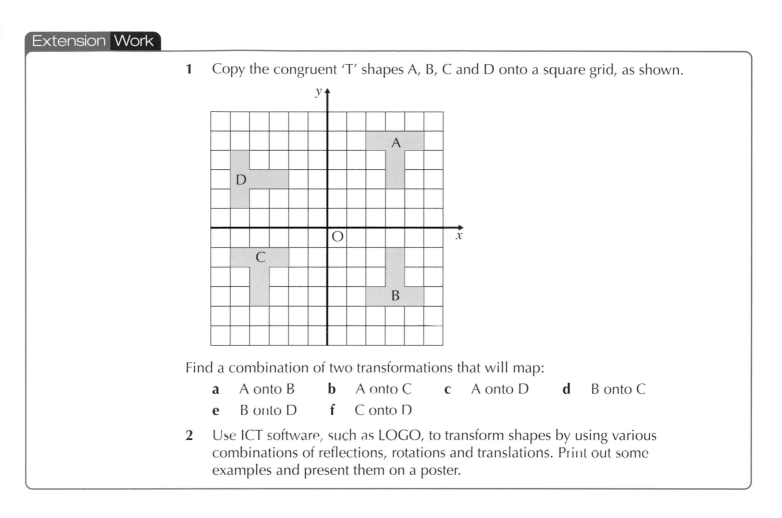

Find a combination of two transformations that will map:

a A onto B **b** A onto C **c** A onto D **d** B onto C

e B onto D **f** C onto D

2 Use ICT software, such as LOGO, to transform shapes by using various combinations of reflections, rotations and translations. Print out some examples and present them on a poster.

Enlargements

The three transformations you have met so far (reflections, rotations and translations) do not change the size of the object. You are now going to look at a transformation that does change the size of an object: **an enlargement**. The illustration shows a photograph that has been enlarged.

The diagram shows △ABC enlarged to give △A'B'C':

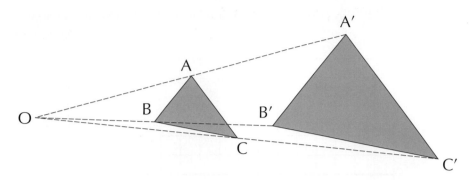

All the sides of △A'B'C' are twice as long as the sides of △ABC. Notice also that OA' = 2 × OA, OB' = 2 × OB and OC' = 2 × OC. We say that △ABC is enlarged by a scale factor of two about the centre of enlargement O to give the image △A'B'C'. The dotted lines are called the guidelines or rays for the enlargement.

To enlarge a shape we need a **centre of enlargement** and a **scale factor**.

Example 9.3 ▷ Enlarge the triangle XYZ by a scale factor of two about the centre of enlargement O:

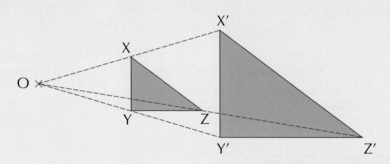

Draw rays OX, OY and OZ. Measure the length of the three rays and multiply each of these lengths by two. Then extend each of the rays to these new lengths measured from O and plot the points X', Y' and Z'. Join X', Y' and Z':

△X'Y'Z' is the enlargement of △XYZ by a scale factor of two about the centre of enlargement O.

Example 9.4 ▷ The rectangle ABCD on the coordinate grid shown has been enlarged by a scale factor of 3 about the origin O to give the image rectangle A'B'C'D'.

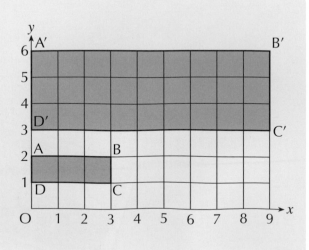

The coordinates of the object are: A(0, 2), B(3, 2), C(3, 1) and D(0, 1). The coordinates of the image are: A'(0, 6), B'(9, 6), C'(9, 3) and D'(0, 3). Notice that if a shape is enlarged by a scale factor about the origin on a coordinate grid, the coordinates of the enlarged shape are multiplied by the scale factor.

1 Draw copies of (or trace) the shapes below and enlarge each one by the given scale factor about the centre of enlargement O.

    a   Scale factor 2   **b**   Scale factor 3   **c**   Scale factor 2   **d**   Scale factor 3

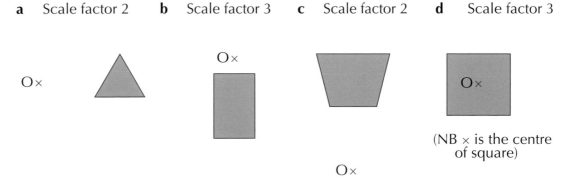

(NB × is the centre of square)

2 Copy the diagrams below onto centimetre-squared paper and enlarge each one by the given scale factor about the origin O.

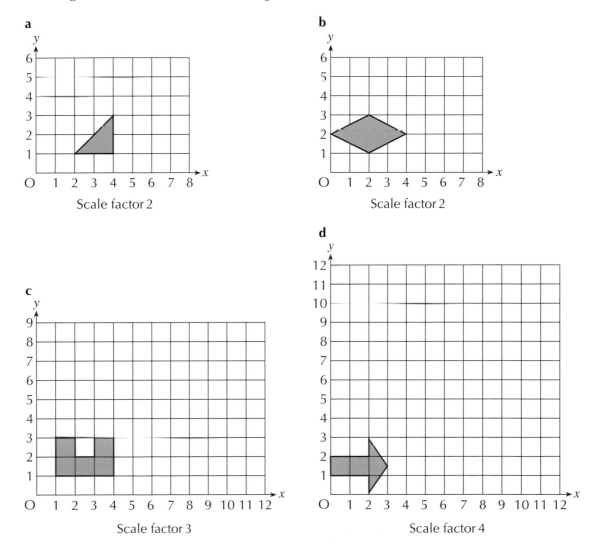

3 Draw axes for x and y from 0 to 10 on centimetre-squared paper. Plot the points A(4, 6), B(5, 4), C(4, 1) and D(3, 4) and join them together to form the kite ABCD. Enlarge the kite by a scale factor of 2 about the point (1, 2).

4 Copy the diagram shown onto centimetre-squared paper.

a Enlarge the square ABCD by a scale factor of two about the point (5, 5). Label the square A′B′C′D′. Write down the coordinates of A′, B′, C′ and D′.

b On the same grid, enlarge the square ABCD by a scale factor of three about the point (5, 5). Label the square A″B″C″D″. Write down the coordinates of A″, B″, C″ and D″.

c On the same grid, enlarge the square ABCD by a scale factor of four about the point (5, 5). Label the square A‴B‴C‴D‴. Write down the coordinates of A‴, B‴, C‴ and D‴.

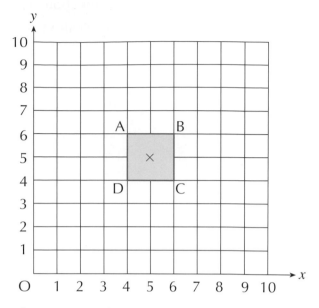

d What do you notice about the coordinate points that you have written down?

5 Copy the diagram shown onto centimetre-squared paper.

a What is the scale factor of the enlargement?

b By adding suitable rays to your diagram, find the coordinates of the centre of enlargement.

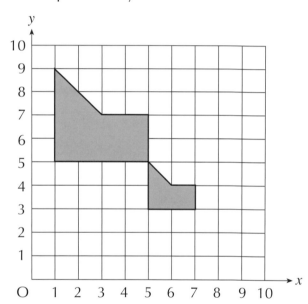

6 a Draw axes for x and y from 0 to 12 on centimetre-squared paper. Plot the points A(1, 3), B(3, 3), C(3, 1) and D(1, 1), and then join them together to form the square ABCD.

b Write down the area of the square.

c Enlarge the square ABCD by a scale factor of 2 about the origin. What is the area of the enlarged square?

d Enlarge the square ABCD by a scale factor of 3 about the origin. What is the area of the enlarged square?

e Enlarge the square ABCD by a scale factor of 4 about the origin. What is the area of the enlarged square?

f Write down anything you notice about the increase in area of the enlarged squares. Can you write down a rule to explain what is happening?

g Repeat the above using your own shapes. Does your rule still work?

1   Working in pairs or groups, design a poster to show how the 'stick-man' shown can be enlarged by different scale factors about any convenient centre of enlargement.

2   The triangle ABC is mapped onto triangle A'B'C' by an enlargement of scale factor $\frac{1}{2}$ about O, as shown. Draw some diagrams of your own to show how shapes can be enlarged by a scale factor of $\frac{1}{2}$.

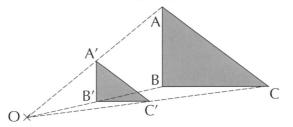

3   Use reference books or the Internet to explain how each of the following use enlargements:

    a   slide projectors   **b**   telescopes   **c**   microscopes

4   Use ICT software, such as LOGO, to enlarge shapes by different scale factors and with different centres of enlargement.

Shape and ratio

Ratio can be used to compare lengths, areas and volumes of 2-D and 3-D shapes, as the following examples show.

Example 9.5

A ══════ B   C ═══════════════════════════ D
   12 mm   4.8 cm

To find the ratio of the length of the line segment AB to the length of the line segment CD, change the measurements to the smallest unit and then simplify the ratio. So the ratio is 12 mm : 4.8 cm = 12 mm : 48 mm = 1 : 4. Remember that ratios have no units in the final answer.

Example 9.6

4 cm ⌐ A ⌐ 3 cm   8 cm ⌐ B ⌐ 5 cm

Find the ratio of the area of rectangle A to the area of rectangle B, giving the answer in its simplest form.

The ratio is 12 cm² : 40 cm² = 3 : 10.

Example 9.7 ▶

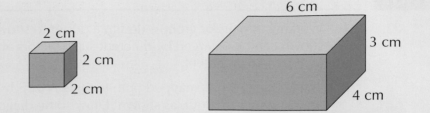

Find the ratio of the volume of the cube to the volume of the cuboid, giving the answer in its simplest form.

The ratio is 8 cm³ : 72 cm³ = 1 : 9.

Exercise 9D

1 Express each of the following ratios in its simplest form.

    a 10 mm : 25 mm   **b** 2 mm : 2 cm   **c** 36 cm : 45 cm

    d 40 cm : 2 m   **e** 500 m : 2 km

2 For the two squares shown, find each of the following ratios, giving your answers in their simplest form:

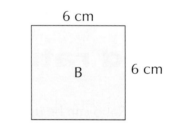

    a The length of a side of square A to the length of a side of square B.

    b The perimeter of square A to the perimeter of square B.

    c The area of square A to the area of square B.

3 Three rectangles A, B and C are arranged as in the diagram. The ratio of the length of A to the length of B to the length of C is 3 cm : 6 cm : 9 cm = 1 : 2 : 3.

    a Find each of the following ratios in the same way, giving your answers in their simplest form:

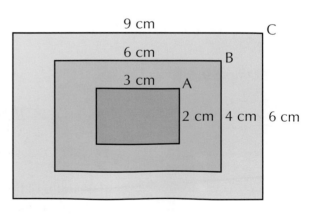

        i The width of A to the width of B to the width of C.

        ii The perimeter of A to the perimeter of B to the perimeter of C.

        iii The area of A to the area of B to the area of C.

    b Write down anything you notice about the three rectangles.

4 In the diagram, Flag X is mapped onto Flag Y by a reflection in mirror line 1. Flag X is also mapped onto Flag Z by a reflection in mirror line 2.

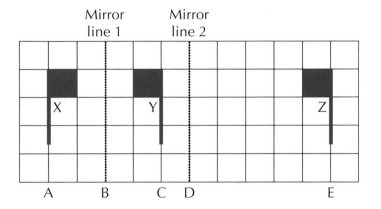

Find the ratio of each of the following lengths, giving your answers in their simplest form:

    a   AB : BC   **b**   AB : AE   **c**   AC : AE   **d**   BD : CE

5 **a**   Find the ratio of the area of the pink square to the area of the yellow surround, giving your answer in its simplest form.

     b   Express the area of the pink square as a fraction of the area of the yellow surround.

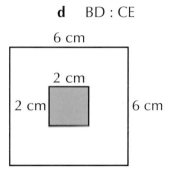

6 The dimensions of lawn A and lawn B are given on the diagrams.

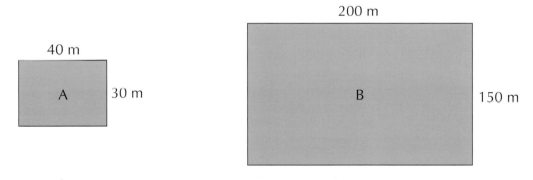

    a   Calculate the area of lawn A, giving your answer in square metres.

    b   Calculate the area of lawn B giving your answer in:

        i   square meters   **ii**   hectares (1 hectare − 10 000 m²)

    c   Find the ratio of the length of lawn A to the length of lawn B, giving your answer in its simplest form.

    d   Find the ratio of the area of lawn A to the area of lawn B, giving your answer in its simplest form.

    e   Express the area of lawn A as a fraction of the area of lawn B.

7 The dimensions of a fish tank are given on the diagram:

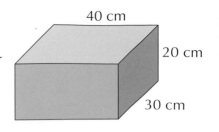

40 cm

20 cm

30 cm

a Calculate the volume of the fish tank, giving your answer in litres (1 litre = 1000 cm³).

b The fish tank is filled with water to a depth of $\frac{3}{4}$ of the height. Calculate the volume of water in the fish tank, giving your answer in litres.

c Find the ratio of the volume of water in the fish tank to the total volume of the fish tank, giving your answer in its simplest form.

Extension Work

1

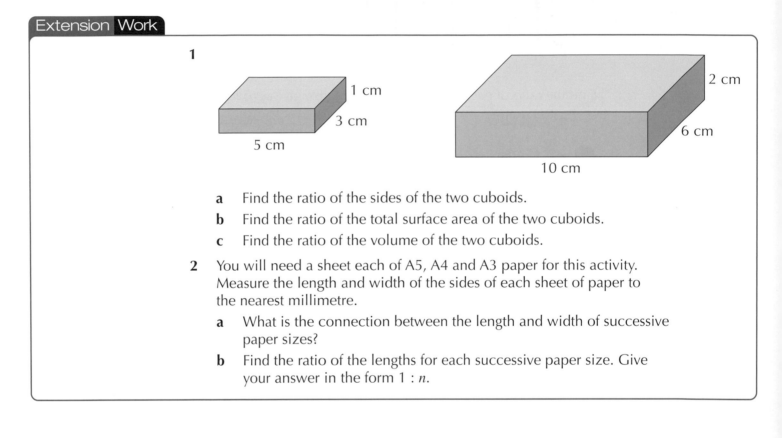

1 cm

3 cm

5 cm

2 cm

6 cm

10 cm

a Find the ratio of the sides of the two cuboids.

b Find the ratio of the total surface area of the two cuboids.

c Find the ratio of the volume of the two cuboids.

2 You will need a sheet each of A5, A4 and A3 paper for this activity. Measure the length and width of the sides of each sheet of paper to the nearest millimetre.

a What is the connection between the length and width of successive paper sizes?

b Find the ratio of the lengths for each successive paper size. Give your answer in the form 1 : *n*.

What you need to know for level 5

- How to recognise congruent shapes
- How to recognise and visualise simple transformations of 2-D shapes
- How to solve problems using ratio

What you need to know for level 6

- How to transform 2-D shapes by a combination of reflections, rotations and translations
- How to enlarge a 2-D shape by a scale factor

National Curriculum SATs questions

LEVEL 5

1   *2002 Paper 1*

Four squares join together to make a bigger square.

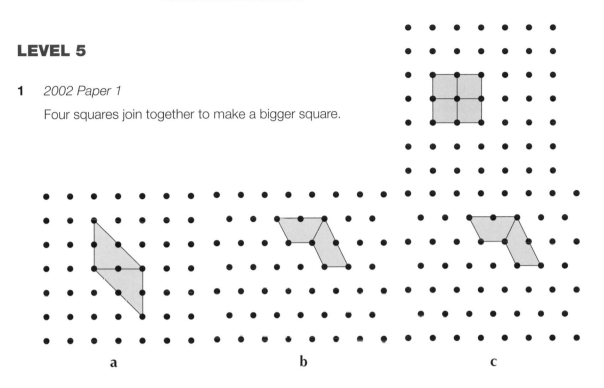

a   b   c

a   **Four** congruent triangles join together to make a bigger triangle. On a copy of the diagram, draw **two more** triangles to complete the drawing of the bigger triangle.

b   Four congruent trapezia join to make a bigger trapezium. On a copy of the diagram, draw **two more** trapezia to complete the drawing of the bigger trapezium.

c   Four congruent trapezia join together to make a **parallelogram**.
On a copy of the diagram, draw **two more** trapeziums to complete the drawing of the parallelogram.

LEVEL 6

2   *1996 Paper 1*

Julie has written a computer program to transform pictures of tiles. There are **only two instructions** in her program:

Reflect vertical or **Rotate 90° clockwise**.

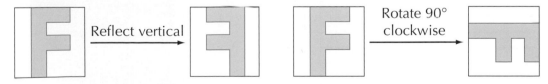

a Julie wants to transform the first pattern to the second pattern:

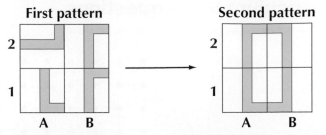

Copy and complete the instructions to transform the tiles B1 and B2. You must use only **Reflect vertical** or **Rotate 90° clockwise**.

A1 Tile is in the correct position.

A2 Reflect vertical, and then Rotate 90° clockwise.

B1 Rotate 90° clockwise, and then ……

B2 ……

b Paul starts with the first pattern that was on the screen:

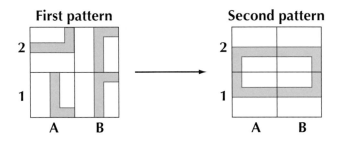

Copy and complete the instructions for the transformations of A2, B1 and B2 to make Paul's pattern. You must use only **Reflect vertical** or **Rotate 90° clockwise**.

A1 Reflect vertical, and then Rotate 90° clockwise.

A2 Rotate 90° clockwise, and then……

B1 ……

B2 ……

3 *2002 Paper 2*

On a copy of the grid, draw an **enlargement** of **scale factor 2** of the arrow. Use **point C** as the centre of the enlargement.

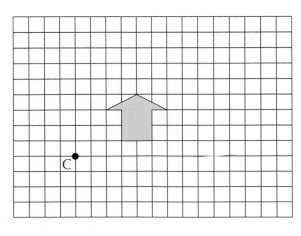

4 *2001 Paper 1*

Two parts of this square design are shaded black. Two parts are shaded pink.

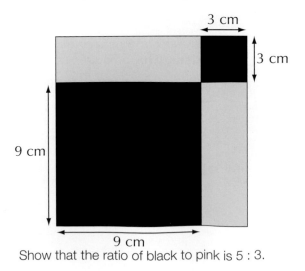

Show that the ratio of black to pink is 5 : 3.

This chapter is going to show you

- how to solve more difficult equations
- how to substitute into a formula
- how to create your own expressions and formulae

What you should already know

- How to add, subtract and multiply negative numbers

Solving equations

The equations you are going to meet will contain an unknown value, often written as x. This is called the **unknown** of the equation. Solving the equation means finding the actual value of the x, which we can do in several different ways.

For example, there are many ways you could go about solving the equation $5x - 3 = 27$, but by carefully using the methods you will practise below, you can solve this sort of equation quickly and correctly every time.

Example 10.1

Solve the equation $5x - 3 = 27$.

Add 3 to both sides: $5x - 3 + 3 = 27 + 3$

$5x = 30$

Divide both sides by 5: $\dfrac{5x}{5} = \dfrac{30}{5}$

$x = 6$

Example 10.2

Solve the equation $4(2z + 1) = 64$.

Expand the bracket: $8z + 4 = 64$

Subtract 4 from both sides: $8z + 4 - 4 = 64 - 4$

$8z = 60$

Divide both sides by 8: $z = 7.5$

Exercise 10A

1 Solve the following equations.

a $2x + 3 = 17$	**b** $4x - 1 = 19$	**c** $5x + 3 = 18$
d $2y - 3 = 13$	**e** $4z + 5 = 17$	**f** $6x - 5 = 13$
g $10b + 9 = 29$	**h** $2r - 3 = 9$	**i** $3x - 11 = 1$
j $7p + 5 = 82$	**k** $5x + 7 = 52$	**l** $9x - 8 = 55$

2 Solve the following equations.

a $3 + 2x = 11$ **b** $1 + 3w = 16$ **c** $5 + 4g = 17$

d $4 + 5x = 24$ **e** $7 + 4j = 23$ **f** $3 + 2x = 13$

g $2 + 3x = 38$ **h** $8 + 5x = 13$ **i** $3 + 4m = 11$

j $6 + 2n = 20$ **k** $4 + 3x = 31$ **l** $7 + 5x = 52$

3 Solve the following equations.

a $2x + 5 = 12$ **b** $2s - 3 = 10$ **c** $2t + 3 = 14$

d $2g - 5 = 12$ **e** $4x + 3 = 13$ **f** $4x - 5 = 13$

g $4v + 9 = 39$ **h** $4x - 3 = 11$ **i** $6x - 1 = 8$

j $6q + 5 = 26$ **k** $6x + 7 = 34$ **l** $6p - 8 = 37$

4 Solve the following equations. Start by expanding the brackets.

a $2(x + 3) = 16$ **b** $4(x - 1) = 16$ **c** $5(x + 3) = 20$

d $4(x + 1) = 12$ **e** $6(x - 5) = 18$ **f** $30 = 2(x + 9)$

5 Solve the following equations. Start by expanding the brackets.

a $2(3x + 1) = 14$ **b** $4(2x - 1) = 36$ **c** $5(2x + 3) = 55$

d $4(3x + 5) = 32$ **e** $6(4x - 5) = 42$ **f** $110 = 10(2x + 9)$

6 Each of the functions below has an expression involving x as its input, and a number as its output. By writing down an equation, find the value of x in each case. The first one has been done for you.

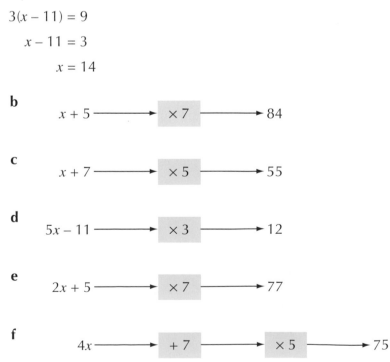

a

$$x - 11 \longrightarrow \boxed{\times 3} \longrightarrow 9$$

Multiplying the input by 3 gives an output of 9, so we can write down the following equation and then solve it as normal:

$3(x - 11) = 9$

$\quad x - 11 = 3$

$\qquad x = 14$

b

$$x + 5 \longrightarrow \boxed{\times 7} \longrightarrow 84$$

c

$$x + 7 \longrightarrow \boxed{\times 5} \longrightarrow 55$$

d

$$5x - 11 \longrightarrow \boxed{\times 3} \longrightarrow 12$$

e

$$2x + 5 \longrightarrow \boxed{\times 7} \longrightarrow 77$$

f

$$4x \longrightarrow \boxed{+ 7} \longrightarrow \boxed{\times 5} \longrightarrow 75$$

An alternative method for solving the equation from Example 10.1 is to start off by dividing both sides by 4:

$$4(2z + 1) = 64$$

Divide both sides by 4:
$$2z + 1 = 16$$
$$2z + 1 - 1 = 16 - 1$$
$$2z = 15$$
$$z = 7.5$$

Use this method, rather than expanding brackets, to solve the equations in Questions 4 and 5 of Exercise 10A.

Equations involving negative numbers

The equations that you met in the last lesson all had solutions that were positive numbers. This is not always the case, and the exercise below will give you practice at solving equations involving negative numbers.

Example 10.3

Solve the equation $5x + 11 = 1$.

Subtract 11 from each side: $5x + 11 - 11 = 1 - 11$
$$5x = -10$$

Divide both sides by 5:
$$\frac{5x}{5} = \frac{-10}{5}$$
$$x = -2$$

Example 10.4

Solve the equation $-5x = 10$.

Divide both sides by -5:
$$\frac{-5x}{-5} = \frac{10}{-5}$$

Example 10.5

Solve the equation $8 - 3x = 20$.

Subtract 8 from each side: $8 - 3x - 8 = 20 - 8$
$$-3x = 12$$

Divide both sides by -3:
$$\frac{-3x}{-3} = \frac{12}{-3}$$
$$x = -4$$

Exercise 10B

1 Solve the following equations.

a $2x + 3 = 1$	**b** $3x + 5 = 2$	**c** $2x + 9 = 5$
d $3h + 8 = 2$	**e** $3d + 4 = 19$	**f** $5x + 25 = 10$
g $4x + 15 = 3$	**h** $2x + 13 = 5$	**i** $2 = 3x + 11$
j $6n + 3 = 15$	**k** $12 = 5r + 27$	**l** $9x + 30 = 3$

2 Solve the following equations.

a	$13 + 2x = 5$	**b**	$21 + 3j = 6$	**c**	$15 + 4x = 7$
d	$24 + 5x = 4$	**e**	$27 + 4x = 31$	**f**	$15 + 2s = 9$
g	$22 + 3x = 28$	**h**	$18 + 5x = 3$	**i**	$33 + 4p = 9$
j	$17 + 2x = 1$	**k**	$12 = 24 + 3x$	**l**	$2 = 17 + 5y$

3 Solve the following equations.

a	$3x + 6 = -12$	**b**	$4x - 2 = -10$	**c**	$3x + 1 = -14$
d	$2x - 4 = -12$	**e**	$4j + 3 = -13$	**f**	$2k - 7 = -1$
g	$2x + 9 = -39$	**h**	$3x - 2 = -11$	**i**	$6x - 2 = -8$
j	$2m + 6 = -26$	**k**	$-34 = 5x + 6$	**l**	$3x - 10 = -37$

4 Solve the following equations.

a	$-4x = 20$	**b**	$-10x = 20$
c	$-2x = 12$	**d**	$-6x = 54$
e	$-7x = 42$	**f**	$9 = -3x$
g	$-9x = 99$	**h**	$8 = -2x$
i	$-x = 13$	**j**	$-5x = -20$

5 Solve the following equations.

a	$15 - 2x = 19$	**b**	$11 - 3x = 14$
c	$15 - 4x = 27$	**d**	$29 - 5x = 14$
e	$15 - 4e = 3$	**f**	$13 - 2x = 23$
g	$20 - 3x = 29$	**h**	$16 - 5x = 36$
i	$20 = 40 - 4f$	**j**	$10 = 16 - 2w$

6 Solve the following equations.

a	$2(x + 3) = 4$	**b**	$4(x - 1) = -16$	**c**	$5(x + 3) = 5$
d	$4(x + 5) = 8$	**e**	$6(z - 5) = -36$	**f**	$10(y + 9) = 20$
g	$3(t - 11) = -15$	**h**	$21 = 7(x + 5)$		

7 Solve the following equations.

a	$2(3x + 1) = -10$	**b**	$4(2x - 1) = -28$	**c**	$5(2x + 3) = 5$
d	$4(3x + 5) = 8$	**e**	$-26 = 2(4d - 5)$	**f**	$10(2a + 9) = 230$
g	$3(5v - 11) = 27$	**h**	$7(2x + 5) = -7$		

8 Victoria has made a mistake somwhere in her working for each of the equations shown opposite. Can you spot on which line the error occurs and work out the correct solution to each one?

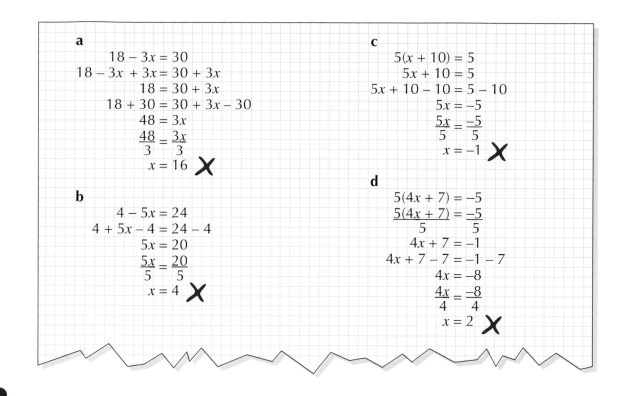

a
$$18 - 3x = 30$$
$$18 - 3x + 3x = 30 + 3x$$
$$18 = 30 + 3x$$
$$18 + 30 = 30 + 3x - 30$$
$$48 = 3x$$
$$\frac{48}{3} = \frac{3x}{3}$$
$$x = 16 \quad \textbf{X}$$

b
$$4 - 5x = 24$$
$$4 + 5x - 4 = 24 - 4$$
$$5x = 20$$
$$\frac{5x}{5} = \frac{20}{5}$$
$$x = 4 \quad \textbf{X}$$

c
$$5(x + 10) = 5$$
$$5x + 10 = 5$$
$$5x + 10 - 10 = 5 - 10$$
$$5x = -5$$
$$\frac{5x}{5} = \frac{-5}{5}$$
$$x = -1 \quad \textbf{X}$$

d
$$5(4x + 7) = -5$$
$$\frac{5(4x + 7)}{5} = \frac{-5}{5}$$
$$4x + 7 = -1$$
$$4x + 7 - 7 = -1 - 7$$
$$4x = -8$$
$$\frac{4x}{4} = \frac{-8}{4}$$
$$x = 2 \quad \textbf{X}$$

Extension Work

1 The following equations each have two possible solutions, one where x is positive, and one where x is negative. Use a spreadsheet to help you find the positive solution to each equation by trial and improvement. Give your answers to one decimal place.

a $x(x + 5) = 32$

b $x(x - 4) = 25$

2 Use a spreadsheet to help you solve $x(x + 8) = -11$ by trial and improvement. There are two answers, both negative, one greater than -4, the other less than -4. Give your answers to one decimal place.

Equations with unknowns on both sides

Sometimes there are unknown terms on both sides of an equation. You need to add or subtract terms in order to create an equation with the unknown term on one side only.

Example 10.6 ▷

Solve the equation $5x - 4 = 2x + 14$.

Subtract $2x$ from both sides: $\quad 5x - 4 - 2x = 2x + 14 - 2x$

$$3x - 4 = 14$$

Add 4 to both sides: $\qquad\quad 3x - 4 + 4 = 14 + 4$

$$3x = 18$$

Divide both sides by 3: $\qquad\quad \frac{3x}{3} = \frac{18}{3}$

$$x = 6$$

Example 10.7 ▶

Solve the equation $4x + 2 = 7 - x$.

Add x to each side:

$$4x + 2 + x = 7 - x + x$$
$$5x + 2 = 7$$

Subtract 2 from both sides:

$$5x + 2 - 2 = 7 - 2$$
$$5x = 5$$

Divide each side by 5:

$$\frac{5x}{5} = \frac{5}{5}$$
$$x = 1$$

Exercise 10C

1 Solve the following equations.

a	$2x = 4 + x$	**b**	$3x = 12 + x$	**c**	$4x = 15 + x$
d	$5x = 12 + x$	**e**	$3x = 19 + 2x$	**f**	$5x = 10 + 3x$
g	$4x = 14 + 2x$	**h**	$5x = 15 + 2x$	**i**	$7x = 12 + 4x$
j	$6x = 15 + 9x$	**k**	$5x = 12 + 2x$	**l**	$9x = 30 + 12x$

2 Solve the following equations.

a	$5x + 3 = x + 15$	**b**	$4x + 5 = x + 20$	**c**	$6x + 4 = x + 14$
d	$4x - 2 = 2x + 8$	**e**	$5x - 3 = 2x + 9$	**f**	$8x - 6 = 3x + 14$
g	$2x - 5 = 6x - 9$	**h**	$7x - 10 = 3x - 2$	**i**	$4x - 6 = 9x - 21$

3 Solve the following equations.

a	$4x + 3 = 9 + x$	**b**	$8x + 5 = 19 + x$	**c**	$5x + 4 = 12 + x$
d	$6x - 4 = 12 - 2x$	**e**	$7x - 3 = 17 + 2x$	**f**	$4x - 5 = 7 + 2x$
g	$7 - 5x = 2x - 14$	**h**	$5 + 4x = 11 + 2x$	**i**	$7 + 3x = 15 + 7x$

4 Solve the following equations. Begin by expanding the brackets.

a	$2(x + 3) = 14 + x$	**b**	$3(2x + 5) = 25 + x$
c	$5(3x - 4) = 12 + 7x$	**d**	$6x - 4 = 2(4 + 2x)$
e	$9x + 3 = 3(8 + 2x)$	**f**	$8x - 10 = 2(3 + 2x)$
g	$2(5x + 7) = 3(7 + x)$	**h**	$3(8 + 4x) = 4(9 + 2x)$
i	$2(7x - 6) = 3(1 + 3x)$		

Extension Work

Solve the equations   **a** $\dfrac{2x + 1}{x + 5} = 1$ **b** $\dfrac{5x + 3}{x + 6} = 2$ **c** $\dfrac{10x - 1}{2x + 5} = 3$

Substituting into expressions

Replacing the letters in an expression by numbers is called **substitution**. Substituting different numbers will give an expression different values. You need to be able to substitute negative numbers as well as positive numbers into expressions.

Example 10.8 ▷ What is the value of $5x + 7$ when   **i** $x = 3$ **ii** $x = -4$.

i   when $x = 3$, $5x + 7 = 5 \times 3 + 7 = 22$

ii   when $x = -4$, $5x + 7 = 5 \times (-4) + 7 = -20 + 7 = -13$

Exercise 10D

1 Write down the value of each expression for each value of x.

a	$3x + 5$	**i**	$x = 3$	**ii**	$x = 7$	**iii**	$x = -1$
b	$4x - 2$	**i**	$x = 4$	**ii**	$x = 5$	**iii**	$x = -3$
c	$8 + 7x$	**i**	$x = 2$	**ii**	$x = 6$	**iii**	$x = -2$
d	$93 - 4x$	**i**	$x = 10$	**ii**	$x = 21$	**iii**	$x = -3$
e	$x^2 + 3$	**i**	$x = 4$	**ii**	$x = 5$	**iii**	$x = -3$
f	$x^2 - 7$	**i**	$x = 6$	**ii**	$x = 2$	**iii**	$x = -10$
g	$21 + 3x^2$	**i**	$x = 7$	**ii**	$x = 3$	**iii**	$x = -5$
h	$54 - 2x^2$	**i**	$x = 3$	**ii**	$x = 5$	**iii**	$x = -1$
i	$5(3x + 4)$	**i**	$x = 5$	**ii**	$x = 4$	**iii**	$x = -2$
j	$3(5x - 1)$	**i**	$x = 3$	**ii**	$x = 2$	**iii**	$x = -6$

2 If $a = 2$ and $b = 3$ find the value of each of the following.

a $3a + b$ **b** $a \quad 3b$

c $3(b + 4a)$ **d** $5(3b - 2a)$

3 If $c = 5$ and $d = -2$ find the value of each of the following.

a $2c + d$ **b** $6c - 2d$

c $2(3d + 7c)$ **d** $4(3c - 5d)$

4 If $e = 4$ and $f = -3$ find the value of each of the following.

a $e^2 + f^2$ **b** $e^2 - f^2$

c $ef + 3e^2 - 2f^2$ **d** $e(4f^2 - e^2)$

5 If $g = 6$, $h = -4$ and $j = 7$ find the value of each of the following.

a $gh + j$ **b** $g - hj$

c ghj **d** $(g + h)(h + j)$

Extension Work

1   What values of n can be substituted into n^2 that give n^2 a value less than 1?

2   What values of n can be substituted into $(n - 4)^2$ that give $(n - 4)^2$ a value less than 1?

3   What values of n can be substituted into $1/n$ that give $1/n$ a value less than 1?

4   Find at least five different expressions that give the value 10 when $x = 2$ is substituted into them.

Substituting into formulae

Formulae occur in all sorts of situations, often when converting between two sorts of quantity. Some examples are converting between degrees Celsius and degrees Fahrenheit, or between different currencies, such as from pounds (£) to euros (€).

Example 10.9 ▷

The formula for converting degress Celsius (°C) to degress Fahrenheit (°F) is:

$$F = \frac{9C}{5} + 32$$

Convert 35 °C to °F.

Substituting $C = 35$ into the formula gives:

$$F = \frac{9 \times 35}{5} + 32 = 63 + 32 = 95$$

So 35 °C = 95 °F.

Example 10.10 ▷

The formula for the area, A, of a triangle with base length b, and height h, is given by $A = \frac{1}{2}bh$.

Calculate the base length (b) of a triangle whose area is 14 cm² and whose height is 7cm.

Substitute the values that you know into the formula:

$$14 = \frac{1}{2} \times b \times 7$$

Rearrange to get the unknown (b) by itself on one side:

$$14 \div 7 = \frac{1}{2} \times b \times 7 \div 7$$

$$2 = \frac{1}{2} \times b$$

$$2 \times 2 = \frac{1}{2} \times b \times 2$$

$$4 = b$$

So the base is 4 cm long.

Exercise 10E

1 If $A = LB$, find A when   **i** $L = 8$ and $B = 7$ **ii** $L = 6$ and $B = 1.5$

2 If $A = 6rh$, find A when   **i** $r = 6$ and $h = 17$ **ii** $r = 2.5$ and $h = 12$

3 If $A = 180(n - 2)$, find A when   **i** $n = 7$ **ii** $n = 12$

4 If $V = u + ft$

     a   find V when   **i** $u = 40, f = 32$ and $t = 5$ **ii** $u = 12, f = 13$ and $t = 10$

     b   find u when $V = 5, f = 1$ and $t = 2$

5 If $D = \frac{M}{V}$

     a   find D when   **i** $M = 28$ and $V = 4$ **ii** $M = 8$ and $V = 5$

     b   find M when $D = 7$ and $V = 3$

6 A magician charges £25 for every show he performs, plus an extra £10 per hour spent on stage. The formula for calculating his charge is $C = 10t + 25$, where C is the charge in pounds and t is the length of the show in hours.

    a How much does he charge for a show lasting

        i   1 hour   **ii**   3 hours   **iii** $2\frac{1}{2}$ hours?

    b The magician charges £30 for one of his shows. How long did the show last?

7 The area (A) of the trapezium shown is given by the formula $A = \dfrac{h(a + b)}{2}$.

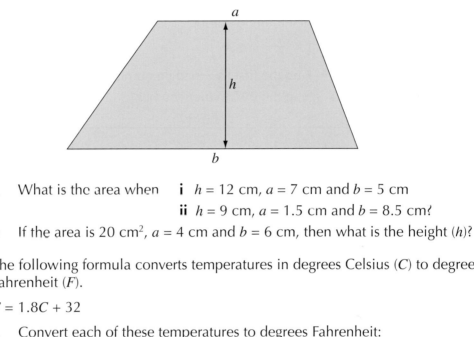

    a What is the area when   **i** $h = 12$ cm, $a = 7$ cm and $b = 5$ cm

                             ii $h = 9$ cm, $a = 1.5$ cm and $b = 8.5$ cm?

    b If the area is 20 cm², $a = 4$ cm and $b = 6$ cm, then what is the height (h)?

8 The following formula converts temperatures in degrees Celsius (C) to degrees Fahrenheit (F).

    $F = 1.8C + 32$

    a Convert each of these temperatures to degrees Fahrenheit:

        i   45 °C   **ii**   40 °C   **iii**   65 °C   **iv**   100 °C

    b Convert each of these temperatures to degrees Celsius:

        i   50 °F   **ii**   59 °F   **iii**   41 °F   **iv**   23 °F

9 If $N = h(A^2 - B^2)$, find N when **i** $h = 7$, $A = 5$ and $B = 3$ **ii** $h = 15$, $A = 4$ and $B = 2$

10 If $V = hr^2$, find V when   **i** $h = 5$ and $r = 3$ **ii** $h = 8$ and $r = 5$

11 The volume (V) of the cuboid shown is given by the formula:

    $V = abc$

    The surface area (S) of the cuboid is given by the formula:

    $S = 2ab + 2bc + 2ac$

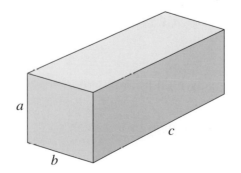

a Find   **i** the volume and

  ii the surface area, when $a = 3$ m, $b = 4$ m and $c = 5$ m.

b Find   **i** the volume and

  ii the surface area when $a = 3$ cm, and a, b and c are all the same length. What name is given to this cuboid?

12 The triangle numbers are given by the following formula:

$$T = \frac{n(n + 1)}{2}$$

The first triangle number is found by substituting in $n = 1$, which gives
$T = 1 \times \frac{(1 + 1)}{2} = 1$.

a Find the first five triangle numbers.

b Find the 99th triangle number.

Extension Work

1 If $\frac{1}{F} = \frac{1}{U} - \frac{1}{V}$

Calculate   **i** F when $U = 4$ and $V = 5$ **ii** V when $F = 2$ and $U = 3$

2 If $\frac{1}{T} = \frac{1}{A} + \frac{1}{B}$

Calculate   **i** T when $A = 3$ and $B = 2$ **ii** A when $T = 2$, $B = 8$

Creating your own expressions and formulae

The last lesson showed you some formulae that could be used to solve problems. In this lesson you will be given problems and have to write down your own formulae to help solve them.

You will need to choose a letter to represent each variable in a problem, and use these when you write the formula. Usually these will be the first letters of the words they represent, e.g., V often represents volume and A is often used for area.

Example 10.11 ▷

Find an expression for the sum, S, of any three consecutive whole numbers.

Let the smallest number be n.

The next number is $(n + 1)$ and the biggest number is $(n + 2)$.

So $S = n + (n + 1) + (n + 2)$

$S = n + n + 1 + n + 2$

$S = 3n + 3$

Example 10.12 ▷

How many months are there in   **i** 5 years

  ii t years?

There are 12 months in a year, so   **i** in 5 years there will be $12 \times 5 = 60$ months

  ii in t years there will be $12 \times t = 12t$ months

1 Using the letters suggested, construct a simple formula in each case.

   a The sum, S, of three numbers a, b and c.

   b The product, P, of two numbers x and y.

   c The difference, D, between the ages of two people; the eldest one being a years old and the other b years old.

   d The sum, S, of four consecutive integers.

   e The number of days, D, in W weeks.

   f The average age, A, of three boys whose ages are m, n and p years.

2 How many days are there in:

   a 3 weeks   **b** w weeks?

3 A girl is now 13 years old.

   a How many years old will she be in:

      i 5 years   **ii** t years?

   b How many years old was she:

      i 3 years ago   **ii** m years ago?

4 A car travels at a speed of 30 mph. How many miles will it travel in:

   a 2 hours   **b** t hours?

5 How many grams are there in:

   a 5 kg   **b** x kg?

6 How many minutes are there in m hours?

7 Write down the number that is half as big as b.

8 Write down the number that is twice as big as T.

9 If a boy runs at b miles per hour, how many miles does he run in k hours?

10 **a** What is the cost, in pence, of 6 papers at 35 pence each?

    b What is the cost, in pence, of k papers at 35 pence each?

    c What is the cost, in pence, of k papers at q pence each?

11 A boy is b years old and his mother is 6 times as old:

   a Find the mother's age in terms of b.

   b Find the sum of their ages in y years time.

12 Mr Speed's age is equal to the sum of the ages of his three sons. The youngest son is aged x years, the eldest is 10 years older than the youngest and the middle son is 4 years younger than the eldest. How old is Mr Speed?

Extension Work

1 A man is now three times as old as his daughter. In 10 years time, the sum of their ages will be 76 years. How old was the man when his daughter was born?

2 Find three consecutive odd numbers for which the sum is 57.

3 A group of pupils had to choose between playing football and badminton. The number of pupils that chose football was three times the number that chose badminton. The number of players for each game would be equal if 12 pupils who chose football were asked to play badminton. Find the total number of pupils.

What you need to know for level 5

- How to construct expressions and formulae
- How to use simple formulae

What you need to know for level 6

- Solve linear equations with unknown values on both sides
- Interpret the terms in expressions and formulae

National Curriculum SATs questions

LEVEL 5

1 *2002 Paper 1*

Look at this table:

	Age in years
Ann	a
Ben	b
Cindy	c

Copy the table below and write in words the meaning of each equation. The first one is done for you.

a	$b = 30$	Ben is 30 years old
b	$a + b = 69$	
c	$b = 2c$	
d	$\dfrac{a + b + c}{3} = 28$	

2 **a** Copy the expressions below and work out their values when $x = 5$.

  i $2x + 13$

  ii $5x - 5$

  iii $3 + 6x$

  b When $2y + 11 = 17$, work out the value of y. Show your working.

3 You can often use algebra to show why a number puzzle works.
Copy the diagram below and fill in the missing expressions.

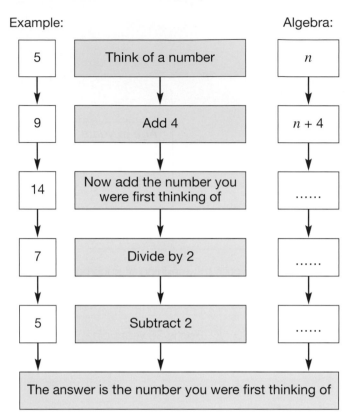

Example: Algebra:

5	Think of a number	n
9	Add 4	$n + 4$
14	Now add the number you were first thinking of	......
7	Divide by 2	......
5	Subtract 2	......

The answer is the number you were first thinking of

LEVEL 6

4 *2002 Paper 1*

Solve the equation $9y - 3 = 5y + 13$.
Show your working.

5 Look at these equations:

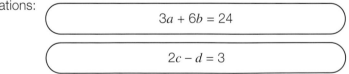

$$3a + 6b = 24$$

$$2c - d = 3$$

a Use the equations above to work out the value of the expressions below.
The first one is done for you, (copy and complete the others).

$8c - 4d = $ _____12_____

i $a + 2b$ = _____

ii $d - 2c$ = _____

b Use one or both of the equations above to write an expression that has a value of 21.

This chapter is going to show you

- how to write questions for a questionnaire
- how to collect data
- how to use two-way tables
- how to construct statistical diagrams for discrete data
- when to use range, mean, median and mode
- how to construct stem and leaf diagrams

What you should already know

- How to interpret data from tables, graphs and charts
- How to find mode, median, mean and range for small data sets
- How to write a short report of a statistical survey
- How to design a data-collection sheet

Statistical surveys

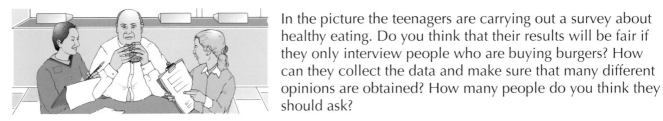

In the picture the teenagers are carrying out a survey about healthy eating. Do you think that their results will be fair if they only interview people who are buying burgers? How can they collect the data and make sure that many different opinions are obtained? How many people do you think they should ask?

Example 11.1

Here are some questions that might be used in a survey. Give a reason why each question is not very good and then write a better question.

a How old are you?   **b** Do you eat lots of fruit or vegetables?

c Don't you agree that exercise is good for you?

d If you go to a sports centre with your friends and you want to play badminton, do you usually play a doubles match or do you just practise?

a This is a personal question. If you want to find out about the ages of people use answer boxes and group several ages together.

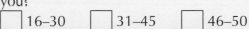

How old are you?

☐ 0–15   ☐ 16–30   ☐ 31–45   ☐ 46–50   ☐ More than 50

b This question is asking about two different items, so the answers may be confusing. It may be awkward to answer with a yes or a no, it is better to have two separate questions:

Do you eat fruit?   Do you eat vegetables?

c This question is trying to force you to agree. It is a leading question. A better question would be:

Is exercise good for you?

d This question is too long. There is too much information, which makes it difficult to answer. It should be split up into several smaller questions.

Choose one of the problem statements given below for your statistical survey, or make up your own and get your teacher to check it. For the problem you choose:

- Write down a hypothesis for the problem.
- Write down three or four good questions for your questionnaire or decide how you will make your observations.
- Make a data-collection sheet.
- Collect information from at least 30 people/observations.

1 Do girls spend more on clothes than boys?

2 Do old people use libraries more than teenagers?

3 When people decide where to shop, does the type of transport they use affect their decision? For example, people who use local shops might walk, people who use town centres might travel by bus and people who use out-of-town shopping centres might be car users.

4 If people holiday abroad one year, do they tend to stay in Britain the following year?

5 Do pupils who enjoy playing sports eat healthier foods?

6 Do sports teams tend to score more towards the end of matches, as the opponents become tired?

7 Do taller people have longer hair?

8 Do more men wear glasses than women?

9 Do families eat out more than they used to?

Extension Work

Take each problem statement from the exercise and write down how you would collect the data required. For example, would you collect the data using a questionnaire or by carrying out an experiment, or would you collect the data from books, computer software or the internet? Also, write a short report to explain the advantages and disadvantages of each method of data collection.

Stem-and-leaf diagrams

The speeds of vehicles in a 30 mile-per-hour limit are recorded. The speeds are sorted into order and put into a stem-and-leaf diagram. The slowest speed is 23 miles per hour. The fastest speed is 45 miles per hour. How can you tell this from the stem-and-leaf diagram?

```
2 | 3  7  7  8  9  9
3 | 1  2  3  5  5  5  7  9
4 | 2  2  5                         Key: 2 | 3 means 23 miles per hour
```

How many cars are breaking the speed limit?

Example 11.2 ▷ A teacher asked 25 pupils how many pieces of homework they were given in one week. The results are shown in the stem-and-leaf diagram:

```
0 | 1  1  2  2  2  2  3  5  7  7  7  8  9
1 | 0  0  1  1  1  2  4  4  5  6
2 | 1  3                          Key: 1 | 2 means 12 homeworks
```

Use the stem-and-leaf diagram to find:

a the median   **b** range   **c** mode

a As there are 25 pupils, the middle value is the thirteenth, so the median = 9.

b The most homeworks is the last value, 23, and the least homeworks is the first value, 1.

The range = biggest value – smallest value
= 23 – 1
= 22 homeworks

c The mode occurs the most, so the mode = 2 homeworks because it occurs 4 times.

Exercise 11B

1 15 sales people have a competition to find out who sells the most items in one day. Here are the results:

```
1 | 2  2  3  7  7
2 | 1  4  4  4  5  5  6
3 | 0  2  5                        Key: 1 | 2 means 12 items
```

a How many items did the winner sell?   **b** What is the mode?
c Find the range   **d** Work out the median

2 35 Year 8 pupils are asked to estimate how many text messages they send on their mobile phones each week. Their replies are put into a stem-and-leaf diagram.

```
0 | 5  5  6  7  8  8
1 | 0  0  0  0  0  1  1  4  4
1 | 8  9  9  9
2 | 0  0  1  3  3  3  4
2 | 5  6
3 | 0  0  4
3 | 5  6  6                        Key: 0 | 5 means 5 text messages
```

Work out:

a The mode   **b** the smallest estimate   **c** the range   **d** the median

3 A farmer records the number of animals of each type on his farm. His results are shown in the stem-and-leaf diagram:

```
5 │ 2  6  8
6 │ 5  9
7 │ 5
```
                                    Key: 5 | 2 represents 52 animals of one type

a He has more sheep than any other type of animal. How many sheep does he have?

b How many animals has he altogether?

c Explain why a stem-and-leaf diagram may not be the best way to represent these data.

4 The ages of 30 people at a disco are as shown:

32	12	47	25	23	23	17	36	42	17
31	15	24	49	19	31	23	34	36	45
47	12	39	11	26	23	22	38	48	17

a Put the ages into a stem-and-leaf diagram (remember to show a key).

b State the mode.

c Work out the range.

Pie charts

In the picture, which colour represents 'unfit adults'? How do you know? The pie chart is used because it shows the proportion of the whole amount and is quite easy to interpret.

Sometimes you will have to interpret pie charts that are already drawn and sometimes you will be asked to construct a pie chart.

Example 11.3 ▷ Draw a pie chart to represent the following set of data showing how a group of people travel to work.

Type of travel	Walk	Car	Bus	Train	Cycle
Frequency	24	84	52	48	32

It is easier to set out your workings in a table.

Type of travel	Frequency	Calculation	Angle
Walk	24	$\frac{24}{240} \times 360 = 36°$	36°
Car	84	$\frac{84}{240} \times 360 = 126°$	126°
Bus	52	$\frac{52}{240} \times 360 = 78°$	78°
Train	48	$\frac{48}{240} \times 360 = 72°$	72°
Cycle	32	$\frac{32}{240} \times 360 = 48°$	48°
TOTAL	240		360°

We work out the angle for each sector using

$$\frac{\text{Frequency}}{\text{Total frequency}} \times 360°$$

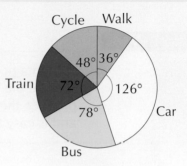

Example 11.4

The pie chart shows the types of housing on a new estate. Altogether there were 540 new houses built.

How many are
a detached?   b semi-detached?
c bungalows?   d terraced?

You need to work out the fraction of 540 that each sector represents.

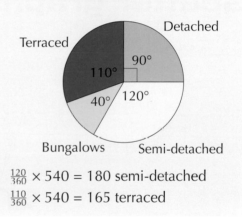

a $\frac{90}{360} \times 540 = 135$ detached
b $\frac{120}{360} \times 540 = 180$ semi-detached
c $\frac{40}{360} \times 540 = 60$ bungalows
d $\frac{110}{360} \times 540 = 165$ terraced

1 Draw pie charts to represent the following data:

a The favourite subject of 36 pupils

Subject	Maths	English	Science	Languages	Other
Frequency	12	7	8	4	5

b The type of food that 40 people usually eat for breakfast

Food	Cereal	Toast	Fruit	Cooked	Other	None
Frequency	11	8	6	9	2	4

c The number of goals scored by an ice-hockey team in 24 matches

Goals	0	1	2	3	4	5 or more
Frequency	3	4	7	5	4	1

d   The favourite colour of 60 Year 8 pupils

Colour	Red	Green	Blue	Yellow	Other
Frequency	17	8	21	3	11

2   The pie chart shows the results of a survey of 216 children about their favourite foods.

How many chose

a   chips?   **b**   burgers?

c   fish fingers?   **d**   curry?

Extension Work

Design a poster to show information about the pupils in your class. Either include pie charts that you have drawn yourself or use a spreadsheet to produce the pie charts. Make sure that any pie chart you produce has labels and is easy to understand.

Scatter graphs

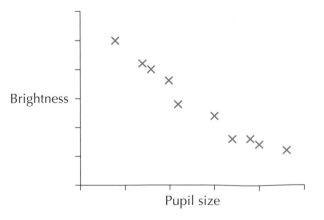

A doctor records the size of the pupils of people's eyes and the brightness of the sunlight. He then plots the results on a graph. What can you tell about the connection between the brightness and the pupil size of the people?

Example 11.5 ▷ Below are three scatter graphs. Describe the relationships in each graph.

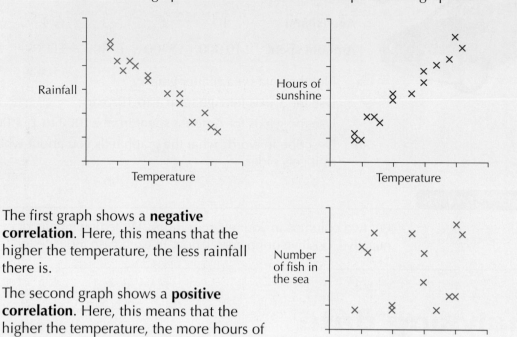

The first graph shows a **negative correlation**. Here, this means that the higher the temperature, the less rainfall there is.

The second graph shows a **positive correlation**. Here, this means that the higher the temperature, the more hours of sunshine there are.

The third graph shows **no correlation**. Here, this means that there is no connection between the temperature and the number of fish in the sea.

Exercise 11D

1 A survey is carried out to compare pupils' ages with the amount of money that they spend each week.

Age (year)	11	16	14	13	13	18	10	12	14	15
Amount spent	£3	£3.50	£6	£5	£6.50	£12	£2.50	£4	£8	£7.50

a Plot the data on a scatter graph:
Use the x-axis for Age from 10 to 20 years;
Use the y-axis for Amount spent from £0 to £15.

b Describe in words what the graph tells you and what sort of correlation there is.

2 The table shows how much time pupils spend watching television and how long they spend on homework per week.

Time watching TV (hours)	12	8	5	7	9	3	5	6	10	14
Time spent on homework (hours)	4	7	10	6	5	11	9	6	6	3

a Plot the data on a scatter graph (take each axis as Time from 0 to 15 hours).

b Describe in words what the graph tells you and what sort of correlation there is.

3 The table shows the value of a car and the age of the car.

Age (years)	1	2	3	4	5	6	7
Amount spent	£10 000	£8300	£7500	£6000	£5300	£4200	£3400

a Plot the data on a scatter graph:

Use the *x*-axis for Age from 1 to 10 years;

Use the *y*-axis for Amount spent from £1000 to £11 000.

b Describe in words what the graph tells you about what happens to a car's value as it gets older.

Extension Work

Put two columns in your exercise book. Write down pairs of events that have negative, positive or no correlation. In each case indicate the type of correlation.

Analysing data

Suppose that you want to put some data into the form of diagrams or tables. How do you choose which form to use? Ask yourself a few questions. Will my diagram be easy to understand? If I use a pie chart will there be too many sectors? Am I comparing two sets of data?

Exercise 11E

For each question below, write down whether the best way to collect data is by:

- Questionnaire;
- Controlled experiment;
- Data from textbooks or the internet.

1 Do more men attend sports events than women?

2 Does it always snow in December?

3 Is a dice fair?

4 Which soap powder is most popular?

5 What percentage of 13-year-old children have mobile phones?

6 How popular is a particular restaurant?

7 How many people have had an illness in the past 2 months?

8 Do Year 8 girls prefer Brad Pitt or Tom Cruise?

9 How many people visit a shopping centre on a Sunday?

10 How many lorries use a road between 8.00AM and 9.00AM?

Now you are ready to analyse and write a report on the data that you collected for Exercise 11A.

Your report should consist of:

- A brief statement of what you expect to show. This is called a hypothesis.
- A section that explains how you collected your data.
- A copy of any questionnaires you may have used.
- Completed data-collection sheets or tally charts.
- Suitable diagrams to illustrate your data.
- Calculated statistics, such as mean, median, mode and range.
- A brief conclusion that refers back to your hypothesis.

You may wish to use some or all of the following sorts of diagrams if you think they are appropriate: bar charts, pie charts, stem-and-leaf diagrams, scatter graphs.

Extension Work

The extension work is to finish writing up your report, including as much detail as possible using the guidelines given in this chapter.

What you need to know for level 5

- How to use, collect and record discrete data
- How to interpret graphs and diagrams, including pie charts and draw conclusions
- To understand that different outcomes may result from repeating an experiment

What you need to know for level 6

- How to use, collect and record continuous data
- How to construct pie charts
- How to draw conclusions from scatter diagrams and have a basic understanding of correlation
- When dealing with a combination of two experiments, identify all possible outcomes using diagrams and tables

National Curriculum SATs questions

LEVEL 5

1 *2001 Paper 1*

There are 60 pupils in a school. 6 of these pupils wear glasses.

a The pie chart is not drawn accurately.

What should the angles be? Show your working.

b Exactly half of the 60 pupils in the school are boys.

From this information, is the percentage of boys in this school that wear glasses 5%, 6%, 10%, 20%, 50% or not possible to tell?

2 *2001 Paper 2*

A teacher asked two different classes: 'What type of book is your favourite?'

a Results from class A (total 20 pupils):

Type of book	Frequency
Crime	3
Non-fiction	13
Fantasy	4

Draw a pie chart to show this information. Show your working and draw your angles accurately.

b The pie chart on the right shows the results from all of class B.

Each pupil had only one vote.

The sector for non-fiction represents 11 pupils.

How many pupils are in class B?

Show your working.

3 *1999 Paper 1*

The scatter diagram shows the heights and masses of some horses.

The scatter diagram also shows a line of best fit.

a What does the scatter diagram show about the relationship between the height and mass of horses?

b The height of a horse is 163 cm.

Use the line of best fit to estimate the mass of the horse (in kg).

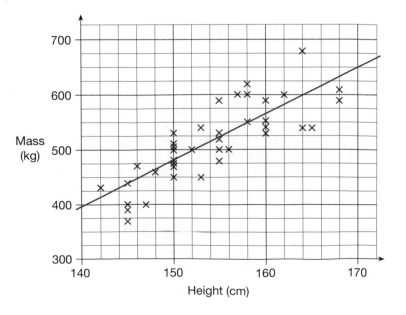

c   A different horse has a mass of 625 kg.

Use the line of best fit to estimate the height of the horse (in cm).

d   A teacher asks his class to investigate this statement:

'The length of the back leg of a horse is always less than the length of the
front leg of a horse.'

What might a scatter graph look like if the statement is correct? Take the x-axis as the
Length of front leg from 70 to 110 cm.

Take the y-axis to be Length of back leg from 70 to 110 cm.

4   *1998 Paper 2*

A competition has three different games.

a   Jeff plays two games.

To win, Jeff needs a mean score of 60.

	Game A	Game B	Game C
Score	62	53	

How many points does he need to score in Game C? Show your working.

b   Imran and Nia play the three games.

Their scores have the same mean.

The range of Imran's scores is twice
the range of Nia's scores. Copy the table above and fill in the missing scores.

Imran's scores		40	
Nia's scores	35	40	45

The scatter diagrams show the scores of everyone who plays all 3 games.

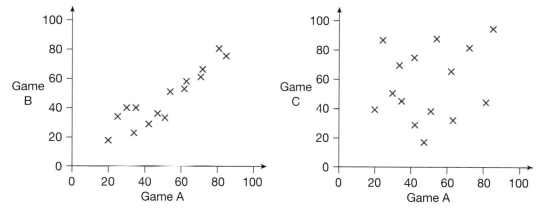

c   Look at the scatter diagrams.

Which statement most closely describes the relationship between the games?

Game A and Game B				
perfect negative	negative	no relationship	positive	perfect positive

Game A and Game C				
perfect negative	negative	no relationship	positive	perfect positive

d   What can you tell about the relationship between the scores on Game B and the scores on
Game C?

Game B and Game C				
perfect negative	negative	no relationship	positive	perfect positive

This chapter is going to show you

- how to add and subtract fractions with any denominators
- how to use BODMAS with more complex problems
- how to solve problems using decimals, fractions, percentages and units of measurement

What you should already know

- How to add and subtract fractions with the same denominator
- How to find equivalent fractions
- How to use the four operations with decimals

Fractions

This section recalls some of the rules you have already met about fractions.

Example 12.1

Work out:

a How many sevenths are in 4 whole ones.

b How many fifths are in $3\frac{3}{5}$.

a There are 7 sevenths in one whole, so there are $4 \times 7 = 28$ sevenths in 4 whole ones.

b There are $3 \times 5 = 15$ fifths in 3 whole ones, so there are $15 + 3 = 18$ fifths in $3\frac{3}{5}$.

Example 12.2

Write the following as mixed numbers:

a $\frac{48}{15}$ **b** The fraction of a kilometre given by 3150 metres

a $48 \div 15 = 3$ remainder 3, so $\frac{48}{15} = 3\frac{3}{15}$, which can cancel to $3\frac{1}{5}$. (Note: it is usually easier to cancel after the fraction has been written as a mixed number rather than before.)

b 1 kilometre is 1000 metres, so the fraction is $\frac{3150}{1000} = 3\frac{150}{1000} = 3\frac{3}{20}$.

Exercise 12A

1 Find the missing number in each of these fractions:

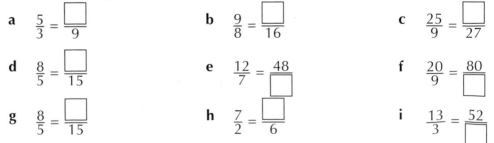

a $\frac{5}{3} = \frac{\square}{9}$

b $\frac{9}{8} = \frac{\square}{16}$

c $\frac{25}{9} = \frac{\square}{27}$

d $\frac{8}{5} = \frac{\square}{15}$

e $\frac{12}{7} = \frac{48}{\square}$

f $\frac{20}{9} = \frac{80}{\square}$

g $\frac{8}{5} = \frac{\square}{15}$

h $\frac{7}{2} = \frac{\square}{6}$

i $\frac{13}{3} = \frac{52}{\square}$

2 **a** How many sixths are in $3\frac{5}{6}$?   **b** How many eighths are in $4\frac{1}{2}$?

     c How many tenths are in $2\frac{2}{5}$?   **d** How many ninths are in $5\frac{7}{9}$?

3 Write each mixed number in Question 2 as a top-heavy fraction in its simplest form.

4 Write each of the following as a mixed number in its simplest form:

     a $\frac{14}{12}$ **b** $\frac{15}{9}$ **c** $\frac{24}{21}$ **d** $\frac{35}{20}$

     e $\frac{28}{20}$ **f** $\frac{70}{50}$ **g** $\frac{28}{24}$ **h** $\frac{26}{12}$

     i $\frac{44}{24}$ **j** $\frac{32}{10}$ **k** $\frac{36}{24}$ **l** $\frac{75}{35}$

5 Write these fractions as mixed numbers (cancel down if necessary):

     a seven thirds   **b** sixteen sevenths   **c** twelve fifths   **d** nine halves

     e $\frac{20}{7}$ **f** $\frac{24}{5}$ **g** $\frac{13}{3}$ **h** $\frac{19}{8}$ **i** $\frac{146}{12}$ **j** $\frac{78}{10}$ **k** $\frac{52}{12}$ **l** $\frac{102}{9}$

6 Write as fractions:

     a the turn of the minute hand round a clock as it goes from:

         i 7:15 to 9:45   **ii** 8:25 to 10:10   **iii** 6:12 to 7:24

         iv 8:55 to 10:45   **v** 7:05 to 10:20   **vi** 9:36 to 11:24

     b the fraction of a metre given by:

         i 715 cm   **ii** 2300 mm   **iii** 405 cm

         iv 580 cm   **v** 1550 mm   **vi** 225 cm

     c the fraction of a kilogram given by:

         i 2300 g   **ii** 4050 g   **iii** 7500 g

         iv 5600 g   **v** 1225 g   **vi** 6580 g

Extension Work

A gallon is an imperial unit of capacity still in common use. There are 8 pints in a gallon. A litre is about $1\frac{3}{4}$ pints and a gallon is about $4\frac{1}{2}$ litres. Write the missing mixed numbers to make these statements true:

     a 2 litres = ... pints   **b** 10 pints = ... gallons   **c** 5 gallons = ... litres

     d 3 litres = ... pints   **e** 3 gallons = ... litres   **f** 20 pints = ... gallons

Adding and subtracting fractions

This section will give you more practice with adding and subtracting fractions.

Example 12.3

Work out:

     a $\frac{3}{8} + 1\frac{1}{4}$ **b** $1\frac{7}{8} - \frac{3}{4}$

Previously, we used a fraction chart or line to do these. An eigths fraction line is drawn below.

     a Start at 0 and count on $\frac{3}{8}$, then 1 and then $\frac{1}{4}$ to give $\frac{3}{8} + 1\frac{1}{4} = 1\frac{5}{8}$.

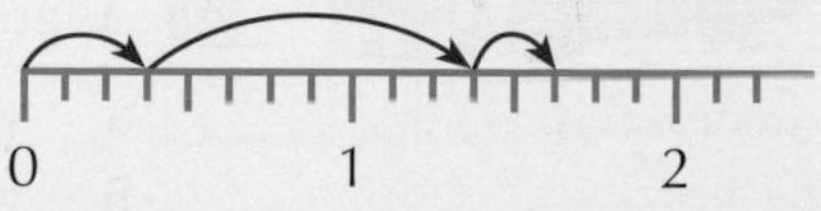

     b Start at $1\frac{7}{8}$ and count back $\frac{3}{4}$ to give $1\frac{7}{8} - \frac{3}{4} = 1\frac{1}{8}$.

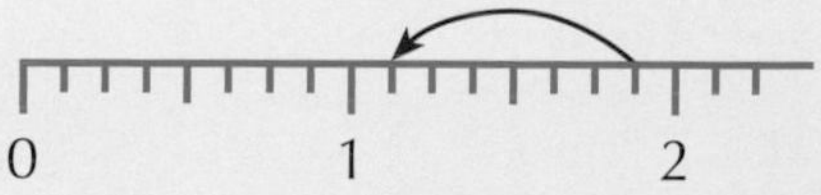

When denominators are not the same, they must be made the same before the numerators are added or subtracted. To do this, we need to find the Lowest Common Multiple (LCM) of the denominators.

Example 12.4 ▷

Work out:

a $\quad \frac{2}{3} + \frac{1}{4}$ b $\quad \frac{8}{9} - \frac{5}{6}$

a The LCM of 3 and 4 is 12, so the two fractions need to be written as twelfths:

$$\frac{2}{3} + \frac{1}{4} = \frac{8}{12} + \frac{3}{12} = \frac{11}{12}$$

b The LCM of 9 and 6 is 18, so the two fractions need to be written as eighteenths:

$$\frac{8}{9} - \frac{5}{6} = \frac{16}{18} - \frac{15}{18} = \frac{1}{18}$$

Exercise 12B

1 Work out the following (the number line on page 147 may help):

a $\quad \frac{5}{8} + \frac{1}{2}$ b $\quad 1\frac{1}{8} + \frac{3}{8}$ c $\quad 2\frac{3}{8} + 1\frac{5}{8}$ d $\quad \frac{3}{8} + 1\frac{1}{2} + 1\frac{3}{4}$

e $\quad \frac{5}{8} - \frac{1}{2}$ f $\quad 2\frac{1}{8} - \frac{5}{8}$ g $\quad 2\frac{3}{8} - 1\frac{5}{8}$ h $\quad 1\frac{3}{4} + 1\frac{1}{2} - 1\frac{7}{8}$

2 Work out the following. Cancel down answers to lowest terms and convert top-heavy fractions to mixed numbers.

a $\quad \frac{1}{3} + \frac{1}{3}$ b $\quad \frac{5}{6} + \frac{5}{6}$ c $\quad \frac{3}{10} + \frac{3}{10}$ d $\quad \frac{3}{7} + \frac{5}{7} + \frac{2}{7}$

e $\quad \frac{14}{15} - \frac{2}{15}$ f $\quad \frac{7}{9} - \frac{4}{9}$ g $\quad \frac{11}{12} - \frac{5}{12}$ h $\quad \frac{3}{10} + \frac{9}{10} - \frac{5}{10}$

3 Firstly, convert the following fractions to equivalent fractions with a common denominator, and then work out the answer, cancelling down or writing as a mixed number as appropriate:

a $\quad \frac{1}{3} + \frac{1}{4}$ b $\quad \frac{1}{6} + \frac{1}{3}$ c $\quad \frac{3}{10} + \frac{1}{4}$ d $\quad \frac{1}{9} + \frac{5}{6}$

e $\quad \frac{4}{15} + \frac{3}{10}$ f $\quad \frac{7}{8} + \frac{5}{6}$ g $\quad \frac{7}{12} + \frac{1}{4}$ h $\quad \frac{3}{4} + \frac{1}{3} + \frac{1}{2}$

i $\quad \frac{1}{3} - \frac{1}{4}$ j $\quad \frac{5}{6} - \frac{1}{3}$ k $\quad \frac{3}{10} - \frac{1}{4}$ l $\quad \frac{8}{9} - \frac{1}{6}$

m $\quad \frac{4}{15} - \frac{1}{10}$ n $\quad \frac{7}{8} - \frac{5}{6}$ o $\quad \frac{7}{12} - \frac{1}{4}$ p $\quad \frac{3}{4} + \frac{1}{3} - \frac{1}{2}$

4 A magazine has $\frac{1}{3}$ of its pages for advertising, $\frac{1}{12}$ for letters and the rest is for articles:

a What fraction of the pages is for articles?

b If the magazine has 120 pages, how many are used for articles?

5 A survey of students showed that $\frac{1}{5}$ of them walked to school, $\frac{2}{3}$ came by bus and the rest came by car:

a What fraction came by car?

b If there were 900 pupils in the school, how many came by car?

6 A farmer plants $\frac{2}{7}$ of his land with wheat and $\frac{3}{8}$ with maize; the rest is used for cattle:

a What fraction of the land is used to grow crops?

b What fraction is used for cattle?

Consider the series $\frac{1}{2} + \frac{1}{4} + \frac{1}{8} + \frac{1}{16} + \frac{1}{32} + \frac{1}{64} + \frac{1}{128}$ ... If we write down the first term, then add the first two terms, then add the first three terms, we obtain the series $\frac{1}{2}, \frac{3}{4}, \frac{7}{8}, \ldots$

a Continue this sequence for another four terms.

b What total will the series reach if it continues for an infinite number of terms?

c Repeat with the series $\frac{1}{3} + \frac{1}{9} + \frac{1}{27} + \frac{1}{81} + \frac{1}{243} + \frac{1}{729} + \frac{1}{2187}$ ...

BODMAS

You have met BODMAS in Year 7. It gives the order in which mathematical operations are carried out.

B	– Brackets
O	– pOwers
DM	– Division and Multiplication
AS	– Addition and Subtraction

Example 12.5 ▷ Evaluate:

a $2 \times 3^2 + 6 \div 2$ **b** $(2 + 3)^2 \times 8 - 6$

Show each step of the calculation.

a Firstly, work out the power, which gives $2 \times 9 + 6 \div 2$

Secondly, the division, which gives $2 \times 9 + 3$

Thirdly, the multiplication, which gives $18 + 3$

Finally, the addition to give 21

b Firstly, work out the bracket, which gives $5^2 \times 8 - 6$

Secondly, the power, which gives $25 \times 8 - 6$

Thirdly, the multiplication, which gives $200 - 6$

Finally, the subtraction to give 194

Note that if we have a calculation that is a string of additions and subtractions, or a string of multiplications and divisions, then we do the calculation from left to right.

Example 12.6 ▷ Calculate:

a $\dfrac{(2 + 6)^2}{2 \times 4^2}$ **b** $3.1 + [4.2 - (1.7 + 1.5) \div 1.6]$

a $\dfrac{(2 + 6)^2}{2 \times 4^2} = \dfrac{8^2}{2 \times 16} = \dfrac{64}{32} = 2$

b $3.1 + [4.2 - (1.7 + 1.5) \div 1.6] = 3.1 + (4.2 - 3.2 \div 1.6) = 3.1 + (4.2 - 2) = 3.1 + 2.2 = 5.3$

Note that if there are 'nested brackets', then the inside ones are calculated first.

1 Write the operation that you do first in each of these calculations, and then work out each one:

a $5 + 4 \times 7$ **b** $18 - 6 \div 3$ **c** $7 \times 7 + 2$ **d** $16 \div 4 - 2$

e $(5 + 4) \times 7$ **f** $(18 - 6) \div 3$ **g** $7 \times (7 + 2)$ **h** $16 \div (4 - 2)$

i $5 + 9 - 7 - 2$ **j** $2 \times 6 \div 3 \times 4$ **k** $12 - 15 + 7$ **l** $12 \div 3 \times 6 \div 2$

2 Work out the following, showing each step of the calculation:

a $3 + 4 + 4^2$ **b** $3 + (4 + 4)^2$ **c** $3 \times 4 + 4^2$ **d** $3 \times (4 + 4)^2$

e $5 + 3^2 - 7$ **f** $(5 + 3)^2 - 7$ **g** $2 \times 6^2 + 2$ **h** $2 \times (6^2 + 2)$

i $\dfrac{200}{4 \times 5}$ **j** $\dfrac{80 + 20}{4 \times 5}$ **k** $\sqrt{(4^2 + 3^2)}$ **l** $\dfrac{(2 + 3)^2}{6 - 1}$

m $3.2 - (5.4 + 6.1) + (5.7 - 2.1)$ **n** $8 \times (12 \div 4) \div (2 \times 2)$

3 Write out each of the following and insert brackets to make the calculation true:

a $3 \times 7 + 1 = 24$ **b** $3 + 7 \times 2 = 20$ **c** $2 \times 3 + 1 \times 4 = 32$

d $2 + 3^2 = 25$ **e** $5 \times 5 + 5 \div 5 = 26$ **f** $5 \times 5 + 5 \div 5 = 10$

g $5 \times 5 + 5 \div 5 = 30$ **h** $5 \times 5 + 5 \div 5 = 6$ **i** $15 - 3^2 = 144$

4 Work out the following (calculate the inside bracket first):

a $120 \div [25 - (3 - 2)]$ **b** $120 \div (25 - 3 - 2)$ **c** $5 + [8 \times (6 - 3)]$

d $5 + (8 \times 6 - 3)$ **e** $[120 \div (60 - 20)] + 20$ **f** $(120 \div 60 - 20) + 20$

g $[120 \div (20 \div 4)] + 3$ **h** $(120 \div 20 \div 4) + 3$ **i** $[(3 + 4)^2 - 5] \times 2$

Extension Work

By putting brackets in different places, one calculation can be made to give many different answers. For example:

$$4 \times 6 + 4 - 3 \times 8 + 1 = 24 + 4 - 24 + 1 = 5$$

without brackets or with brackets, it could be:

$$4 \times (6 + 4) - 3 \times (8 + 1) = 4 \times 10 - 3 \times 9 = 40 - 27 = 13$$

1 By putting brackets into the appropriate places in the calculation above, obtain answers of:

     a 33   **b** 17   **c** 252

2 Similarly, put brackets into $12 \div 6 - 2 \times 1 + 5 \times 3$ to make:

     a 54   **b** 15   **c** 0

Multiplying decimals

This section will give you more practice on multiplying integers and decimals.

Example 12.7 ▷

Find:

a 0.02×0.03 **b** 400×0.008 **c** $20 \times 0.06 \times 0.009$

a $2 \times 3 = 6$. There are four decimal places in the multiplication, so there are four in the answer. So, $0.02 \times 0.03 = 0.0006$.

b Rewrite the problem as equivalent products, that is $400 \times 0.008 = 40 \times 0.08 = 4 \times 0.8 = 3.2$.

c Calculate this in two parts. Firstly, $20 \times 0.06 = 2 \times 0.6 = 1.2$.

Secondly, rewrite 1.2×0.009 as $9 \times 12 = 108$, but with four decimal places in the answer. So:

$20 \times 0.06 \times 0.009 = 0.0108$

Example 12.8 ▷

A sheet of paper is 0.005 cm thick. How thick is a pack of paper containing 3000 sheets?

This is a multiplication problem:

$0.005 \times 3000 = 0.05 \times 300 = 0.5 \times 30 = 15$ cm

Exercise 12D

1 Without using a calculator, write down the answers to:

a 0.2×0.3	**b** 0.4×0.2	**c** 0.6×0.6	**d** 0.7×0.2
e 0.02×0.4	**f** 0.8×0.04	**g** 0.06×0.1	**h** 0.3×0.03
i 0.7×0.8	**j** 0.07×0.08	**k** 0.9×0.3	**l** 0.006×0.9
m 0.5×0.09	**n** 0.5×0.5	**o** 0.8×0.005	**p** 0.06×0.03

2 Without using a calculator, work out:

a 300×0.8	**b** 0.06×200	**c** 0.6×500	**d** 0.02×600
e 0.03×400	**f** 0.004×500	**g** 0.007×200	**h** 0.002×9000
i 0.005×8000	**j** 200×0.006	**k** 300×0.01	**l** 800×0.06
m 500×0.5	**n** 400×0.05	**o** 300×0.005	**p** 200×0.0005

3 Without using a calculator, work out:

a $0.006 \times 400 \times 200$	**b** $0.04 \times 0.06 \times 50\,000$	**c** $0.2 \times 0.04 \times 300$
d $300 \times 200 \times 0.08$	**e** $20 \times 0.008 \times 40$	**f** $0.1 \times 0.07 \times 2000$

4 Screws cost £0.06. An engineering company orders 20 000 screws. How much will this cost?

5 A grain of sand weighs 0.006 grams. How much would 500 000 grains weigh?

6 A kilogram of uranium ore contains 0.000 002 kg of plutonium:

    a   How much plutonium is in a tonne of ore?

    b   In a year, 2 million tonnes of ore are mined. How much plutonium will this give?

Extension Work

Work out:

a 0.1×0.1 **b** $0.1 \times 0.1 \times 0.1$ **c** $0.1 \times 0.1 \times 0.1 \times 0.1$

Using your answers, write down the answers to:

d 0.1^5 **e** 0.1^6 **f** 0.1^7 **g** 0.1^{10}

Write down the answers to:

h 0.2^2 **i** 0.3^2 **j** 0.4^2 **k** 0.5^2 **l** 0.8^2

m 0.2^3 **n** 0.3^3 **o** 0.4^3 **p** 0.5^3 **q** 0.8^3

Dividing decimals

This section gives more practice on dividing integers and decimals.

Example 12.9

Work out:

a $0.08 \div 0.2$ **b** $20 \div 0.05$

a Rewrite the sum as equivalent divisions, $0.08 \div 0.2 = 0.8 \div 2 = 0.4$. You must multiply both numbers by 10 at a time, to keep the calculation equivalent.

b Rewriting this as equivalent divisions gives:

$$20 \div 0.05 = 200 \div 0.5 = 2000 \div 5 = 400$$

Example 12.10

Work out:

a $4.8 \div 80$ **b** $24 \div 3000$

a Divide both numbers by 10 to make the calculation easier:

$$4.8 \div 80 = 0.48 \div 8 = 0.06$$

It may be easier to set this out as a short-division problem: $8\overline{)0.48}$, $\ 0.06$

b $24 \div 3000 = 2.4 \div 300 = 0.24 \div 30 = 0.024 \div 3 = 0.008$

Both numbers are divided by 1000 overall, then the equivalent calculation is done as a short-division problem: $3\overline{)0.024}$, $\ 0.008$

1 Without using a calculator, work out:

a	0.4 ÷ 0.02	b	0.8 ÷ 0.5	c	0.06 ÷ 0.1	d	0.9 ÷ 0.03
e	0.2 ÷ 0.01	f	0.06 ÷ 0.02	g	0.09 ÷ 0.3	h	0.12 ÷ 0.3
i	0.16 ÷ 0.2	j	0.8 ÷ 0.02	k	0.8 ÷ 0.1	l	0.24 ÷ 0.08
m	0.2 ÷ 0.2	n	0.08 ÷ 0.8	o	0.9 ÷ 0.09	p	0.4 ÷ 0.001

2 Without using a calculator, work out:

a	200 ÷ 0.4	b	300 ÷ 0.2	c	40 ÷ 0.08	d	200 ÷ 0.02
e	90 ÷ 0.3	f	40 ÷ 0.04	g	50 ÷ 0.1	h	400 ÷ 0.2
i	300 ÷ 0.5	j	400 ÷ 0.05	k	400 ÷ 0.1	l	200 ÷ 0.01
m	30 ÷ 0.5	n	50 ÷ 0.5	o	60 ÷ 0.5	p	400 ÷ 0.5

3 Without using a calculator, work out:

a	3.2 ÷ 20	b	2.4 ÷ 400	c	12 ÷ 400	d	3.6 ÷ 90
e	24 ÷ 800	f	2.4 ÷ 2000	g	1.4 ÷ 70	h	1.6 ÷ 40
i	32 ÷ 2000	j	0.18 ÷ 300	k	0.24 ÷ 0.2	l	0.032 ÷ 4000

4 Bolts cost £0.03. How many can I buy with £6000?

5 Grains of salt weigh 0.002 g. How many grains are in a kilogram of salt?

6 How many gallons of sea water will produce 3 kg of gold if each gallon contains 0.000 002 g of gold?

Extension Work

1 Given that 46 × 34 = 1564, write down the answers to:

    a 4.6 × 34   b 4.6 × 3.4   c 1564 ÷ 3.4   d 15.64 ÷ 0.034

2 Given that 57 × 32 = 1824, write down the answers to:

    a 5.7 × 0.032   b 0.57 × 32 000   c 5700 × 0.32   d 0.0057 × 32

3 Given that 2.8 × 0.55 = 1.540, write down the answers to:

    a 28 × 55   b 154 ÷ 55   c 15.4 ÷ 0.028   d 0.028 × 5500

What you need to know for level 5

- How to manipulate fractions and mixed numbers
- The order in which the four operations must be used
- How to multiply and divide integers and decimals

What you need to know for level 6

- How to add and subtract fractions with different denominators
- The order in which brackets and powers must be used
- How to use the power and/or cube and cube root keys on your calculator

National Curriculum SATs questions

LEVEL 5

1 *2001 Paper 2*

Some people use yards to measure length. The diagram shows one way to change yards to metres.

number of yards $\longrightarrow$ ✕ 36 $\longrightarrow$ ✕ 2.54 $\longrightarrow$ ÷ 100 $\longrightarrow$ number of metres

a Change 100 yards to metres.

b Change 100 metres to yards.

LEVEL 6

2 *2002 Paper 1*

$\frac{1}{3}, \frac{1}{8}, \frac{1}{5}$ are all examples of unit fractions.

The ancient Egyptians used only unit fractions.

For example, for $\frac{3}{4}$, they wrote the sum $\frac{1}{2} + \frac{1}{4}$.

a For what fraction did they write the sum $\frac{1}{2} + \frac{1}{5}$?

b They wrote $\frac{9}{20}$ as the sum of two unit fractions. One of them was $\frac{1}{4}$. What was the other?

All units fractions must have:

$\dfrac{1}{3}$ ←— a numerator of 1

←— a denominator that is an integer greater than 1

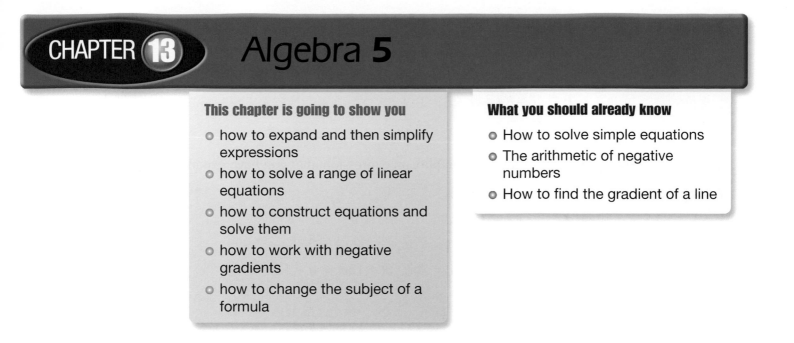

This chapter is going to show you

- how to expand and then simplify expressions
- how to solve a range of linear equations
- how to construct equations and solve them
- how to work with negative gradients
- how to change the subject of a formula

What you should already know

- How to solve simple equations
- The arithmetic of negative numbers
- How to find the gradient of a line

Expand and simplify

In algebra we often have to rearrange expressions and formulae. You have met two methods for doing this before, *expansion* and *simplification*.

Expansion means removing the brackets from an expression by multiplying each term inside the brackets by the term outside the brackets.

Example 13.1 ▷

Expand:

a $2(x + 3y)$ **b** $m(5p - 2)$

a $2(x + 3y) = 2x + 6y$

b $m(5p - 2) = 5mp - 2m$

We need to be careful if there is a negative term in front of the bracket because, in effect, that will then change the sign of the term in the expansion.

Example 13.2 ▷

Expand:

a $4 - (a + b)$ **b** $10 - (2x - 3y)$ **c** $T - 3(2m + 4n)$

a $4 - (a + b) = 4 - a - b$

b $10 - (2x - 3y) = 10 - 2x + 3y$

c $T - 3(2m + 4n) = T - 6m - 12n$

Simplification means gathering together all the like terms in an expression to write it as simply as possible.

Example 13.3 ▷

Simplify:

a $5a + b + 2a + 5b$ **b** $4c + 3d - c - 2d$ **c** $4x - 2y + 2x - 3y$

a $5a + b + 2a + 5b = 7a + 6b$

b $4c + 3d - c - 2d = 3c + d$

c $4x - 2y + 2x - 3y = 6x - 5y$

You can sometimes simplify an expression after you have expanded the brackets.

Example 13.4 ▷

Expand and simplify:

a $3a + c + 2(a + 3c)$ **b** $10t - 3(2t - 4m)$

a $3a + c + 2(a + 3c) = 3a + c + 2a + 6c = 5a + 7c$

b $10t - 3(2t - 4m) = 10t - 6t + 12m = 4t + 12m$

Exercise 13A

1 Simplify the following:

    a $2a + 3a$ **b** $5b - 3b$ **c** $4c + 3c - 2c$

    d $8d - 3d + 5d$ **e** $4x + x$ **f** $6t - t$

    g $m + 3m - 2m$ **h** $3d - 5d$ **i** $t - 4t$

    j $2n - 5n + 4n$ **k** $3a - 5a - 7a$ **l** $a - a - a + a$

2 Simplify the following:

    a $3m + 2k + m$ **b** $2p + 3q + 5p$ **c** $4t + 3d - t$

    d $5k + g - 2k$ **e** $5p + 2p + 3m$ **f** $2w + 5w + k$

    g $m + 3m - 2k$ **h** $3x + 5x - 4t$ **i** $3k + 4m + 2m$

    j $2t + 3w + w$ **k** $5x + 6m - 2m$ **l** $4y - 2p + 5p$

3 Expand the following:

    a $3(2a + 3b)$ **b** $2(4t - 3k)$ **c** $5(n + 3p)$

    d $4(2q - p)$ **e** $a(3 + t)$ **f** $b(4 + 3m)$

    g $x(5y - t)$ **h** $y(3x - 2n)$ **i** $a(m + n)$

    j $a(3p - t)$ **k** $x(6 + 3y)$ **l** $t(2k - p)$

4 Expand and simplify the following:

    a $3x + 2(4x + 5)$ **b** $8a - 3(2a + 5)$ **c** $12t - 2(3t - 4)$

    d $4x + 2(3x - 4)$ **e** $5t - 4(2t - 3)$ **f** $12m - 2(4m - 5)$

    g $6(2k + 3) - 5k$ **h** $5(3n - 2) - 4n$ **i** $2(6x + 5) - 7x$

5 Expand and simplify the following:

    a $2(3k + 4) + 3(4k + 2)$ **b** $5(2x + 1) + 2(3x + 5)$

    c $3(5m + 2) + 4(3m + 1)$ **d** $5(2k + 3) - 2(k + 3)$

    e $4(3t + 4) - 3(5t + 4)$ **f** $2(6k + 7) - 3(2k + 3)$

    g $4(3 + 2m) - 2(5 + m)$ **h** $5(4 + 3d) - 3(4 + 2d)$

    i $3(5 + 4k) - 2(3 + 5k)$

In a magic square, each row and each column add up to the same amount.

1 Show that the square below is a magic square.

$x + m$	$x + y - m$	$x - y$
$x - y - m$	x	$x + y + m$
$x + y$	$x - y + m$	$x - m$

2 Create another magic square using the variables A, B and C.

Solving equations

You have met a number of different types of linear equation so far. We solve them by adding, subtracting, multiplying or dividing both sides of the equation by the same thing, to leave the variable on its own on one side of the equation.

Example 13.5

Solve each of the equations:

a $3x = 15$ **b** $2 = \dfrac{12}{n}$ **c** $4t - 3 = 17$ **d** $3(2x + 4) = 54$

a $3x = 15$

Divide both sides by 3, to give:

$x = 5$

b $2 = \dfrac{12}{n}$

Multiply both sides by n to give:

$2n = 12$

Now divide both sides by 2, to give:

$n = 6$

c $4t - 3 = 17$

Add 3 to both sides, to give:

$4t = 20$

Now divide both sides by 4, to give:

$t = 5$

c $3(2x + 4) = 54$

Divide both sides by 3, to give

$2x + 4 = 18$

Now subtract 4 from both sides, to give:

$2x = 14$

Now divide both sides by 2, to give:

$x = 7$

1 Solve the following equations:

a	$4x = 12$	**b**	$5x = 30$	**c**	$2m = 14$
d	$3n = 15$	**e**	$2x = 7$	**f**	$2x = 11$
g	$10x = 8$	**h**	$10x = 13$	**i**	$5x = 3$
j	$5x = 8$	**k**	$5x = 21$	**l**	$4x = 15$

2 Solve the following equations:

a	$4 = \dfrac{12}{n}$	**b**	$5 = \dfrac{15}{x}$	**c**	$3 = \dfrac{18}{m}$
d	$7 = \dfrac{21}{x}$	**e**	$2 = \dfrac{10}{x}$	**f**	$4 = \dfrac{20}{m}$
g	$5 = \dfrac{45}{x}$	**h**	$2 = \dfrac{7}{n}$	**i**	$2 = \dfrac{25}{k}$
j	$10 = \dfrac{17}{x}$	**k**	$5 = \dfrac{13}{x}$	**l**	$4 = \dfrac{17}{n}$

3 Solve the following equations:

a	$3(2t + 5) = 33$	**b**	$2(5m + 3) = 36$	**c**	$5(2m + 1) = 45$
d	$4(3k + 2) = 56$	**e**	$2(2t - 3) = 18$	**f**	$4(3x - 2) = 28$
g	$3(5t - 4) = 18$	**h**	$5(9 - 2x) = 15$	**i**	$3(2k + 7) = 9$
j	$4(2m + 9) = 8$	**k**	$5(3 - 2x) = 55$	**l**	$3(5 - 4k) = 45$

4 Solve the following equations:

a	$1.5x + 3.6 = 5.4$	**b**	$2.4x + 7.1 = 13.1$	**c**	$3.4m - 4.3 = 7.6$
d	$5.6k - 2.9 = 5.5$	**e**	$4.5n - 3.7 = 12.5$	**f**	$1.8t + 7.1 = 18.8$
g	$28 - 3.6x = 11.8$	**h**	$31.3 - 2.8x = 27.1$	**i**	$2.4 - 1.8m = 8.7$

5 Solve the following equations:

a	$3(x + 1) + 2(x - 1) = 21$	**b**	$4(x + 3) + 3(x - 2) = 41$
c	$4(2x + 1) + 5(3x + 2) = 83$	**d**	$5(2x + 3) - 2(3x + 1) = 29$
e	$4(6x + 5) - 2(4x + 3) = 54$	**f**	$3(4x + 5) - 5(2x - 3) = 37$

Extension Work

Solve the following equations:

a $\dfrac{6x + 7}{4x - 1} = 2$ **b** $\dfrac{4x + 5}{x + 6} - 2 = 0$ **c** $\dfrac{11 - 2x}{1 - 4x} = 1.2$

Constructing equations to solve

The first step of solving a problem with algebra is to write down an equation. This is called **constructing** an equation.

You need to choose a letter to stand for each variable in the problem. This might be x or the first letter of a suitable word. For example, t is often used to stand for time.

Example 13.6 ▷ I think of a number, add 7 to it, multiply it by 5 and get the answer 60. What is the number I first thought of?

Let my number be x.

"Add 7 to it" gives $x + 7$.

"Multiply it by 5" gives $5(x + 7)$.

"I get the answer 60" allows us to form the equation $5(x + 7) = 60$

We can solve this now:

$$5(x + 7) = 60$$

Divide both sides by 5: $\qquad x + 7 = 12$

Subtract 7 from both sides: $\qquad x = 5$

Exercise 13C

1 Write an expression for each of the following:

a Two numbers add up to 100. If one of the numbers is x, write an expression for the other.

b The difference between two numbers is 8. If the smaller of the two numbers is y, write down an expression for the larger number.

c Jim and Ann have 18 marbles between them. If Jim has p marbles, how many marbles has Ann?

d Lenny rides a bike at an average speed of 8 km/h. Write down an expression for the distance he travels in t hours.

e If n is an even number, find an expression for the next consecutive even number.

2 Solve each of the following problems by creating an equation and then solving it:

a A mother is four times as old as her son now. If the mother was 46 years old two years ago, find the son's age now.

b If n is an odd number:

  i Write an expression for the next three consecutive odd numbers.

  ii If the sum of these four numbers is 32, find n.

c The sum of two consecutive even numbers is 54, find the numbers.

d If the sum of two consecutive odd numbers is 208, what are the numbers?

e John weighs 3 kg more than his brother. The total weight is 185 kg. How much does John weigh?

f Joy's Auntie Mary is four times as old as Joy. If the sum of their ages is 70, find their ages.

g A teacher bought 20 books in a sale. Some cost £8 each and the others cost £3 each. She spent £110 in all. How many of the £3 books did she buy?

h The sum of six consecutive even numbers is 174. What is the smallest of the numbers?

i The sum of seven consecutive odd numbers is 133. What is the largest of the numbers?

1   The sum of two numbers is 56, and their difference is 14. What is their product?

2   The sum of two numbers is 43, and their product is 450. What is their difference?

3   The difference of two numbers is 12, and their product is 448. What is their sum?

4   The sum of two numbers is 11, and twice the first plus half the second is 10. Find the product of the two numbers.

Problems with graphs

In Chapter 7 it was found that the graph of any linear equation is a straight line, and the equation written in the form $y = mx + c$ tells us the *gradient* of the line (m) and the *y-axis intercept* (c).

The gradient of a straight line is found by dividing the vertical rise of the line by its corresponding horizontal run.

The gradient is positive if it runs from the bottom left to the top right and negative if it runs from top left to bottom right.

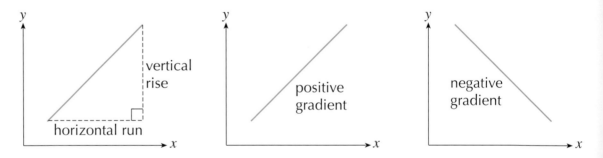

Exercise 13D   **1**   Each diagram shows the horizontal run and the vertical rise of a straight line. Find the gradient of each line:

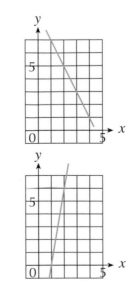

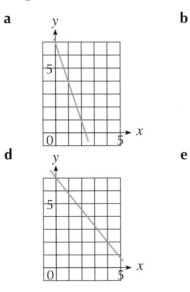

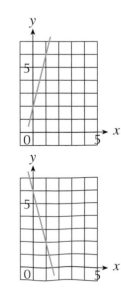

2 Find the gradient of the straight line that joins the following pairs of coordinates:

   a   (0, 3) and (2, 9)   **b**   (2, 5) and (6, 17)
   c   (2, 10) and (3, 4)   **d**   (3, 9) and (5, 3)
   e   (−1, 2) and (1, 8)   **f**   (−3, 8) and (−1, −2)

3 Find the gradient and the y-axis intercept of each of the following equations:

   a $y = 4x + 1$ **b** $y = 3x − 1$ **c** $y = 5x$ **d** $y = −2x + 3$

4 Write the equation of the line in the form $y = mx + c$, where:

   a $m = 3$ and $c = 2$ **b** $m = 4$ and $c = −3$ **c** $m = −2$ and $c = 5$
   d $m = −4$ and $c = −1$ **e** $m = 4$ and $c = 0$ **f** $m = 0$ and $c = 8$

5 Find the gradient, the y-intercept and the equation of each linear graph shown:

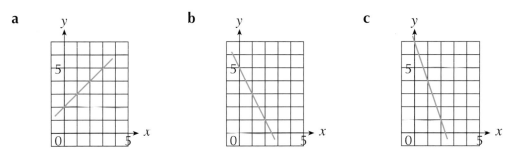

a   **b**   **c**

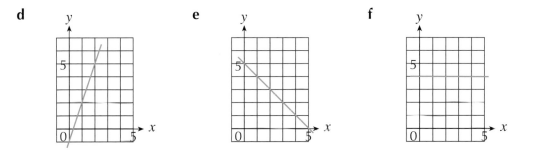

d   **e**   **f**

6 Draw graphs from the following equations by using the gradient and the y-axis intercept (that is, do not use substitution to find other coordinates).

   a $y = 2x + 3$ **b** $y = 3x − 2$ **c** $y = −2x + 6$

7 Look at the following equations:

   i $y = 2x + 5$ **ii** $y = 3x + 2$ **iii** $y = 2x − 3$
   iv $y = 2 − x$ **v** $y + 5 = 3x$ **vi** $y = x$

   Which of the graphs described by these equations satisfy the following conditions?

   a   Passes through the origin.
   b   Has a gradient of 2.
   c   Passes through the point (0, 2).
   d   Has a gradient of 1.
   e   Are parallel to each other.

1   Rewrite each of the following equations in the form $y = mx + c$:

   a $x + y = 2$ b $4y + 8x = 12$

   c $5 = 2y - 4x$ d $3x + 4y - 8 = x - y + 2$

   e $3 + 4x = \frac{1}{2}y$

2   Draw the graph for each of the following equations:

   a $x + y = 7$ b $2y + x = 6$ c $12x = 4y + 8$

   d $16 = 4x - 4y$ e $x - y = 10$ f $\frac{x + y}{x - y} = 5$

Real-life graphs

Graphs are used to show a relationship that exists between two variables.

Example 13.7 ▷

Draw a sketch graph to illustrate that a hot cup of tea will take about 20 minutes to go cold.

The graph is as shown. The two axes needed are temperature and time, with time on the horizontal axis.

The temperature starts hot at 0 minutes, and is at cold after 20 minutes.

The graph needs a negative gradient.

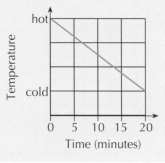

Exercise 13E   ①   Sketch graphs to illustrate the following comments, clearly labelling each axis:

   a   The more sunshine we have, the hotter it becomes.

   b   The longer the distance, the longer it takes to travel.

   c   In 2 hours all the water in a saucer had evaporated.

   d   My petrol tank starts a journey full, with 40 litres of petrol in. When my journey has finished, 300 miles later, my tank is nearly empty. It just has 5 litres of petrol left in it.

2 The graph shows a car park's charges.

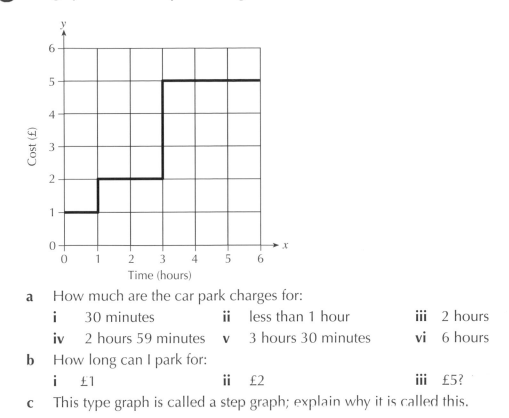

a How much are the car park charges for:

    i   30 minutes   **ii** less than 1 hour   **iii** 2 hours

    iv 2 hours 59 minutes **v** 3 hours 30 minutes **vi** 6 hours

b How long can I park for:

    i   £1   **ii** £2   **iii** £5?

c This type graph is called a step graph; explain why it is called this.

3 A country's parcel post costs are given in the table shown.

Weight	Home country	Abroad
0 grams to 500 grams	£1.40	£3.50
Above 500 grams and up to 1 kg	£2.50	£4.60
Above 1 kg and up to 2 kg	£3.20	£5.90
Above 2 kg and up to 3 kg	£4.60	£7.00
Above 3 kg and up to 5 kg	£5.50	£9.50
Above 5 kg and up to 10 kg	£6.00	£12.00
Above 10 kg and up to 20 kg	£8.00	£15.00

Draw step graphs to show charges against weight for:

a   The home country   **b**   Abroad

4 A taxi's meter reads £2 at the start of every journey. Once two miles has been travelled, an extra £3 is added to the fare. The reading then increases in steps of £3 for each whole mile covered up to five miles. For journeys over five miles, an extra £1 is added per mile over the five

a How much is charged for the following journeys?

    i   Half a mile   **ii** 1 mile   **iii** 3 miles

    iv 5 miles   **v** 6 miles   **vi** 10 miles

b Draw a step graph to show the charges for journeys up to 10 miles.

5 Look at each of the following graphs and write a short story to go with each.

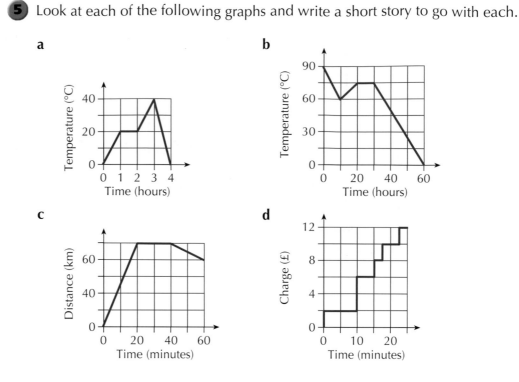

a

b

c

d

Extension Work

1   I drop a stone into a well. The three possibilities are shown below:

   a   The well is 20 feet deep and empty at the bottom.

   b   The well is 30 feet deep, but the bottom 10 feet are filled with mud.

   c   The well is 30 feet deep, but the bottom 10 feet are filled with water.

   For each possibility draw the following graphs:

   i   Distance dropped against time.

   ii   Speed of the stone against time.

Change of subject

Look at the following formula:

$P = 4a + 2b$

The formula states the value of the variable P, in terms of a and b.

We say P is the **subject** of the formula. Often we need to rearrange a formula to make another variable into the subject.

This is done in a very similar way to how we solve equations, by adding, subtracting, multiplying or dividing both sides of the equation by the same amount.

Example 13.8 ▷ Change the formula $E = 5t + 3$, to make t the subject.

The formula needs altering so that t is on its own on the left-hand side of the formula.

Subtract 3 from both sides: $\qquad\qquad\qquad\qquad\qquad E - 3 = 5t$

Divide both sides by 5: $\qquad\qquad\qquad\qquad\qquad \dfrac{E - 3}{5} = t$

Turn it round so that t is on the left-hand side: $\qquad t = \dfrac{E - 3}{5}$

Example 13.9 ▷ Rewrite the formula $N = 5(2m - p)$, and express m in terms of N and P.

Expand the bracket first: $\qquad\qquad\qquad\qquad\qquad N = 10m - 5p$

Add $5p$ to both sides of the equation: $\qquad\qquad N + 5p = 10m$

Divide both sides by 10: $\qquad\qquad\qquad\qquad \dfrac{N + 5p}{10} = m$

Turn it round so that m is on the left-hand side: $\qquad m = \dfrac{N + 5P}{5}$

m is now the subject of the formula.

Exercise 13F

1 Rewrite each of the following formulae as indicated:

 a $A = wk$; express w in terms of A and k.

 b $A = \dfrac{hb}{2}$; express h in terms of A and b.

 c $C = 2\pi rh$; express r in terms of C and h.

 d $A = 3(x + y)$; express x in terms of A and y.

2 Rewrite each of the following formulae as indicated:

 a $C = \pi D$; make D the subject of the formula.

 b $P = 2(a + b)$; make a the subject of the formula.

 c $S = 3r(h + 1)$; make h the subject of the formula.

 d $V = \pi r^2 h$; make h the subject of the formula.

 e $S = 5t + 4$; make t the subject of the formula.

3 $E = 5n + 8$

 a Find E when $n = 15$.

 b Make n the subject of the formula.

 c Find n when $E = 23$.

4 $S = a + 3t$

 a Find S when $a = 7$ and $t = 4$.

 b Make t the subject of the formula.

 c Find t when $S = 24$ and $a = 6$.

5 $y = 5x - m$

    a   Find y when $x = 2$ and $m = 3$.

    b   Make m the subject of the formula.

    c   Find m when $x = 12$ and $y = 5$.

6 $T = \dfrac{R + Q}{R}$

    a   Find T when $R = 20$ and $Q = 8$.

    b   Make Q the subject of the formula.

    c   Find Q when $R = 16$ and $T = 2$.

7 $V = 12rh$

    a   Find V when $r = 5$ and $h = 2$.

    b   Make r the subject of the formula.

    c   Find r when $V = 36$ and $h = 2$.

8 Use the formula $S = 7m + 8k$ to find the value of k when $m = 3$ and $S = 33$.

9 Use the formula $I = \dfrac{PTR}{100}$ to find the value of T when $P = 4$, $I = 10$ and $R = 20$.

10 Use the formula $A = \dfrac{h(a + b)}{2}$ to find the value of b when $h = 8$, $a = 3$ and $A = 60$.

Extension Work

1 Make n the subject of this equation: $5 = \dfrac{n + 3}{n + m}$.

2 A father complained about the cost of foreign telephone calls his two children made. The two calls together lasted 10 minutes, and the short one cost 40p a minute more than the longer one. The cost of the longer call was £11.55, and the other was £3.75. How long was each call?

What you need to know for level 5

- Construct and use simple formulae
- Solve simple linear equations
- Simplify expressions that involve simple, like terms

What you need to know for level 6

- Construct and solve linear equations
- Sketch graphs of real-life situations
- Expand and simplify expressions

National Curriculum SATs questions

LEVEL 5

1 *2000 Paper 2*

Joanne is cooking dinner.
Her rule for working out how much rice to cook is:

number of spoonfuls of rice = double the number of
people and then add one.

For example: For **three** people I cook **seven** spoonfuls of rice

Write Joanne's rule as a formula.

Use S for the number of spoonfuls of rice and P for the number of people.

2 *1999 Paper 1*

The diagram shows a rectangle $(n + 3)$ cm long and $(n + 2)$ cm wide.
It has been split into four smaller rectangles.

Copy the diagram and write a number or an expression for the area of each small rectangle.

One has been done for you:

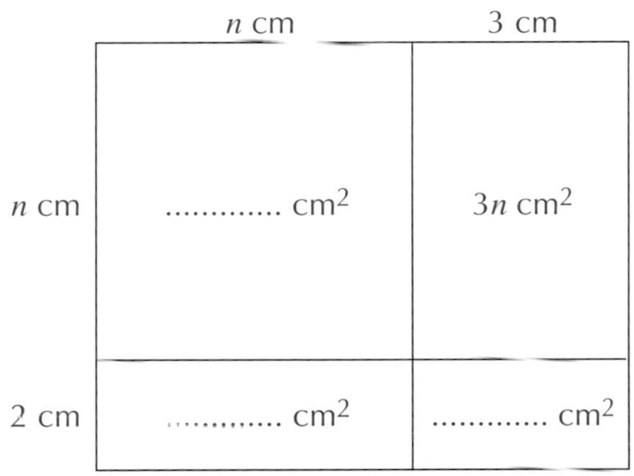

	n cm	3 cm
n cm	.... cm^2	$3n$ cm^2
2 cm	.... cm^2	.... cm^2

LEVEL 6

3 *2000 Paper 2*

Solve the following equations:

a $9 - 3x = 3$

b $3 + 2x + 7 = 2x + 7 + 3x$

c $5x - 2 = 2x + 5$

4 *2002 Paper 2*

Each point on the straight line $x + y = 12$ has an x-coordinate and a y-coordinate that add together to make 12.

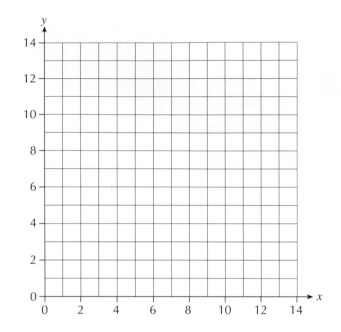

Copy the graph below (or use your own graph paper) and draw the straight line $x + y = 12$

5 *2002 Paper 2*

I went for a walk.

The distance–time graph shows information about my walk.

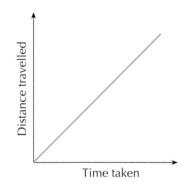

Which of the statements below describes my walk?

a I was walking faster and faster.

b I was walking slower and slower.

c I was walking north-east.

d I was walking at a steady speed.

e I was walking uphill.

This chapter is going to show you

- how to investigate problems involving numbers and measures
- how to identify important information in a question
- how to interpret information from graphs
- how to use examples to prove a statement is true or false
- how to divide a quantity using proportion or ratio

What you should already know

- When to use symbols, words or algebra to describe a problem
- When to use tables, diagrams and graphs
- How to break down a calculation into simpler steps
- How to solve simple problems using ratio and proportion

Number and measures

A newspaper has 48 pages. The pages have stories, adverts or both on them. 50% of the pages have both. Twice as many pages have adverts only as have stories only. How many pages have stories only?

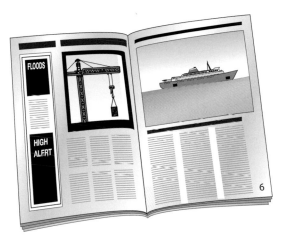

Example 14.1

Use the digits 1, 2, 3 and 4 once only to make the largest possible product.

To make large numbers, the larger digits need to have the greatest value.

So try a few examples:

$$41 \times 32 = 1312$$
$$42 \times 31 = 1302$$
$$43 \times 21 = 903$$
$$431 \times 2 = 862$$

There are other possibilities, but these all give smaller answers.

The biggest product is $41 \times 32 = 1312$.

Exercise 14A

1 Three consecutive numbers add up to 75. What are the numbers?

2 a Copy and complete the table.

Powers of 3	Answer	Units digit
3^1	3	3
3^2	9	9
3^3	27	7
3^4	81	1
3^5	243	
3^6		
3^7		

b What is the units digit of 3^{44}?

3 A dog and a cat run around a circular track of length 48 m. They both set off in the same direction from the starting line at the same time. The dog runs at 6 m per second and the cat runs at 4 m per second. How long is it before the dog and the cat are together again?

4 a Find two consecutive odd numbers with a product of 1763.

b Use the digits 1, 3, 6 and 7 once each to form the largest possible product of two numbers.

For example $13 \times 67 = 871$

$137 \times 6 = 822$

5 Here is a magic square in which each row, column and diagonal add up to 15:

8	1	6
3	5	7
4	9	2

Complete the magic squares on the right so that each row, column and diagonal adds up to 15.

6 Amy is 6 years older than Bill. Two years ago Amy was three times as old as Bill. How old will Amy be in 4 years' time?

7 A map has a scale of 1 cm to $2\frac{1}{2}$ km. The road between two towns is 5 cm on the map, to the nearest centimetre.

a Calculate the shortest possible actual distance between the two towns.

b Calculate the difference between the shortest and longest possible distances between the two towns.

8 Which is the greater mass, 3 kg or 7 pounds (lb)? Explain your answer.

9 Which is the greater length, 10 miles or 15 kilometres? Explain your answer.

10 Which is the greater area, 1 square mile or 1 square kilometre? Explain your answer.

Extension Work

Make up a recipe in imperial units (e.g., 6 ounces of flour, 2 pints of water, etc). Use metric conversions and rewrite the recipe in metric units. If you need to find out the conversions, use a textbook or the internet.

Using algebra, graphs and diagrams to solve problems

Of three chickens (A, B and C), A and B have a total mass of 4.1 kg, A and C have a total mass of 5.8 kg, and B and C have a total mass of 6.5 kg. What is the mass of each chicken?

Example 14.2

A gardener has a fixed charge of £5 and an hourly rate of £3 per hour. Write down an equation for the total charge £C when the gardener is hired for *n* hours. State the cost of hiring the gardener for 6 hours.

The formula is:

$C = 5$ (for the fixed charge) plus $3 \times n$ (for the hours worked)

$C = 5 + 3n$

If $n = 6$ then the total charge $C = 5 + (3 \times 6)$

$$C = 23$$

So the charge is £23.

Example 14.3

I think of a number, add 3 and then double it. The answer is 16. What is the number?

| ? | → | + 3 | → | × 2 | → | 16 |

Working this flowchart backwards

| 5 | ← | − 3 | ← | ÷ 2 | ← | 16 |

The answer is 5.

Exercise 14B

1 A man and his suitcase weigh 84 kg, to the nearest kilogram. The suitcase weighs 12 kg to the nearest kilogram. What is the heaviest that the man could weigh?

2 The sum of two numbers is 43 and the difference is 5. What are the two numbers?

3 a A tool-hire company has a fixed charge of £12 plus £5 per day to hire a tool. Write the total hire charge, £C, as a formula in terms of *n*, the number of days.

b Work out the cost for 10 days.

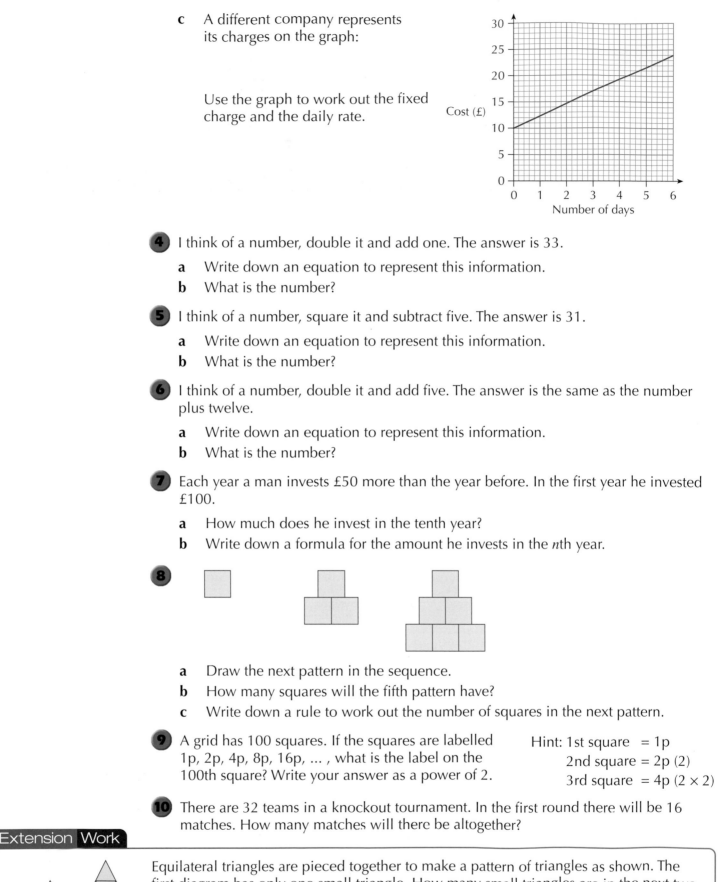

c A different company represents its charges on the graph:

Use the graph to work out the fixed charge and the daily rate.

Cost (£)

Number of days

4 I think of a number, double it and add one. The answer is 33.

    a Write down an equation to represent this information.

    b What is the number?

5 I think of a number, square it and subtract five. The answer is 31.

    a Write down an equation to represent this information.

    b What is the number?

6 I think of a number, double it and add five. The answer is the same as the number plus twelve.

    a Write down an equation to represent this information.

    b What is the number?

7 Each year a man invests £50 more than the year before. In the first year he invested £100.

    a How much does he invest in the tenth year?

    b Write down a formula for the amount he invests in the nth year.

8

    a Draw the next pattern in the sequence.

    b How many squares will the fifth pattern have?

    c Write down a rule to work out the number of squares in the next pattern.

9 A grid has 100 squares. If the squares are labelled 1p, 2p, 4p, 8p, 16p, ... , what is the label on the 100th square? Write your answer as a power of 2.

Hint: 1st square = 1p
2nd square = 2p (2)
3rd square = 4p (2 × 2)

10 There are 32 teams in a knockout tournament. In the first round there will be 16 matches. How many matches will there be altogether?

Extension Work

Equilateral triangles are pieced together to make a pattern of triangles as shown. The first diagram has only one small triangle. How many small triangles are in the next two patterns? Extend the patterns to see if you can work out a formula for the number of small triangles in the tenth pattern. What is the special name given to this pattern?

Logic and proof

Look at the recipe, which is for four people. How much of each ingredient is needed to make a chocolate cake for six people?

Chocolate cake
500g flour
100g sugar
35g cocoa powder
60g butter

Example 14.4 ▷

Take any three consecutive numbers. Multiply the first number by the third number and square the middle number. Work out the difference between the two answers. Example:

7, 8, 9

$7 \times 9 = 63$

$8^2 = 8 \times 8 = 64$

Difference = 1

Note: Whichever numbers you choose, you will always get an answer of 1.

Example 14.5 ▷

Prove that the sum of three odd numbers is always odd.

Call the three odd numbers x, y and z.

$x + y$ is an even number because odd + odd = even.

$(x + y) + z$ is odd, because even + odd = odd.

This is true whatever odd numbers x, y and x actually are.

Exercise 14C

1 Copy and complete the following number problems, filling in the missing digits:

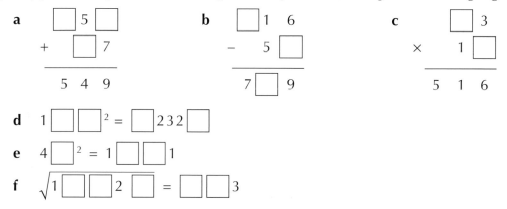

a
```
  [ ] 5 [ ]
+   [ ] 7
-----------
    5 4 9
```

b
```
  [ ] 1 6
-   5 [ ]
-----------
  7 [ ] 9
```

c
```
    [ ] 3
×   1 [ ]
-----------
  5 1 6
```

d $\quad 1[\ ][\ ]^2 = [\ ]232[\ ]$

e $\quad 4[\ ]^2 = 1[\ ][\ ]1$

f $\quad \sqrt{1[\ ][\ ]2[\ ]} = [\ ][\ ]3$

2 Give an example to show that the sum of three odd numbers is always odd.

3 Prove that the sum of two consecutive whole numbers is always odd.

4 Prove that the product of three consecutive numbers is divisible by 6.

5 Explain why the only even prime number is 2.

6 Show that the product of two consecutive numbers is always even.

7 a Find the three numbers below 30 that have exactly three factors.

b What do you notice about these numbers?

8 Find the six factors of 18.

9 Find the twelve factors of 60.

10 Which bottle is the best value for money?

11 Which is the better value for money?

    a   6 litres for £7.50 or 3 litres for £3.80.

    b   4.5 kg for £1.80 or 8 kg for £4.00.

    c   200 g for £1.60 or 300 g for £2.10.

    d   Six chocolate bars for £1.50 or four chocolate bars for 90p.

12 A recipe uses 750 g of meat and makes a meal for five people. How many grams of meat would be needed if the meal was for eight people?

Extension Work

Invent your own recipes for two people. Rewrite them for four people and then for five people. Remember that you cannot have half an egg!

Proportion

Look at the picture.
Can you work out how many pints are in 3 litres?

A litre of water is a pint and three-quarters

Example 14.6

A café sells 200 cups of tea, 150 cups of coffee and 250 other drinks in a day.

What proportion of the drinks sold are

    a   cups of tea   **b**   cups of coffee?

    a   There are 200 cups of tea out of 600 cups altogether, so the proportion of cups of tea is $\frac{200}{600} = \frac{1}{3}$.

    b   There are 150 cups of coffee out of 600 cups altogether, so the proportion of cups of coffee is $\frac{150}{600} = \frac{1}{4}$.

Exercise 14D

1 An orange drink is made using one part juice to four parts water. What proportion of the drink is juice? Give your answer as a fraction, decimal or percentage.

2 A woman spends £75 on food and £25 on clothing. What proportion of her spending is on food?

3 A supermarket uses $\frac{3}{4}$ of its space for food and the rest for non-food items. What is the ratio of food to non-food items?

4 A green paint is made by mixing blue and yellow paint in the ratio 3 : 7. How many litres of blue and yellow paint are needed to make:

    a   20 litres of green paint   **b**   5 litres of green paint?

5 5 miles is approximately 8 km:

    a   How many miles are equal to 24 km?
    b   How many kilometres are equal to 25 miles?

6 30 cm is approximately 1 foot.

    a   How many feet is 75 cm?
    b   How many feet is 45 cm?

7 Four cakes cost £10. What will six cakes cost?

8 Six towels cost £18. What will four towels cost?

9 10 candles cost £12. What will 15 candles cost?

10 A lorry travels at 60 miles per hour on the motorway:

    a   How far will it travel in 15 minutes?
    b   How far will it travel in 1 hour and 15 minutes?

11 In 15 minutes a car travelled 12 km. If it continues at the same speed, how far will it travel in:

    a   30 minutes?   **b**   45 minutes?   **c**   20 minutes?

12 In 30 minutes, 40 litres of water runs through a pipe. How much water will run through the pipe in 12 minutes?

13 Roast ham costs 80p for 100 grams. How much will 250 grams cost?

Extension Work

Design a spreadsheet that a shopkeeper could use to increase the price of items by 20%.

Ratio

John and Mary are sharing out the sweets. John wants twice as many sweets as Mary, and there are 21 sweets altogether. Can you work out how many sweets they each get?

Example 14.7 ▷ Alice and Michael have 128 CDs altogether. Alice has three times as many as Michael. How many CDs do they each have?

If Alice has three times as many as Michael, then the ratio is 3:1. This means that, altogether, there are 4 (3 + 1) parts to share out.

4 parts is all 128 CDs, so 1 part = 128 ÷ 4 CDs
$$= 32 \text{ CDs}$$

So Michael has 32 CDs and Alice has 32 × 3 = 96 CDs.

You can check your answer by adding 32 and 96. The answer should be 128.

Example 14.8 ▷ James and Briony are two goalkeepers. James has let in twice as many goals as Briony. Altogether they have let in 27 goals. How many goals has James let in?

James has let in twice as many goals as Briony, so we can say that if Briony has let in x goals then James has let in $2x$.

Altogether, this means that $3x = 27$, so $x = 9$ and $2x = 18$

So James has let in 18 goals.

Exercise 14E

1 Simplify the ratios:

a	6 : 4	**b**	10 : 25	**c**	21 : 7
d	6 : 9	**e**	5 : 20	**f**	8 : 2
g	12 : 3	**h**	20 cm : 15 cm	**i**	4 km : 12 km
j	£7.50 : £3.50	**k**	15p : 3p	**l**	1 m : 25 cm
m	400 g : 1 kg	**n**	500 mm : 1 m	**o**	£1 : 70p
p	1 tonne : 750 kg	**q**	2 hours : 30 minutes	**r**	1 day : 6 hours
s	20 mm : 3 cm	**t**	50p : £2.50		

2
a	Divide 32 cm in the ratio 3 : 1	**b**	Divide 20 kg in the ratio 1 : 4
c	Divide £30 in the ratio 3 : 2	**d**	Divide 120 g in the ratio 7 : 5
e	Divide £250 in the ratio 3 : 7	**f**	Divide 40 litres in the ratio 2 : 3
g	Divide 49p in the ratio 4 : 2 : 1	**h**	Divide 20 million in the ratio 2 : 2 : 1

3 Harriet and Richard go shopping and buy 66 items altogether. Harriet buys twice as many items as Richard. How many items does Harriet buy?

4 At a concert the numbers of males to females are in the ratio 3 : 2. There are 350 people altogether. How many females are at the concert?

5 180 people see a film at the cinema. The numbers of children to adults are in the ratio 5 : 4. How many children see the film?

6 In a fishing contest the number of trout caught to the number of carp caught is in the ratio 1 : 2. The total number of trout and carp is 72. How many carp were caught?

A bakery makes 1400 loaves. The ratio of white to brown is 4 : 3. How many brown loaves did the bakery make?

 A do-it-yourself shop sells paints. The ratio of gloss paint to emulsion paint sold on one day is 2 : 3. If they sell 85 litres of paint, how much gloss paint do they sell?

Extension Work

Draw a cube of side 1cm. Double the length of the sides and find the volume of the new cube. Work out the ratio of the new volume to the previous volume. Double the side length several more times, working out the new : previous volume ratio each time.

Repeat this exercise, but triple or quadruple the side length each time instead.

Can you find a connection between the new : previous volume ratio and the new : previous side ratio?

What you need to know for level 5

- How to identify the information you need to solve a problem
- How to check a result to see if it is sensible
- How to describe situations mathematically using symbols, words or diagrams
- How to explain your reasoning

What you need to know for level 6

- How to solve complex problems by breaking them down into smaller, more manageable tasks
- How to interpret and discuss information presented in a variety of forms
- How to justify answers by testing for particular cases
- How to calculate using ratios in appropriate situations

National Curriculum SATs questions

LEVEL 5

1 *1998 Paper 2*

You can make different colours of paint by mixing red, blue and yellow in different proportions.

For example, you can make green by mixing 1 part blue to 1 part yellow.

a To make purple, you mix 3 parts red to 7 parts blue. How much of each colour do you need to make 20 litres of purple paint? Give your answer in litres.

b To make orange, you mix 13 parts yellow to 7 parts red. How much of each colour do you need to make 10 litres of orange paint? Give your answer in litres.

2 *2001 Paper 2*

a You pay £2.40 each time you go swimming. Copy and complete the table.

Number of swims	0	10	20	30
Total cost (£)	0	24		

b Now show this information on a graph with the x axis as the Number of swims from 0 to 30. Take the y-axis to be the Total cost (3) from 0 to 80.

c A different way of paying is to pay a yearly fee of £22. Then you pay £1.40 each time you go swimming.

Copy and complete the table.

Number of swims	0	10	20	30
Total cost (£)	22	36		

d Now show this information on the graph you drew for **b**.

e For how many swims does the graph show that the cost is the same for both ways of paying?

3 *1999 Paper 2*

a Nigel pours one carton of apple juice and three cartons of orange juice into a big jug.

What is the ratio of apple juice to orange juice in Nigel's jug?

b Lesley pours one carton of apple juice and $1\frac{1}{2}$ cartons of orange juice into another big jug.

What is the ratio of apple juice to orange juice in Lesley's jug?

c Tandi pours one carton of apple juice and one carton of orange juice into another big jug.

She wants only half as much apple juice as orange juice in her jug. What should Tandi pour into her jug now?

4 You can work out the cost of an advert in a newspaper by using this formula:

$$C = 15n + 75$$

C is the cost in £

n is the number of words in the advert

a An advert has 18 words. Work out the cost of the advert (show your working).

b The cost of an advert is £615. How many words are in the advert? Show your working.

LEVEL 6

5 *1997 Paper 2*

The table shows some information about pupils in a school. There are 408 pupils in the school.

	Left-handed	Right-handed
Girls	32	180
Boys	28	168

a What percentage of the pupils are boys? Show your working.

b What is the ratio of left-handed pupils to right-handed pupils?

Write your ratio in the form 1:…

Show your working.

c One pupil is chosen at random from the whole school.

What is the probability that the pupil chosen is a girl who is right-handed?

6 *1999 Paper 2*

The ship 'Queen Mary' used to sail across the Atlantic Ocean.

The ship's usual speed was 33 miles per hour.

On average, the ship used fuel at the rate of 1 gallon for every 13 feet sailed.

Calculate how many gallons of fuel the ship used in one hour of travelling at the usual speed. (There are 5280 feet in one mile).

Show your working and write down the full calculator display.

Now write your answer correct to two significant figures.

7 A groundsman marks out a football pitch.

a He makes the pitch 93 metres long, to the nearest metre. What is the shortest possible length of the pitch?

b He makes the pitch 50 metres wide, to the nearest metre. What is the shortest possible width of the pitch?

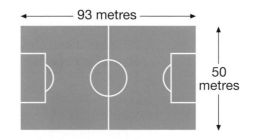

c Des wants to know how many times he should run around the outside of this pitch to be sure of running at least 3km.

Use your answer to parts **a** and **b** to find how many times Des should run around the pitch.

You must show your working.

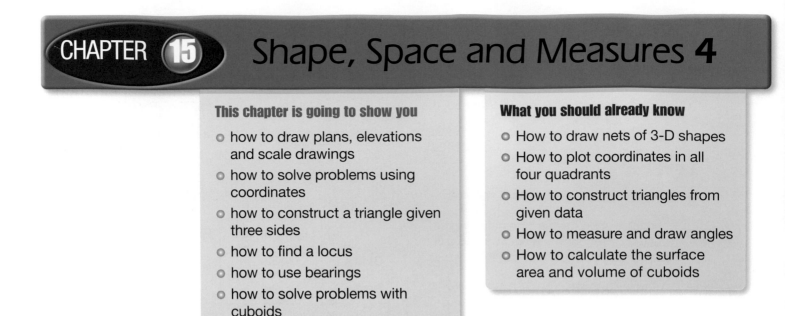

This chapter is going to show you

○ how to draw plans, elevations and scale drawings
○ how to solve problems using coordinates
○ how to construct a triangle given three sides
○ how to find a locus
○ how to use bearings
○ how to solve problems with cuboids

What you should already know

○ How to draw nets of 3-D shapes
○ How to plot coordinates in all four quadrants
○ How to construct triangles from given data
○ How to measure and draw angles
○ How to calculate the surface area and volume of cuboids

Plans and elevations

A **plan** is the view of a 3-D shape when it is looked at from above. An **elevation** is the view of a 3-D shape when it is looked at from the front or from the side.

Example 15.1 ▷

The 3-D shape shown is drawn on centimetre isometric dotted paper. Notice that the paper must be used the correct way round, so always check that the dots form vertical columns.

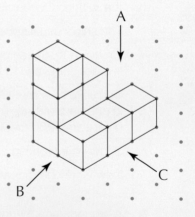

The plan, front elevation and side elevation can be drawn on centimetre-squared paper:

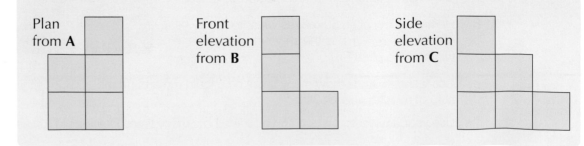

Plan from **A** Front elevation from **B** Side elevation from **C**

1 Draw each of the following cuboids accurately on an isometric grid:

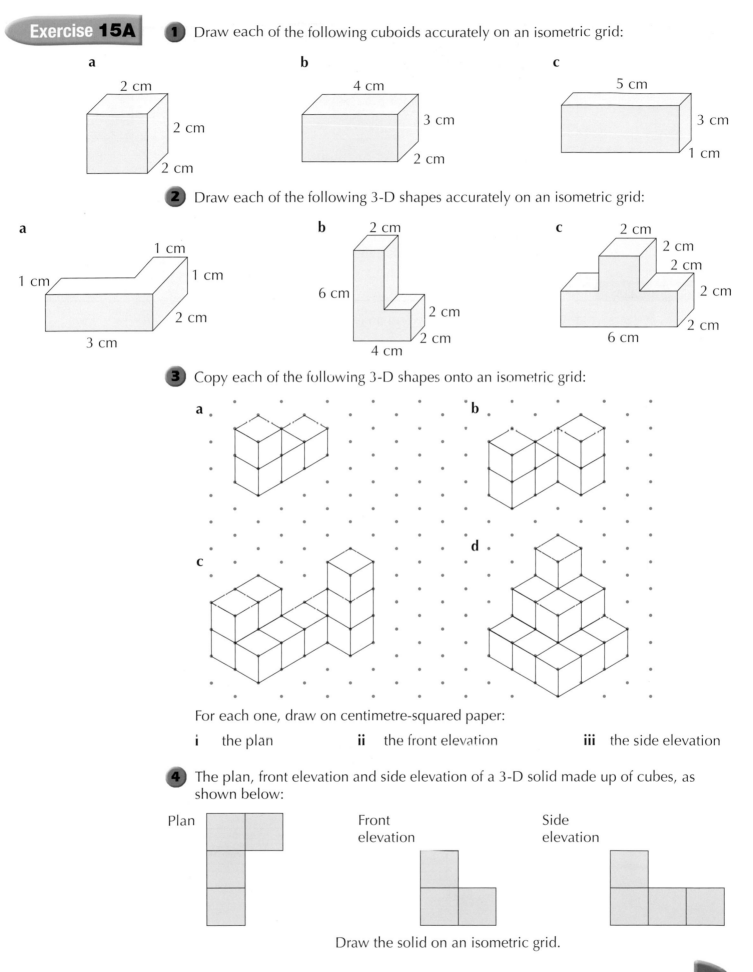

a

2 cm
2 cm
2 cm

b

4 cm
3 cm
2 cm

c

5 cm
3 cm
1 cm

2 Draw each of the following 3-D shapes accurately on an isometric grid:

a

1 cm
1 cm
1 cm
2 cm
3 cm

b

2 cm
6 cm
2 cm
2 cm
4 cm

c

2 cm
2 cm
2 cm
2 cm
2 cm
6 cm

3 Copy each of the following 3-D shapes onto an isometric grid:

a

b

c

d

For each one, draw on centimetre-squared paper:

i the plan   **ii** the front elevation   **iii** the side elevation

4 The plan, front elevation and side elevation of a 3-D solid made up of cubes, as shown below:

Plan

Front elevation

Side elevation

Draw the solid on an isometric grid.

5 The diagrams below are the views of various 3-D shapes from directly above:

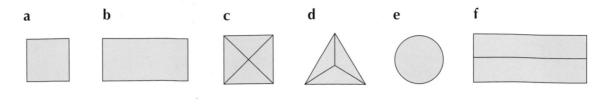

a b c d e f

For each one, write down the name of a 3-D shape that could have this plan.

6 Make a 3-D solid from multi-link cubes. On centimetre-squared paper draw its plan, front elevation and side elevation and show these to a partner. Ask your partner to construct the solid using multi-link cubes. Compare the two solids made.

Extension Work

1 The letter 'T' is drawn on an isometric grid, as shown on the left:

  a Draw other capital letters that can be drawn on an isometric grid.

  b Explain why only certain capital letters can be drawn easily on the grid.

  c Design a poster, using any of these letters, to make a logo for a person who has these letters as their initials.

2 The diagram on the right is another way of representing a cube in 2-D.

This representation is known as a **Schlegel diagram**, named after a famous German mathematician. Investigate Schlegel diagrams, using reference books or the Internet.

Scale drawings

A **scale drawing** is a smaller drawing of an actual object. A scale must always be clearly given by the side of the scale drawing.

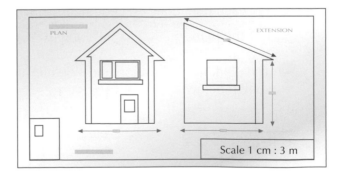

PLAN

EXTENSION

Scale 1 cm : 3 m

Example 15.2 ▷   Shown is a scale drawing of Rebecca's room.

- On the scale drawing, the length of the room is 5 cm, so the actual length of the room is 5 m.

- On the scale drawing, the width of the room is 3.5 cm, so the actual width of the room is 3.5 m.

- On the scale drawing, the width of the window is 2 cm, so the actual width of the window is 2 m.

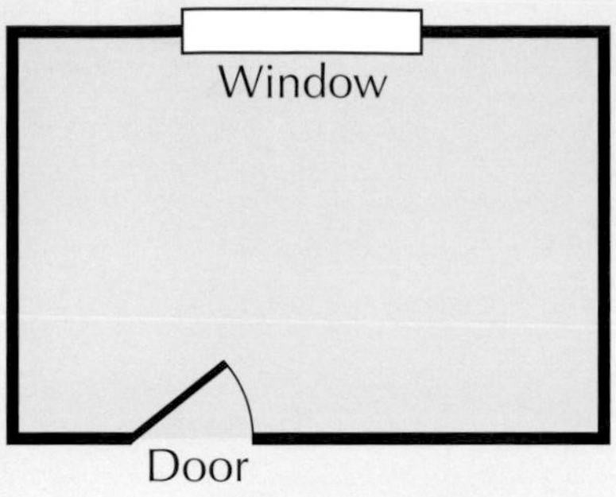

Window

Door

Scale: 1 cm to 1 m

Exercise 15B

1 The lines shown are drawn using a scale of 1 cm to 10 m. Write down the length each line represents:

a   ▬▬▬▬

b   ▬▬▬▬▬▬▬▬▬

c   ▬▬▬▬▬▬

d   ▬▬▬▬▬▬▬▬▬▬▬

e   ▬▬▬▬▬▬▬▬▬

2 The diagram shows a scale drawing for a school hall:

   a   Find the actual length of the hall.

   b   Find the actual width of the hall.

   c   Find the actual distance between the opposite corners of the hall.

3 The diagram shown is Ryan's scale drawing for his Mathematics classroom. Nathan notices that Ryan has not put a scale on the drawing, but he knows that the length of the classroom is 8 m:

   a   What scale has Ryan used?

   b   What is the actual width of the classroom?

   c   What is the actual area of the classroom?

Scale: 1 cm to 5 m

4 Copy and complete the table below for a scale drawing in which the scale is 4 cm to 1 m.

		Actual length	Length on scale drawing
	a	4 m	
	b	1.5 m	
	c	50 cm	
	d		12 cm
	e		10 cm
	f		4.8 cm

5 The plan shown is for a bungalow:

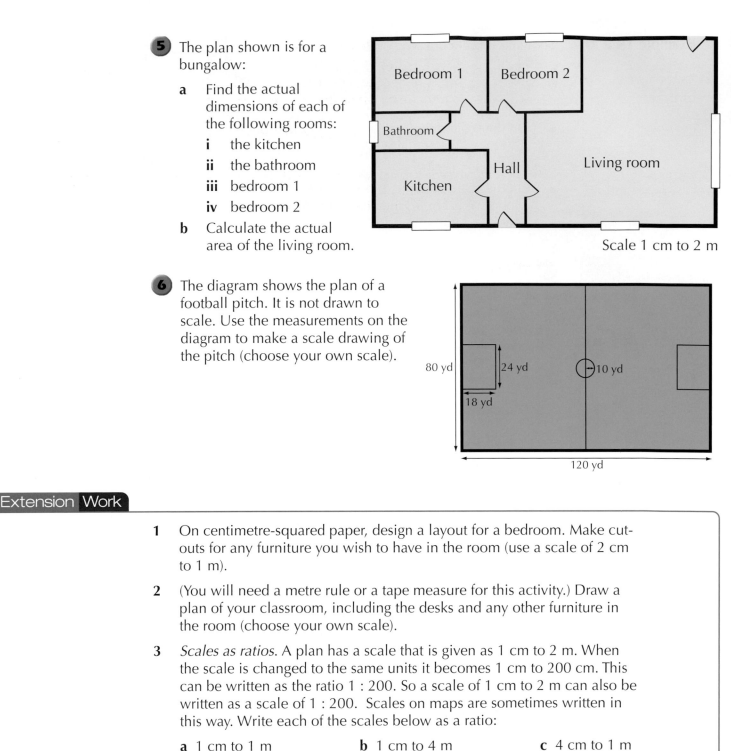

Scale 1 cm to 2 m

a Find the actual dimensions of each of the following rooms:

  i the kitchen

  ii the bathroom

  iii bedroom 1

  iv bedroom 2

b Calculate the actual area of the living room.

6 The diagram shows the plan of a football pitch. It is not drawn to scale. Use the measurements on the diagram to make a scale drawing of the pitch (choose your own scale).

1 On centimetre-squared paper, design a layout for a bedroom. Make cut-outs for any furniture you wish to have in the room (use a scale of 2 cm to 1 m).

2 (You will need a metre rule or a tape measure for this activity.) Draw a plan of your classroom, including the desks and any other furniture in the room (choose your own scale).

3 *Scales as ratios.* A plan has a scale that is given as 1 cm to 2 m. When the scale is changed to the same units it becomes 1 cm to 200 cm. This can be written as the ratio 1 : 200. So a scale of 1 cm to 2 m can also be written as a scale of 1 : 200. Scales on maps are sometimes written in this way. Write each of the scales below as a ratio:

  a 1 cm to 1 m   b 1 cm to 4 m   c 4 cm to 1 m

  d 1 cm to 1 km   e 2 cm to 1 km

Finding the mid-point of a line segment

The next example will remind you how to plot points in all four quadrants using *x*- and *y*-coordinates.

It will also show you how to find the mid-point of a line that joins two points.

Example 15.3 ▶

The coordinates of the points of A, B, C and D on the grid are A(4, 4), B(–2, 4), C(2, 1) and D(2, –3).

The mid-point of the line segment that joins A and B is X (X is usually referred to as the mid-point of AB). From the diagram, the coordinates of X are (1, 4). Notice that the y-coordinates are the same for the three points on the line.

The mid-point of CD is Y. From the diagram, the coordinates of Y are (2, –1). Notice that the x-coordinates are the same for the three points on the line.

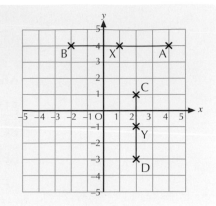

Exercise 15C

1 Copy the grid on the right and plot the points A, B, C, D, E and F.

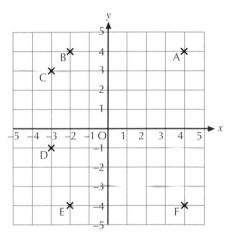

  a Write down the coordinates of the points A, B, C, D, E and F.

  b Using the grid to help, write down the coordinates of the mid-point of each of the following line segments:

   i AB

   ii CD

   iii BE

   iv EF

2 Copy the grid on the right and plot the points P, Q, R and S.

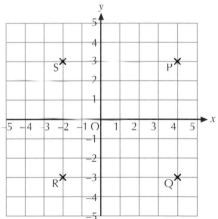

  a Write down the coordinates of the points P, Q, R and S.

  b Join the points to form the rectangle PQRS. Using the grid to help, write down the coordinates of the mid-point of each of the following lines:

   i PQ   **ii** QR
   iii PS   **iv** SR

  c Write down the coordinates of the mid-point of the diagonal PR.

3 a Copy and complete the table on the next page, using the points on the grid to the right. The first row of the table has been completed for you.

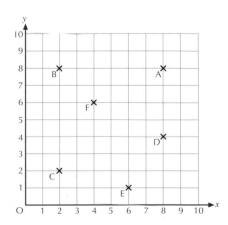

Line segment	Coordinates of the first point on the line segment	Coordinates of the second point on the line segment	Coordinates of the mid-point of the line segment
AB	A(8, 8)	B(2, 8)	(5, 8)
AD			
BC			
BF			
AF			
CE			

b Can you spot a connection between the coordinates of the first and second points and the coordinates of the mid-point? Write down a rule in your own words.

4 By using the rule you found in Question 3 or by plotting the points on a coordinate grid, find the mid-points of the line that joins each of the following pairs of coordinate points:

a A(3, 2) and B(3, 6)   **b** C(4, 6) and D(6, 10)

c E(3, 2) and F(5, 4)   **d** G(8, 6) and H(2, 3)

e I(5, 6) and J(−3 , −2)

Extension Work

To find a formula for the mid-point of a line segment AB:

On the x-axis above, what number lies half way between 4 and 8? Can you see a way of getting the answer without using the number line? The answer of 6 can be found by finding the mean of 4 and 8 or $\frac{4 + 8}{2}$.

Test this rule by trying other numbers.

x_1 and x_2 lie on the x-axis, as shown below. What number lies half way between x_1 and x_2? The answer is the mean of x_1 and x_2, which is $\frac{x_1 + x_2}{2}$.

The same rule will work for numbers on the y-axis:

On the y-axis shown, what number lies half way between y_1 and y_2? The answer is the mean of y_1 and y_2, which is $\frac{y_1 + y_2}{2}$.

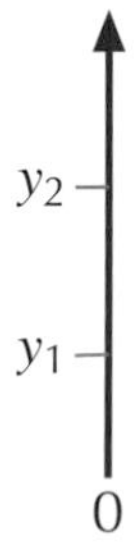

This rule can now be applied to find the coordinates of the mid-point of the line AB on the grid to the right.

Point A has coordinates (x_1, y_1) and point B has coordinates (x_2, y_2). Using the above rule for both axes, we find that the coordinates of the mid-point of AB is given by the formula:

$$\left(\frac{x_1 + x_2}{2}, \frac{y_1 + y_2}{2} \right)$$

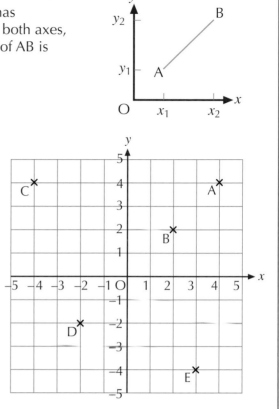

1 Points A, B, C, D and E are plotted on the grid shown. Use the formula above to find the mid-point for each of the following line segments:

 a AB

 b BC

 c CD

 d DE

 e AE

To construct a triangle given three sides

In Year 7, Book 2 showed you how to construct triangles, using a ruler and a protractor, from given data. You were able to construct the following:

- a triangle given two sides and the included angle (SAS):

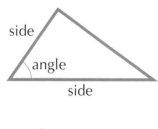

- a triangle given two angles and the included side (ASA):

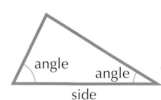

The example below shows you how to construct a triangle given three sides (SSS). You need a ruler and compasses for this construction.

Example 15.4 ▷

To construct the triangle PQR.

Draw line QR 6 cm long. Set compasses to a radius of 4 cm and, with centre at Q, draw a large arc above QR. Set compasses to a radius of 5 cm and, with the centre at R, draw a large arc to intersect the first arc. The intersection of the two arcs is P. Join QP and RP to complete the triangle. Leave your construction lines on the diagram.

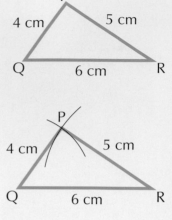

Exercise 15D

1 Construct each of the following triangles (remember to label all the lines):

a
A
3 cm 4 cm
B 5 cm C

b
D
6 cm 3 cm
E 6 cm F

c
G
8 cm
3 cm
H 7 cm I

d
J
6.4 cm 5.7 cm
K 8.6 cm L

2 Construct the ΔXYZ with XY = 6.5 cm, XZ = 4.3 cm and YZ = 5.8 cm.

3 Construct the ΔPQR with PQ = 5 cm, QR = 12 cm and PR = 13 cm. What type of triangle have you drawn?

4 Construct equilateral triangles with sides of length:

    a 3 cm   **b** 5 cm   **c** 4.5 cm

5 Paul thinks that he can construct a triangle with sides of length 3 cm, 4 cm and 8 cm, but finds that he cannot draw it:

    a   Try to construct Paul's triangle.

    b   Explain why it is not possible to draw Paul's triangle.

Extension Work

1 Construct the quadrilaterals shown using only a ruler and compasses:

a
4 cm
5 cm
4 cm
5 cm
6 cm

b
43 mm 52 mm
45 mm
38 mm 74 mm

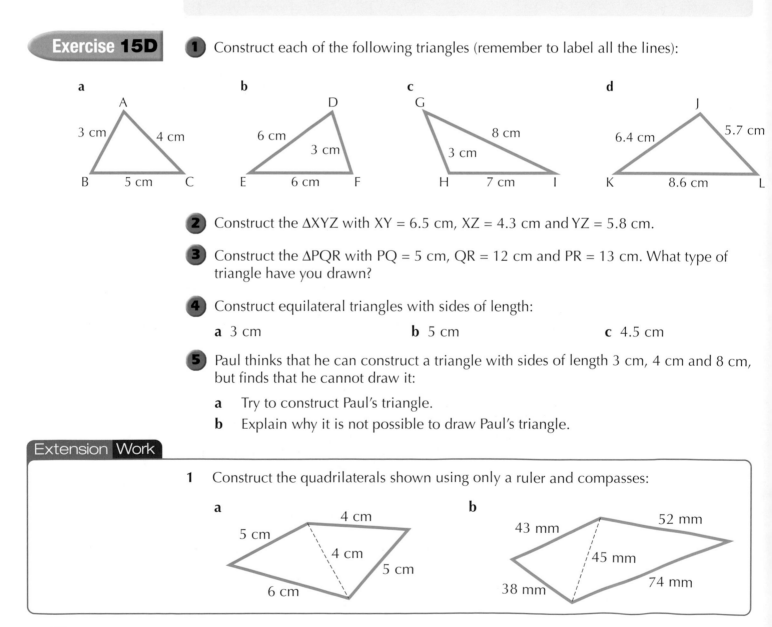

2 a Draw the net below accurately on card. Cut out the net to make a square-based pyramid. Make the square 4 cm × 4 cm, and each equilateral triangle 4 cm × 4 cm × 4 cm.

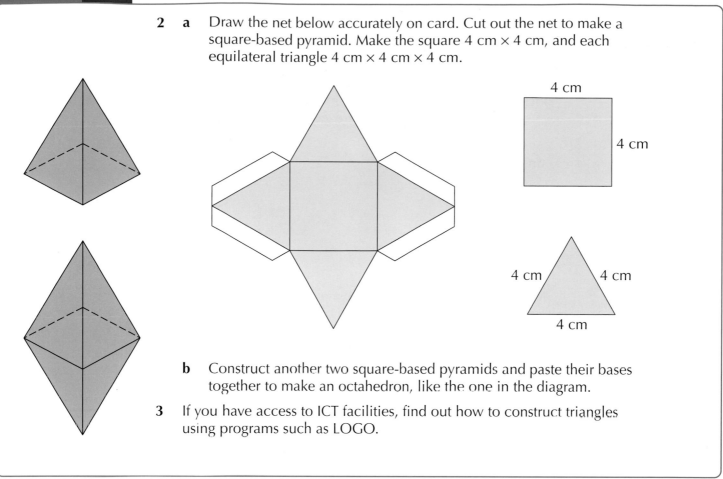

4 cm

4 cm

4 cm   4 cm

4 cm

b Construct another two square-based pyramids and paste their bases together to make an octahedron, like the one in the diagram.

3 If you have access to ICT facilities, find out how to construct triangles using programs such as LOGO.

Loci

The trail from the jet aircraft has traced out a path. The path of the trail is known as a **locus**. A locus (the plural is **loci**) is a set of points that satisfies a given set of conditions or a rule. It is useful to think of a locus as a path traced out by a single moving point.

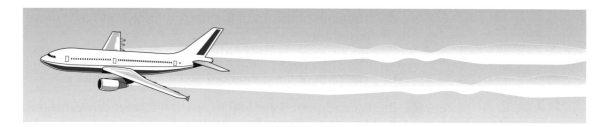

Example 15.5 ▷

Mr Yeates is walking along a straight path that is equidistant from two trees (equidistant means 'the same distance'). The sketch below shows the locus of his walk along the path. The locus can be described as the perpendicular bisector of the line joining the two trees. In some cases, the locus can be drawn accurately if measurements are given.

tree

tree

Example 15.6 ▷

Mr McGinty's goat is tethered to a post by a rope 2 m long. A sketch is shown of the locus of the path of the goat as it moves around the post with the rope remaining taut.

post

2 m

path

The locus can be described as a circle with a radius of 2 m.

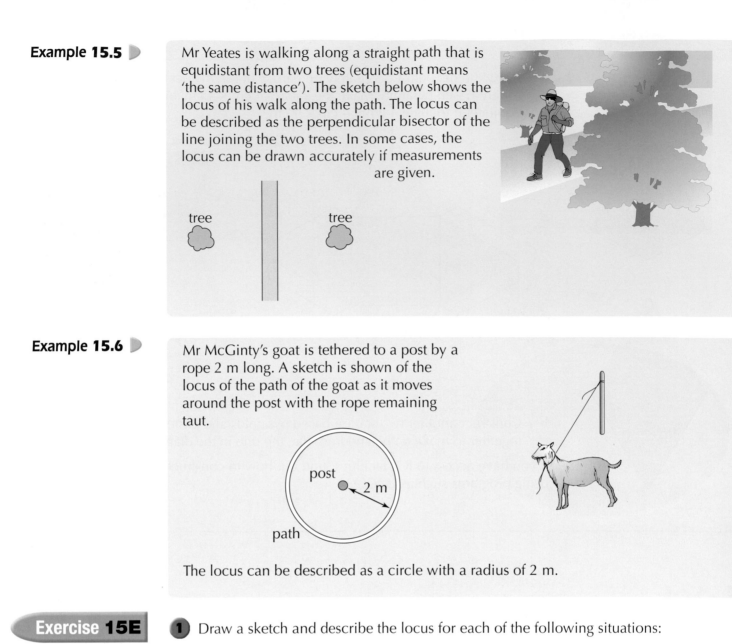

Exercise 15E

1 Draw a sketch and describe the locus for each of the following situations:

a The path of a cricket ball being hit for a six by a batsman.

b The path of the Earth as it orbits the sun.

c The path of a bullet from a rifle.

d The path of the tip of Big Ben's minute hand as it moves from 3 o'clock to half past three.

e The path of a parachutist after jumping from a plane.

f The path of the pendulum of a grandfather clock.

2 Barn A and barn B are 500 m apart. A farmer drives his tractor between the barns so that he is equidistant from each one. On a sketch of the diagram, draw the locus of the farmer.

barn A

barn B

500 m

3 The diagram on the right shows two fences that border a park. Kathryn enters the park at an entrance at X. She then walks through the park so that she is equidistant from each fence.

  a On a sketch of the diagram, draw the locus of Kathryn.

  b Describe Katherine's locus.

X

4 A toy car starts at point A at the edge of a room, and moves so that it is always a fixed distance from point Y.

——————— A ——————— Y ———————

  a On a sketch of the diagram, draw the locus of the car.

  b Describe the locus of the car.

5 The line AB is 20 cm long and C is its mid-point.

A ——————————— C ——————————— B

  a Describe the locus of A if the line is rotated about C.

  b Describe the locus of A if the line is rotated about B.

Extension Work

1 The diagram on the right shows the dimensions of a building. A path is to be laid around the building so that the edge of the path is always 1 m away from the building. Make a scale drawing to show the edge of the path around the building (use a scale of 1 cm to 1 m).

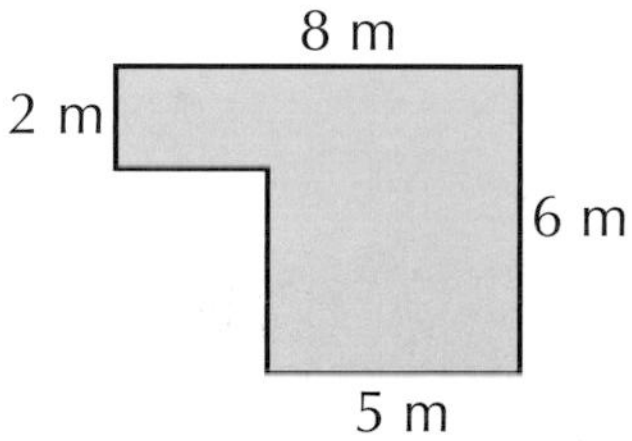

8 m
2 m
6 m
5 m

2 The diagram shows the position of two car-park meters in a large car park in a city centre. When Mrs Kitson buys her parking ticket, she always walks to the nearest meter. On a sketch of the car park, using a ruler and compasses, divide the car park into two regions to show the nearest meter available depending on where she parks.

3 Use reference material or the Internet to find out about contours, isotherms and isobars. How are these related to a locus?

4 If you have access to ICT facilities, find out how to generate shapes and paths, using programs such as LOGO. For example, find out how to draw regular polygons, star shapes and spiral shapes.

Bearings

There are four main directions on a compass – north (N), south (S), east (E) and west (W). These directions are examples of **compass bearings**. A **bearing** is a specified direction in relation to a fixed line. The line that is usually taken is due north. The symbol for due north is: ↑

You have probably seen this symbol on maps in Geography.

Bearings are mainly used for navigation purposes at sea, in the air and in sports such as orienteering. A bearing is measured in degrees (°) and the angle is always measured **clockwise** from the **north line**. A bearing is always given using three digits and is referred to as a **three-digit bearing**. For example, the bearing for the direction east is 090°.

Example 15.7 ▷

On the diagram, the three-figure bearing of B from A is 035° and the three-figure bearing of A from B is 215°.

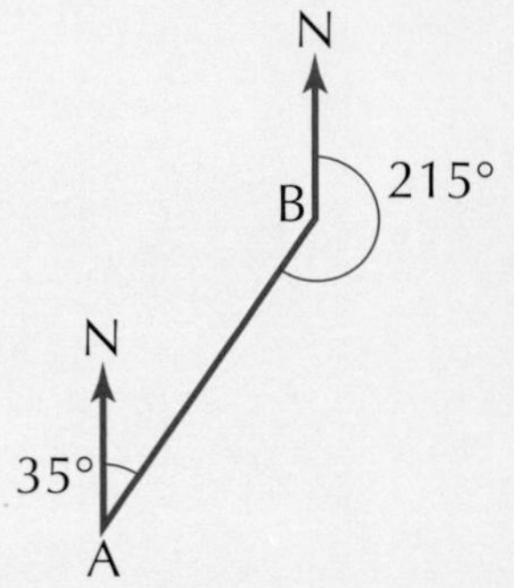

Example 15.8 ▷

The diagram shows the positions of Manchester and Leeds on a map.

The bearing of Leeds from Manchester is 050° and the bearing of Manchester from Leeds is 230°. To find the bearing of Manchester from Leeds, use the dotted line to find the alternate angle of 50° and then add 180°. Notice that the two bearings have a difference of 180°; such bearings are often referred to as 'back bearings'.

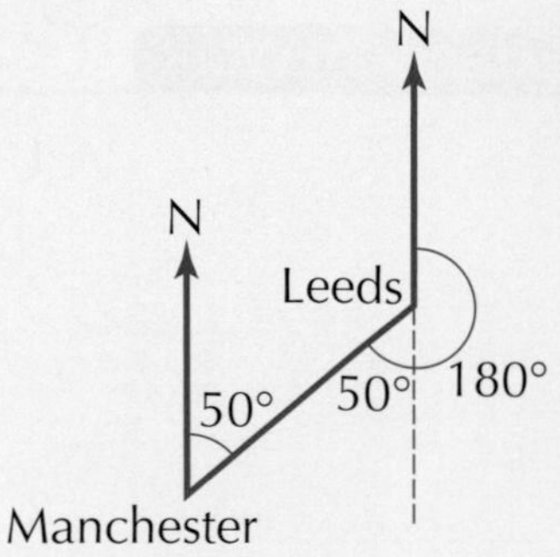

Exercise 15F

1 Write down each of the following compass bearings as three-figure bearings:

    a south   **b** west   **c** north-east   **d** south-west

2 Write down the three-figure bearing of B from A for each of the following:

    a   **b** 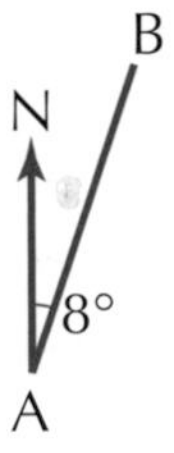   **c** 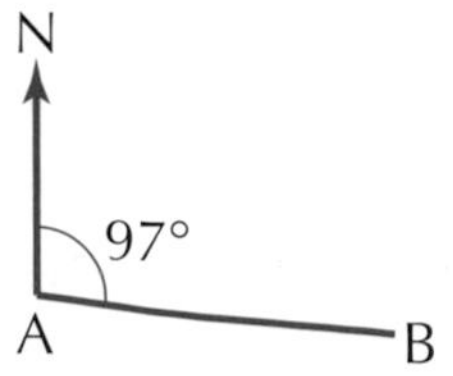   **d**

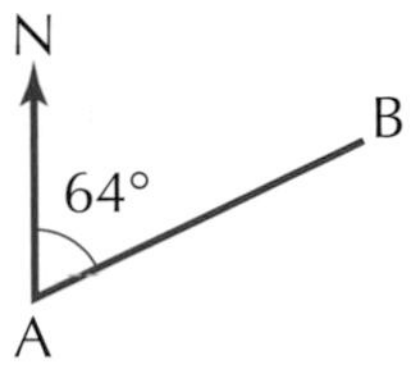

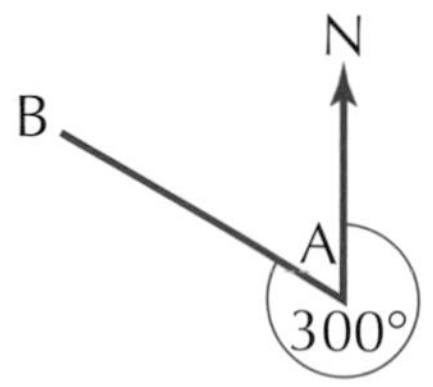

3 Find the three-figure bearing of X from Y for each of the following:

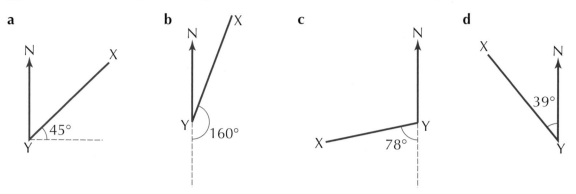

a
b
c
d

4 Draw a rough sketch to show each of the bearings below (mark the angle on each sketch):

    a   From a ship A, the bearing of a light-house B is 030°.

    b   From a town C, the bearing of town D is 138°.

    c   From a gate E, the bearing of a trigonometric point F is 220°.

    d   From a control tower G, the bearing of an aircraft H is 333°.

5 The two diagrams show the positions of towns and cities in England.

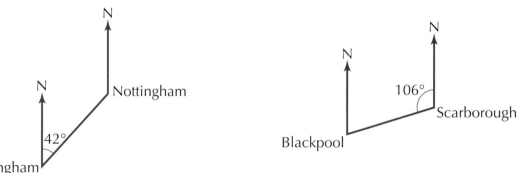

Find the bearing of each of the following:

    a   **i**   Nottingham from Birmingham

          ii   Birmingham from Nottingham

    b   **i**   Scarborough from Blackpool

          ii   Blackpool from Scarborough.

6 Terry and Barbara are planning a walk on Ilkley Moor in Yorkshire. The scale drawing below shows the route they will take, starting from Black Pots.

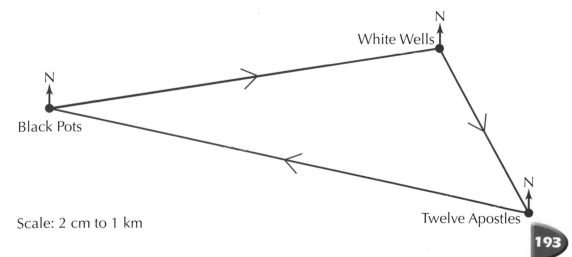

Scale: 2 cm to 1 km

a What is the total distance of their walk if they keep to a direct route between the land marks?

b They have to take three-figure bearings between each land-mark because of poor visibility. Use a protractor to find the bearing of:

i White Wells from Black Pots

ii Twelve Apostles from White Wells

iii Black Pots from the Twelve Apostles.

Extension Work

1 A liner travels from a port X on a bearing of 140° for 120 nautical miles to a port Y. It then travels from port Y on a bearing of 250° for a further 160 nautical miles to a port Z.

a Make a scale drawing to show the journey of the liner (use a scale of 1 cm to 20 nautical miles).

b Use your scale drawing to find:

i the direct distance the liner travels from port Z to return to port X.

ii the bearing of port X from port Z.

2 The diagram shows the approximate direct distances between three international airports:

The bearing of Stansted airport from Heathrow airport is 040°

Stansted   N

65 km

80 km

Heathrow

40 km

Gatwick

a Use this information to make a scale drawing to show the positions of the airports (use a scale of 1 cm to 10 km).

b Use your scale drawing to find:

i the bearing of Gatwick airport from Heathrow airport.

ii the bearing of Gatwick airport from Stansted airport.

A cube investigation

For this investigation you will need a collection of cubes and centimetre isometric dotted paper.

Two cubes can only be arranged in one way to make a solid shape, as shown.

Copy the diagram onto centimetre-isometric dotted paper. The surface area of the solid is 10 cm².

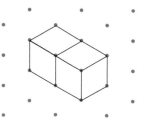

Three cubes can be arranged in two different ways, as shown.

Copy the diagrams onto centimetre isometric dotted paper. The surface area of both solids is 14 cm².

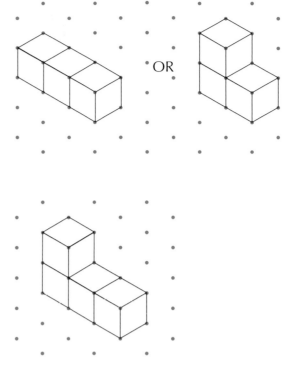

OR

Here is an arrangement of four cubes:
The surface area of the solid is 18 cm².

How many different arrangements can you make using four cubes?

Draw all the different arrangements on centimetre-isometric dotted paper.

What is the greatest surface area for the different solids you have made?

What is the least surface area for the different solids you have made?

Draw a table to show your results and write down anything you notice.

What do you think are the greatest and least surface areas of a solid made from five cubes?

What you need to know for level 5

- How to use coordinates in all four quadrants
- How to make a scale drawing
- How to use three-figure bearings

What you need to know for level 6

- How to draw plans and elevations
- How to construct a triangle from given data
- How to calculate the volume and surface area of shapes made from cubes and cuboids

National Curriculum SATs questions

LEVEL 5

1 *2001 Paper 2*

A plan of a ferry crossing is shown.

a Draw an accurate scale drawing of the ferry crossing (use a scale of 1 cm to 20 m).

b What is the length of the ferry crossing on your diagram?

c The scale is 1 cm to 20 m. Work out the length of the real ferry crossing. Show your working, and write the units with your answer.

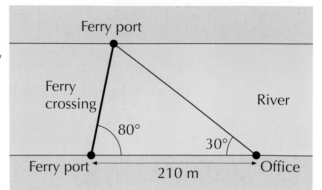

LEVEL 6

2 *1999 Paper 2.*

The diagram shows a model made with nine cubes. Five of the cubes are grey. The other four cubes are white.

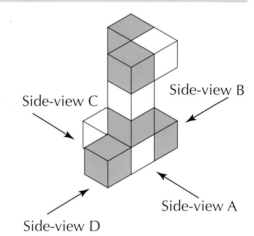

a The drawings below show the four side-views of the model. Which side-view does each drawing show?

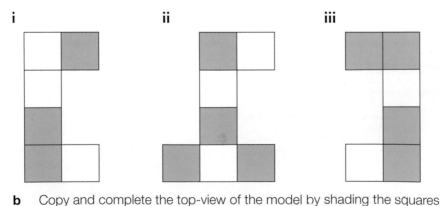

b Copy and complete the top-view of the model by shading the squares that are grey.

Top-view

c Imagine you turn the model upside down. What will the new top-view of the model look like. Copy and complete the new top-view of the model by shading the squares that are grey.

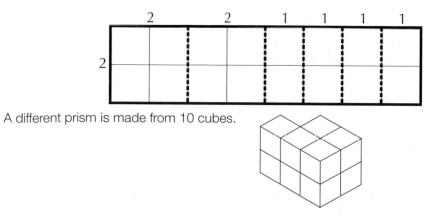

New top-view

3 *1994 Paper 1*

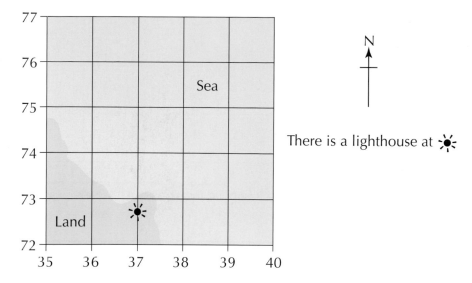

Sea

N

There is a lighthouse at ☀

73

Land

a David is in a boat at 360° east, 750° north. Put a ● on a copy of the map to show David's boat.

b David sees a swimmer in the sea. He looks along a bearing of 235° to see the swimmer. Draw an accurate line on your copy of the map to show the direction David looks along.

c David looks towards the lighthouse. What is the three-figure bearing of the direction David looks along?

4 *1997 Paper 2*

This is a prism made from 6 cubes

The piece of paper below fits exactly around the sides of the prism. The dashed lines are fold lines.

	2		2		1	1	1	1

2

a A different prism is made from 10 cubes.

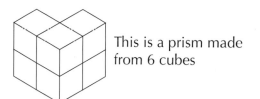

Copy and complete the diagram below to show a piece of paper that fits exactly around the sides of the 10-cube prism.

Show all fold lines as dashed lines.

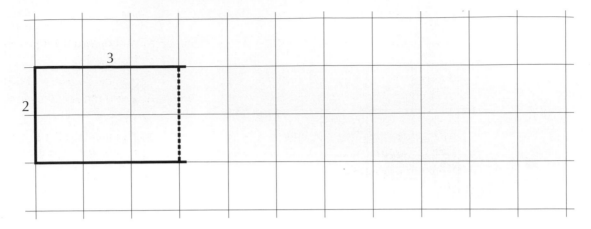

b The piece of paper below fits exactly around the sides of a 14-cube prism.

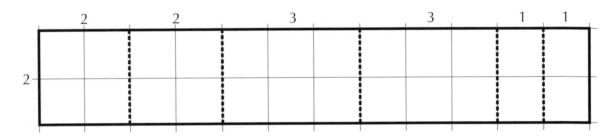

Draw this 14-cube prism on isometric dotted paper.

CHAPTER 16

Handling Data **3**

This chapter is going to show you

- how to calculate statistics from given data
- how to calculate a mean using an assumed mean
- how to construct frequency diagrams for continuous data
- how to construct simple line graphs for time series
- how to compare two distributions by using an average and the range
- how to compare theoretical probabilities with experimental probabilities

What you should already know

- How to construct frequency tables for discrete data
- How to find the mode, median, range and modal class for grouped data
- How to calculate the mean from a simple frequency table
- How to construct graphs and diagrams to represent data
- How to write a short report from a statistical survey

Frequency tables

There are three equal periods in an ice hockey game. Use the picture to work out the time on the clock at the end of each period.

END OF FIRST PERIOD

00.20

Example 16.1

The journey times, in minutes, for a group of 16 railway travellers are shown below:

25, 47, 12, 32, 28, 17, 20, 43, 15, 34, 45, 22, 19, 36, 44, 17

Construct a frequency table to represent the data.

Looking at the data, 10 minutes is a sensible class interval size.

The class intervals are written in the form $10 < T \le 20$.

$10 < T \le 20$ is a way of writing the time interval 10 minutes to 20 minutes, including 20 minutes but not 10 minutes.

There are six times in this group: 12, 17, 15, 19, 20 and 17.
There are three times in the group $20 < T \le 30$: 25, 28, and 22.
There are three times in this group $30 < T \le 40$: 32, 34 and 36.
There are four times in this group $40 < T \le 50$: 47, 43, 45 and 44.

Putting all this information into the table gives:

Time, T (minutes)	Frequency
$10 < T \le 20$	6
$20 < T \le 30$	3
$30 < T \le 40$	3
$40 < T \le 50$	4

Exercise 16A

1 The length of time 25 customers spend in a shop is recorded:

One of the customers was in the shop for exactly 20 minutes. In which class was the customer recorded?

Time, T (minutes)	Frequency
$0 < T \le 10$	12
$10 < T \le 20$	7
$20 < T \le 30$	6

2 The heights (in metres) of 20 people are given below:

1.65, 1.53, 1.71, 1.62, 1.48, 1.74, 1.56, 1.55, 1.80, 1.85, 1.58, 1.61, 1.82, 1.67, 1.47, 1.76, 1.79, 1.66, 1.68, 1.73

Copy and complete the frequency table:

Height, h (metres)	Frequency
$1.40 < h \le 1.50$	
$1.50 < h \le 1.60$	
$1.60 < h \le 1.70$	
$1.70 < h \le 1.80$	
$1.80 < h \le 1.90$	

3 The masses (in kilograms) of fish caught in one day by a fisherman are shown below:

0.3, 5.6, 3.2, 0.4, 0.6, 1.1, 2.4, 4.8, 0.5, 1.6, 5.1, 4.3, 3.7, 3.5

Copy and complete the frequency table:

Mass, M (kilograms)	Frequency
$0 < M \le 1$	
$1 < M \le 2$	
. . .	
. . .	
. . .	
. . .	

4 The temperature (in °C) of 16 towns in Britain is recorded on one day:

12, 10, 9, 13, 12, 14, 17, 16, 18, 10, 12, 11, 15, 15, 12, 13

Copy and complete the frequency table:

Temperature, T (°C)	Frequency
$8 < T \leq 10$	
$10 < T \leq 12$	
. . .	
. . .	
. . .	

Extension Work

Record the number of pages in a large number of school textbooks. Decide on suitable class intervals for the data to be collected together into a frequency table and complete the table. Comment on your results.

Assumed mean and working with statistics

The father's age is double the combined age of his children. Two years ago the children had an average age of 7 years. The difference in the children's ages is 2 years. How old is the father?

Example 16.2 Find the mean of the four numbers 26.8, 27.2, 34.1, 36.4. Use 30 as the assumed mean.

Subtracting 30 from each number gives: –3.2, –2.8, 4.1, 6.4

Adding these numbers up gives: –3.2 + –2.8 + 4.1 + 6.4 = 4.5

So the mean of these numbers is: 4.5 ÷ 4 = 1.125

Adding the 30 back on gives a mean for the original numbers of:

30 + 1.125 = 31.125

Example 16.3 A set of numbers has a mean of 6 and a range of 7.

What happens to the mean and range when the numbers are:

a multiplied by 2? **b** increased by 5?

a As each number has doubled, the mean will also double. For example, if the numbers were 3, 5 and 10, then the new numbers would be 6, 10 and 20.

The old mean is $\frac{3 + 5 + 10}{3} = 6$ and the new mean is $\frac{6 + 10 + 20}{3} = 12$.

The old range is 7 and the new range is 20 – 6 = 14, which is also double.

b As each number has increased by 5, then the mean will also increase by 5. For example, if the numbers were 3, 5 and 10, then the new numbers would be 8, 10 and 15

The old mean is $\dfrac{3 + 5 + 10}{3} = 6$ and the new mean is $\dfrac{8 + 10 + 15}{3} = 11$.

The old range is 6 and the new range is $15 - 8 = 6$, which is still the same.

Exercise 16B

1 Find the mean of 34, 35, 37, 39, 42. Use 37 as the assumed mean.

2 Find the mean of 18, 19, 20, 21, 27. Use 20 as the assumed mean.

3 The heights, in centimetres, of five brothers are 110, 112, 115, 119 and 124. Find their mean height using an assumed mean of 110 cm.

4 Four students each use a trundle wheel to measure the length of their school field in metres. Their results are 161.0, 164.5, 162.5 and 165.0. Find the mean of their results using an assumed mean of 160 m.

5 A box of matches has 'Average contents 600' written on it. Sunil counts the matches in 10 boxes and obtains the following results: 588, 592, 600, 601, 603, 603, 604, 605, 605, 607. Calculate the mean number of matches using an assumed mean of 600. Comment on your answer.

6 The mean of five numbers 5, 9, 10, 20 and x is 10. Find the value of x.

7 Write down three numbers with a mean of 7 and a range of 4.

8 Write down three numbers with a median of 6 and a range of 3.

9 The mean of five numbers is 7, the mode is 10 and the range is 7. What are the five numbers?

10 The mean of a set of numbers is 5 and the range is 6. The numbers are now doubled.

  a What is the new mean?
  b What is the new range?

11 The mean of a set of numbers is 11 and the range is 8. The numbers are now increased by 5.

  a What is the new mean?
  b What is the new range?

12 The mode of a set of numbers is 15 and the range is 6. The numbers are now halved.

  a What is the new mode?
  b What is the new range?

Extension Work

Draw two straight lines of different lengths. Ask other pupils to estimate the lengths of the lines. Record the results and calculate the mean and range for each line. Compare the accuracy of the estimates for the two lines. You could then extend this by repeating for two curved lines and compare the accuracy of the estimates for straight and curved lines.

Drawing frequency diagrams

Look at the picture. How could the organisers record the finishing times to find out when most of the runners finish?

Example 16.4

Construct a frequency diagram for the following data about journey times:

Journey times, t (minutes)	Frequency
$0 < t \le 15$	4
$15 < t \le 30$	5
$30 < t \le 45$	10
$45 < t \le 60$	6

It is important that the diagram has a title and labels, as shown right:

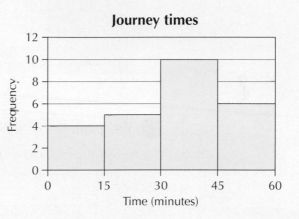

Example 16.5

Look at the graph for ice cream sales. In which month were sales at their highest? Give a reason why you think this happened.

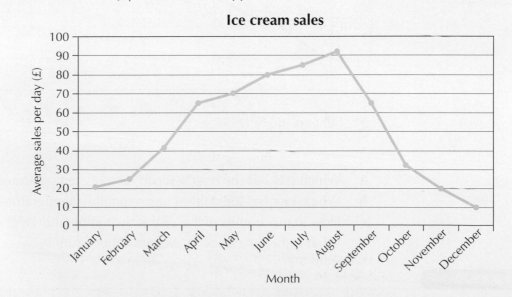

The highest sales were in August (£92 per day). This was probably because the weather was warmer, as people tend to buy ice creams in warm weather.

1 For each frequency table, construct a frequency diagram.

a Aircraft flight times:

Time, T (hours)	Frequency
$0 < T \leq 1$	3
$1 < T \leq 2$	6
$2 < T \leq 3$	8
$3 < T \leq 4$	7
$4 < T \leq 5$	4

b Temperatures of capital cities:

Temperature, T (°C)	Frequency
$0 < T \leq 5$	2
$5 < T \leq 10$	6
$10 < T \leq 15$	11
$15 < T \leq 20$	12
$20 < T \leq 25$	7

c Length of metal rods:

Length, l (centimetres)	Frequency
$0 < l \leq 10$	9
$10 < l \leq 20$	12
$20 < l \leq 30$	6
$30 < l \leq 40$	3

d Mass of animals on a farm:

Mass, M (kg)	Frequency
$0 < M \leq 20$	15
$20 < M \leq 40$	23
$40 < M \leq 60$	32
$60 < M \leq 80$	12
$80 < M \leq 100$	6

2 The graph below shows the mean monthly temperature for two cities:

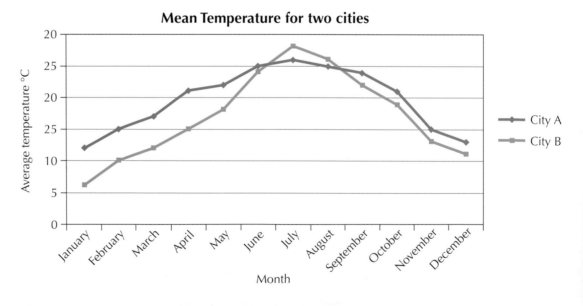

a Which city has the hottest mean monthly temperature?

b Which city has the coldest mean monthly temperature?

c How many months of the year is the temperature higher in City A than City B?

d What is the difference in average temperature between the two cities in February?

Extension Work

Use a travel brochure to compare the temperatures of two European destinations.
Make a poster to advertise one destination as being better than the other.

Comparing data

80m   150m

Look at the picture. What is the range of the golfer's shots?

Example 16.6 The table shows the mean and range of basketball scores for two teams:

	Team A	Team B
Mean	75	84
Range	20	10

Compare the mean and range and explain what they tell you.

The means tell you that the average score for Team B is higher than that for Team A, so they have higher scores generally.

The range compares the difference in their lowest and highest scores; as this is higher for team A, there is more variation in their scores. You could say that they are less consistent.

Exercise 16D

1 The temperature of melting ice is 0°C and the temperature of boiling water is 100°C. What is the range of the two temperatures?

2 The times of four pupils in a 100 metre race are recorded as

     14.2 s   13.8 s   15.1 s   17.3 s

Write down the range of the times.

3 A factory worker records the start and finish times of a series of jobs:

Job Number	1	2	3	4	5
Start time	9.00AM	9.20AM	9.50AM	10.10AM	10.20AM
Finish time	9.15AM	9.45AM	10.06AM	10.18AM	10.37AM

Work out the range of the times taken for each job.

4 The minimum and maximum temperatures are recorded for four counties in England in April:

County	Northumberland	Leicestershire	Oxfordshire	Surrey
Minimum	2°C	4°C	4°C	4.5°C
Maximum	12°C	15°C	16.5°C	17.5°C

a Find the range of the temperatures for each county.

b Comment on any differences you notice.

5 The table shows the mean and range of a set of test scores for Jon and Matt:

	Jon	Matt
Mean	64	71
Range	35	23

Compare the mean and range and explain what they tell you.

6 Fiona recorded how long, to the nearest hour, Everlast, Powercell and Electro batteries lasted in her CD player. She did 5 trials of each make of battery. Her results are given below:

Everlast (£1.00 each)	Powercell (50p each)	Electro (£1.50 each)
6	4	9
5	6	8
6	3	9
6	3	9
7	4	9

a Find the mean and range of the lifetime for each make of battery.

b Which type of battery would you buy and why?

Extension Work

Use an atlas or another data source (the internet or a software program) to compare the populations of the 4 largest cities in China and the United States of America, using the mean and the range.

Which average to use?

Look at the queue of people. Why is it impossible to find the most common height?

This table will help you decide which type of average to use for a set of data.

	Advantages	Disadvantages	Example
Mean	Uses every piece of data. Probably the most used average.	May not be representative if the data contains extreme values.	1, 1, 1, 2, 4, 15 Mean $= \dfrac{1 + 1 + 1 + 2 + 4 + 15}{6} = 4$ which is a higher value than most of the data.
Median	Only looks at the middle values, so it is a better average to use if the data contains extreme values.	Not all values are considered so could be misleading.	1, 1, 3, 5, 10, 15, 20 Median = 4th value = 5. Note that above the median the numbers are a long way from the median but below the median they are very close.
Mode	It is the most common value.	If the mode is an extreme value it is misleading to use it as an average.	Weekly wages of a boss and his 4 staff: £150, £150, £150, £150, £1000. Mode is £150 but mean is £320.
Modal class for continuous data	This is the class with the greatest frequency.	The actual values may not be centrally placed in the class.	<table><tr><td>Time (T) minutes</td><td>Frequency</td></tr><tr><td>$0 < T \le 5$</td><td>2</td></tr><tr><td>$5 < T \le 10$</td><td>3</td></tr><tr><td>$10 < T \le 15$</td><td>6</td></tr><tr><td>$15 < T \le 20$</td><td>1</td></tr></table> The modal class is $10 < T \le 15$, but all 6 values may be close to 15.
Range	It measures how spread out the data is.	It only looks at the two extreme values, which may not represent the spread of the rest of the data.	1, 2, 5, 7, 9, 40. The range is $40 - 1 = 39$ without the last value (40) the range would be only 8.

Exercise 16E

1. Calculate the indicated average for each set of data and explain if that sort of average is sensible or not.

   a 2, 3, 5, 7, 8, 10   Mean   b 0, 1, 2, 2, 2, 4, 6   Mode
   c 1, 4, 7, 8, 10, 11, 12   Median   d 2, 3, 6, 7, 10, 10, 10   Mode
   e 2, 2, 2, 2, 4, 6, 8   Median   f 1, 2, 4, 6, 9, 30   Mean

2. Times (in seconds) to complete a short task are recorded for 15 pupils:

   10.1, 11.2, 11.5, 12.1, 12.3, 12.8, 13.6, 14.4, 14.5, 14.7, 14.9, 15.4, 15.9, 16.6, 17.1

Complete the frequency table and find the modal class.

Explain why the mode is unsuitable for the ungrouped data, but the modal class is suitable for the grouped data.

Time, T (seconds)	Tally	Frequency
$10 < T \leq 12$		
$12 < T \leq 14$		
$14 < T \leq 16$		
$16 < T \leq 18$		

3 Calculate the range for each set of data below and decide whether it is a suitable measure of the spread. Explain your answer.

    a   1, 2, 4, 7, 9, 10   **b**   1, 10, 10, 10, 10   **c**   1, 1, 1, 2, 10

    d   1, 3, 5, 6, 7, 10   **e**   1, 1, 1, 7, 10, 10, 10   **f**   2, 5, 8, 10, 14

Extension Work

Collect a set of data on the attendances at English Premiership football matches over one weekend. Calculate the mean, median and mode.

Repeat this exercise for the Scottish Premier division.

Compare the differences in the distributions of the data. Explain why the mean is probably more suitable for the English league than the Scottish league.

Experimental and theoretical probability

Look at the picture. Would you say the chance of the jigsaw pieces coming out of the box face up is evens or do more pieces come out face down every time?

Example 16.6 ▷ Design and carry out an experiment to test whether drawing pins usually land with the pin pointing up or the pin pointing down.

Count out 50 drawing pins, then drop them onto a table.

Record the number with the pin pointing up and the number with the pin pointing down.

Suppose that 30 point up and 20 point down.

We could then say that the experimental probability of a pin pointing up is: $\frac{30}{50} = \frac{3}{5}$.

Exercise 16F

1 Darren says that if someone is asked to think of a number between 1 and 10 inclusive, they will pick 3 or 7 more often than any other number.

    a   What is the theoretical probability that a person will choose 3 or 7?

    b   Design and carry out an experiment to test out Darren's prediction.

    c   Compare the experimental and theoretical probabilities.

2 **a** What is the theoretical probability that an ordinary fair dice lands on the number 6?

  b What is the theoretical probability that an ordinary fair dice lands on an odd number?

  c Design and carry out an experiment to test these theoretical probabilities.

3 Five cards, numbered 1, 2, 3, 4 and 5, are placed face down in a row as shown. Cards are picked at random.

  a What is the theoretical probability that a person chooses the card with the number 2 on it?

  b A gambler predicts that when people pick a card they will rarely pick the end ones. Design and carry out an experiment to test his prediction.

4 **a** What is the theoretical probability that a coin lands on heads?

  b Design and carry out an experiment to test this theoretical probability.

5 Two fair dice are thrown.

  a Copy and complete the sample space diagram for the total scores:

  b What is the theoretical probability of a total score of 7?

  c Design and carry out an experiment to test whether you think two dice are fair.

First dice

	1	2	3	4	5	6
1						
2						
3						
4						
5						
6						

Second dice

Extension Work

Use computer software to simulate an experiment, for example tossing a coin or rolling a dice. Work out the experimental probabilities after 10, 20, 30 results, and compare with the theoretical probability. Write down any pattern that you notice. Repeat the experiment to see whether any pattern is repeated.

What you need to know for level 5

- How to use a probability scale from 0 to 1
- How to find and justify probabilities based on equally likely outcomes and experimental evidence, as appropriate
- To understand that different outcomes may result from repeating an experiment

What you need to know for level 6

- To collect and record continuous data, choosing appropriate class intervals over a sensible range to create frequency tables
- To construct and interpret frequency diagrams
- When dealing with a combination of two experiments, pupils identify all the outcomes, using diagrams, tables or other forms of communication

National Curriculum SATs questions

LEVEL 5

1 *1997 Paper 1*

Karen and Huw each have three cards,
numbered 2, 3 and 4.

They each take any one of their own cards.

Then they add together the numbers on the two cards.

The table shows all possible answers.

a What is the probability that their answer is
an even number?

b What is the probability that their answer is
a number that is greater than 6?

+	2	3	4
2	4	5	6
3	5	6	7
4	6	7	8

c Both Karen and Huw still have three cards, numbered 2, 3, and 4.

They each take any one of their own cards. Then they multiply together the numbers on the
two cards.

  i Draw a table to show all possible answers.

Copy the sentences below and use your table to fill in the gaps:

  ii The probability that their answer is a number that is less than …… is $\frac{8}{9}$.

  iii The probability that their answer is a number that is less than …… is zero.

2 *2000 Paper 2*

a Paula played four games in a competition.

In three games, Paula scored 8 points each time. In the other game she scored no points.

What was Paula's mean score over the four games?

b Jessie only played two games.

Her mean score was 3 points. Her range was 4 points.

What points did Jessie score in her two games?

c Ali played three games.

His mean score was also 3 points. His range was also 4 points.

What points might Ali have scored in his three games? Show your working.

LEVEL 6

3 *1998 Paper 2*

Some pupils threw three fair dice.

They recorded how many times the numbers on the dice were the same.

Name	Number of throws	Results		
		all different	two the same	all the same
Morgan	40	26	12	2
Sue	140	81	56	3
Zenta	20	10	10	0
Ali	100	54	42	4

a Write the name of the pupil whose data are most likely to give the best estimate of the probability of getting each result. Explain your answer.

b This table show the pupils' results collected together:

Number of throws	Results		
	all different	two the same	all the same
300	171	120	9

Use these data to estimate the probability of throwing numbers that are all different.

4 *1996 Paper 2*

Barry is doing an experiment. He drops 20 matchsticks at random onto a grid of parallel lines.

Barry does the experiment 10 times and records his results. He wants to work out an estimate of probability.

Number of the 20 matchsticks that have fallen across a line

5   7   6   4   6   8   5   3   5   7

a Use Barry's data to work out the probability that a single matchstick when dropped will fall across one of the lines.

Show your working.

b Barry continues the experiment until he has dropped the 20 matchsticks 60 times.

About how many matchsticks in total would you expect to fall across one of the lines?

Show your working.

Published by HarperCollins*Publishers* Limited
77–85 Fulham Palace Road
Hammersmith
London
W6 8JB

Browse the complete Collins catalogue at
www.collinseducation.com

© HarperCollins*Publishers* Ltd 2002
10 9 8 7 6 5 4
ISBN 0 00 713859 8

Keith Gordon, Kevin Evans, Trevor Senior and Brian Speed assert
their moral rights to be identified as the authors of this work.

British Library Cataloguing in Publication Data
A Catalogue record for this publication is available from the
British Library

Edited by John Ormiston
Design and typesetting by Jordan Publishing Design and
Barking Dog Art
Project Management by Sam Holmes
Covers by Tim Byrne
Illustrations by Nigel Jordan, Tony Wilkins and Barking Dog Art
Additional proofreading by Genevieve Sabin and Graham Walker
Production by Jack Murphy
Printed and bound by Printing Express Ltd, Hong Kong

The publishers would like to thank the many teachers and
advisers whose feedback helped to shape *Maths
Frameworking*.

The publishers thank the Qualifications and Curriculum
Authority for granting permission to reproduce questions from
past SAT papers for Key Stage 3.

Every effort has been made to trace copyright holders and to
obtain their permission for the use of copyright material. The
author and publishers will gladly receive any information
enabling them to rectify any error or omission in subsequent
editions.

You might also like to visit:
www.harpercollins.com
The book lover's website